THE SONIC EPISTEME

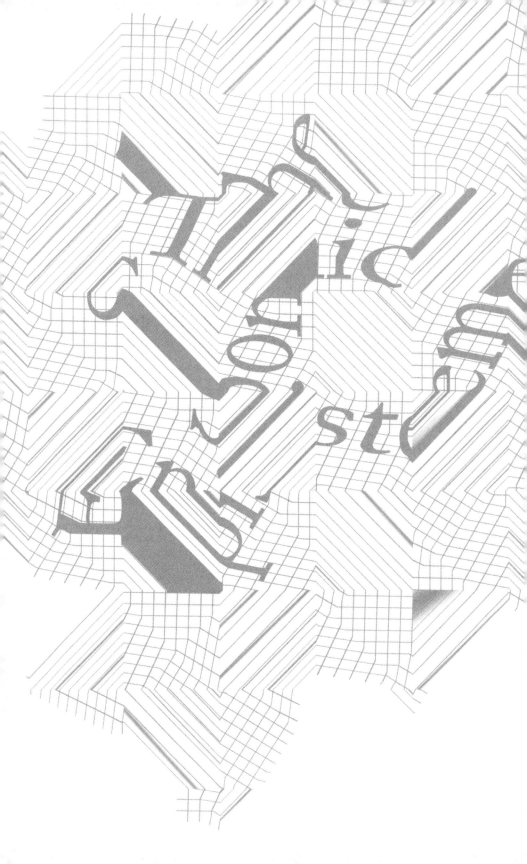

THE
SONIC
EPISTEME

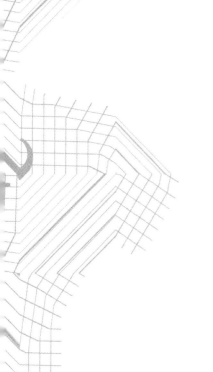

ACOUSTIC
RESONANCE,
NEOLIBERALISM,
AND
BIOPOLITICS

ROBIN JAMES

Duke University Press
Durham and London
2019

© 2019 Duke University Press
All rights reserved
Printed in the United States of America on acid-free paper ∞
Designed by Drew Sisk
Typeset in Garamond Premier Pro and Neuzeit by Tseng Information Systems, Inc.

The Cataloging-in-Publication Data is available at the Library of Congress.

ISBN 9781478007371 (ebook)
ISBN 9781478005780 (hardcover)
ISBN 9781478006640 (paperback)

Cover art by Drew Sisk

CONTENTS

ACKNOWLEDGMENTS

I started working on this book in 2011, when I was rereading Jacques Attali's *Noise* after having just taught Foucault's lectures on neoliberalism. My 2012 *New Inquiry* piece on Attali and Foucault was the germ that sprouted into both this book and *Resilience and Melancholy*, which began, in my head, as the same project. I would like to thank Rob Horning, my editor at *The New Inquiry*, for helping this project get its start. This book also began as my first *Sounding Out!* article on sound and biopolitics. Thanks to Jennifer Stoever and Liana Silva for their work on this and for what has become a long and productive working relationship; I hired Liana as a developmental editor to help me with the final round of manuscript revisions. Everything in this book began as seeds of ideas I shared with my husband, Christian Ryan, over drinks or while walking the dogs. He helped me shape these rough ideas into terms accessible to nonexperts and lent me his college acoustics textbooks so I could double-check and make sure I had the science right. He also took care of all our dogs, plants, and all the housework while I was away giving conference papers and invited talks that would eventually become part of this book. The conditions of capitalism are such that everyone basically needs a "wife," and I am grateful that I have someone who will help me share the reproductive labor it takes just to live, because that's what makes it possible for me to have the time to think and write.

I have shared earlier versions of the work in this book all over the world. Some of the material in the introduction was delivered as talks at the Society for Phenomenology and Existential Philosophy in 2017 and 2018; the 2017 talk was published in the SPEP special issue of the *Journal of Speculative Philosophy*. I lectured on versions of chapter 1 at UCLA's Musicology Colloquium and the Harvard Graduate Music Forum. Versions of the discussion of Rihanna's "BBHMM" in chapter 2 were delivered as lectures at LaSalle University's Philosophy Colloquium, the APA Eastern Division Annual Meeting, Ithaca College's Music Department Colloquium, and the College of Charleston's Aesthetics Working Group. Various parts of chapter 3 were delivered as lectures at the AMS Music and Philosophy Study Group, the University of Virginia Music Department Colloquium, and the SPEP. Versions of chapter 4 were delivered as lectures at the SUNY Stony Brook Sound and Affect conference, University of Groningen Music Department Colloquium, NYU's Music Department Colloquium, the New England Popular Culture Association meeting, the SPEP, IASPM International, IASPM-US, American Philosophies Forum, and the University of Sussex's American Studies Colloquium. Material from throughout the book informed talks I gave at the University of Cardiff and at Goldsmith's.

I am deeply grateful to everyone who invited me to share my work and who engaged with it at these lectures, including Luvell Anderson, Natalia Cecire, Monica Chieffo, Nomi Dave, Hayley Fenn, Joel Garver, the Harvard Graduate Music Forum, Chui Wa Ho, Judy Lockhead, Breena Loraine, Kristin McGee, Eduardo Mendieta, Jonathan Neufeld, Michael O'Brian, Alex Reed, Josh Robinson, Antony Paul Smith, Steven Smith, John Stuhr, Alejandro García Sudo, Olufemi Taiwo, and Marina Vischmitt. I am grateful to other people who gave feedback on various stages of the project, including Marie Thompson, Annie Goh, Ben Tausig, Barry Shank, Louis-Manuel Garcia, my colleagues in the philosophy department at UNC Charlotte, and of course the UNC Charlotte graduate and undergraduate students who read many of the texts I cite in this book in class with me. I would especially thank my spring 2017 Theories of Sound and Music class, as well as my spring 2018 Feminist Theory and Its Applications class. I am also deeply grateful for the thoughtful and constructive feedback provided by the anonymous peer reviewers of this manuscript.

I also owe a lot to my editor at Duke, Elizabeth Ault. She has shepherded this project through a rigorous review process and helped me both with incredibly incisive feedback and with wise advice that helps me get some of my worst writing habits under better control.

I've talked a lot about humans I have to thank, but I also would like to thank the nonhuman members of my family: Sputnik (rest in peace), Laika, Hyperion, and especially Juno, who has sat on my lap or wedged herself between my back and the back of the chair for at least half of the writing of this manuscript. Their emotional support and their drawing me away from the computer to exercise and play helped me be a better writer.

I am grateful to the K-Hole collective for allowing me to reprint a graphic from their 2013 "Youth Mode" report; it appears in chapter 1.

The initial research for chapter 3 was supported by a UNC Charlotte Reassignment of Duties in fall 2014. A portion of this book's production was funded by the UNC Charlotte College of Liberal Arts and Sciences small grants program.

INTRODUCTION

Music . . . first connected the senses to the invisible realm
of mathematical theory. . . . Music harmonized experience
with mathematics.

— Peter Pesic, *Music and the Making of Modern Science*

I. The Sonic Episteme

People use the term "symphony" to explain and put a positive spin on data
analytics so frequently that it's on the fast track to becoming a cliché. Symphony and Symphony Solutions are software companies focused on digital
communication and data analytics. Symphony Health and Symphony Corporation are data analytics firms serving the healthcare industry. Symphony
Retail uses artificial intelligence for retail applications like marketing and
logistics. Data scientists working at these (and other) companies commonly
use ideas of *symphonia* (συμφωνία)—the ancient Greek word for pleasing harmony—to describe the nuts and bolts of what they do. On data science firm
dunnhumby's corporate blog, David Castro-Gavino's post titled "Creating a
Symphony from the Noise of Customer Data" uses the idea of symphony to
explain how data scientists discover useful, meaningful relationships among
individual data points: patterns in the frequency of consumer behaviors interact to form actionable information just as patterns in the frequency of sound
waves interact to form pleasing resonances.[1] Capitalizing on mathematical
similarities between the physics of sound and the metaphysics of predictive
analytics, this comparison appeals to laypeople's musical understanding of
sound to translate the complex math behind data analytics into familiar and
accessible nonquantitative terms.[2]

As the epigraph suggests, Western culture commonly uses music to translate math into qualitative terms. But in the late twentieth and early twenty-
first centuries, the neoliberal, biopolitical push to quantify every last bit of
reality has elevated a specific kind of math—probabilistic statistics—from a

mere tool for describing things to the fundamental structure of reality and knowledge themselves. As philosopher Mary Beth Mader explains, the use of probabilistic statistics to study and govern people has led to "a radical shift in ontological register" from the social to the mathematical. Statistics do not describe relations among people but "a relation between numbers or quantities alone."[3] For example, the Centers for Disease Control reported that the suicide rate in North Carolina from 2014 to 2016 was 15.3 out of 100,000 people. This figure expresses the frequency of one average number (suicides) in relation to another average number (population); it does not represent a count of actual suicides or living people.[4] In addition to showing how this statistic expresses a relation among numbers rather than people, this example highlights that probabilistic statistics reimagine the world as a specific type of mathematical relationship: a frequency ratio. In the "ontological shift" from people to frequency ratios, the rules and principles behind this math come to be taken as the basic rules and principles behind reality itself. Because sound is commonly understood to be a kind of frequency, it is easy to use people's practical knowledge and experience of music to translate that math into down-to-earth terms.

2

These appeals to music and sound don't just dumb down math for nonexperts; they also capture aspects of reality mathematics cannot. As much as states, corporations, and even artistic and academic practices try to quantify everything, people will continue to experience things in qualitative ways, like with their senses or their emotions.[5] And as processes of quantification surpass the grasp of both nonexperts and individual human brains, these qualitative registers of experience may be the most efficient medium in which to perform the ontological shift from people to frequencies in a way that people can easily understand and adapt to. This is where the old music/math trope comes in handy, except here sound isn't just a metaphor for math.

Metaphors draw figurative, counterfactual relationships between things that *aren't actually the same*. However, the introductory examples use "symphony" to translate *the same structure or relationship* from a quantitative medium into a qualitative one. Acoustic resonance (i.e., sound as a frequency or oscillating pattern of variable intensity) and neoliberal, biopolitical statistics are different ways of expressing relationships among frequency ratios: one quantitatively, as a rate; the other qualitatively, as resonant sound. In these cases, acoustically resonant sound and math are two different ways of expressing the same kinds of relationships, two sides of the same coin.

Scholars refer to the quantitative side of this coin as a "neoliberal episteme."[6] For example, philosopher Shannon Winnubst argues that "neoliberalism repeats the themes of liberalism in a different voice"[7] because it articulates liberalism's basic commitments—such as individualism and white supremacy—in terms that are "calculative" rather than "juridical."[8] This rearticulation sets in motion "the fundamental changes in rationality itself that come to dominate the neoliberal iteration of the modern episteme."[9] Though it preserves classical liberalism's fundamental values, it uses different tools and techniques to act on and realize those values—calculative rather than juridical ones. That's why it forms a new type or subtype of episteme. Episteme is Michel Foucault's term for a group of intellectual, economic, and political practices that are tied together by common behind-the-scenes methods, logics, and values. As he explains, "unknown to themselves," the practitioners of a particular episteme "employed the same rules to define the objects proper to their own study, to form their concepts, to build their theories."[10] These "rules" are methods of abstraction, parameters for translating or compressing rich sensory data into words, numbers, images, and other kinds of information. In the neoliberal episteme, probabilistic statistics are the rules used to define objects of knowledge, form concepts, and build theories. That's why Winnubst defines the neoliberal episteme as a calculative rationality.

3

This book is about the neoliberal episteme's complementary qualitative episteme, which I call the sonic episteme. The sonic episteme creates qualitative versions of the same relationships that the neoliberal episteme crafts quantitatively, bringing nonquantitative phenomena in line with the same upgrades to classical liberalism that the neoliberal episteme performs quantitatively. Each of the book's five chapters demonstrates how a specific field or practice (which I call "constituents" of the sonic episteme) uses concepts of acoustic resonance to create qualitative versions of the same updated relations of domination and subordination, and the same mechanisms for policing them, that neoliberalism and biopolitics use probabilistic statistics to make and monitor. In the sonic episteme, those upgrades appear not as the shift from juridical to calculative rationality but as a shift from verbal or visual representation to sound and resonance. Like earlier versions of what sound studies scholar Jonathan Sterne calls "the audiovisual litany,"[11] the sonic episteme misrepresents sociohistorically specific concepts of sound and vision as their universal, "natural" character and uses sound's purported difference from vision to mark its departure from what it deems the West's ocular- and text-centric status quo. Whereas earlier versions of the litany claim sound embodies an originary metaphysical immediacy or "presence" that words and images deny, the sonic episteme

claims sound embodies *material* immediacy and the metaphysics of a probabilistic universe, which modernity's commitments to representationalist abstraction and certainty supposedly occlude.[12]

Appealing to assumptions about sound and music's "minoritarian"[13]
position in Western culture and sound's inherent wholesomeness,[14] the constituents of the sonic episteme I study here claim their use of sound is both
revolutionary (turning Western modernity on its head) and recuperative (recovering what it excluded).[15] In this way, they misrepresent their difference
from the Western modern status quo as progress past it. Although the sonic
episteme presents these upgrades as fixes for modernity's bugs, especially bugs
related to identity-based inequality, it actually repeats these bugs in a voice
that makes those bugs sound and feel like features. Thus, though the sonic
episteme's appeal to sound may appear revolutionary because it frees us from
the conceptual and political baggage we've inherited from Western modernity, it just remakes and renaturalizes all that political baggage in forms more
compatible with twenty-first-century technologies and ideologies — which is
exactly what the neoliberal episteme does with its calculative rationality.

According to Foucault, an episteme's "rules of formation . . . are to be
found only in widely differing theories, concepts, and objects of study."[16] In
order to give a sense of the breadth of the sonic episteme while still staying
within my areas of academic expertise, I focus on some of the constituents of
the sonic episteme found in philosophy (i.e., "theories") and pop culture (i.e.,
"objects of study"). These constituents use concepts of acoustic resonance to
define objects of knowledge, form concepts, build theories, and abstract from
concrete reality to human expression and ideas.

Sometimes their appeal to acoustic resonance is explicit, and sometimes
it's implicit but easy to infer. Jacques Attali's claim that "the laws of acoustics
. . . displa[y] all of the characteristics of the technocracy managing the great
machines of the repetitive [i.e., neoliberal] economy"[17] is one example of an
explicit appeal that directly mentions acoustics. Implicit appeals mention features of acoustic resonance without directly calling them that, such as when
neoliberal economist Milton Friedman implicitly makes the same claim Attali does, arguing that the deregulated, entrepreneurial market is "a system of
proportional representation"[18] that expresses human behavior in statistically
calculated ratios such as probabilities and cost/benefit calculus. Friedman's
proportions are ratios that express the average or normal frequency of a variable, and they are grounded in the same basic mathematical principle we use
to measure sound waves: frequency ratios. This same system of proportional
representation — in particular, the proportional representation of public opin-

ion proffered by polling and, more contemporarily, big data—is the foundation of the "postdemocratic" political ontology philosopher Jacques Rancière critiques in his book *Disagreement*. That's why he calls postdemocracy "the perfect realization of the empty virtue Plato called *sophrosune*"[19] and explicitly—at least for the expert reader—uses sound to translate statistics into nonquantitative terms (in this case, ethics). Plato models *sophrosyne* (generally translated as moderation) on contemporary-to-him understandings of musical harmony as geometric proportion. Rancière uses sophrosyne to describe a society organized by statistically calculated frequency ratios, probabilities, and forecasts, updating Plato's original idea of sophrosyne with twentieth- and twenty-first-century math, which brings us back to Attali's claim that the laws of acoustics look a lot like the principles of neoliberal social order and political ontology.

As I discuss in chapter 4, this same concept of sophrosyne appears in pop culture as an ethical ideal for individuals, corporations, and the state, often implicitly as narratives about personal responsibility. Comparing quantum strings to the strings on a musical instrument, popular science writing about string theory figures such as Brian Greene and Stephon Alexander likewise uses the slippage between ancient Greek concepts of musical harmony and acoustic resonance to translate the math behind its probabilistic models of the universe into terms laypeople can understand. New materialist theorist Karen Barad uses the basic principles of quantum physics as a model for philosophical abstraction and frequently appeals to concepts of "resonance" and "dissonance" to translate the physicists' mathematical models into philosophical concepts and methods.[20] Similarly, Elizabeth Grosz's Deleuzo-Darwinian ontology treats "vibrations, waves, oscillations, resonances" as the fundamental elements of existence.[21]

From neoliberalism to new materialism and beyond, acoustically resonant sound is the "rule" these otherwise divergent practices use "to define the objects proper to their own study, to form their concepts, to build their theories."[22] Because this rule is the qualitative version of the quantitative rules neoliberal market logics and biopolitical statistics use to organize society, the sonic episteme is, in the terms of the well-known Adorno/Foucault meme, possibly bad and definitely dangerous.[23]

The sonic episteme is dangerous, but thankfully it's not the only way to think with and through sound—i.e., to use sound to define concepts and other objects of knowledge, build theories, and abstract from sensory reality to human expressions. Sound, and even resonance, can be a productive model for theorizing if and only if it models intellectual and social practices that are

5

designed to avoid and/or oppose the systemic relations of domination that classical liberalism and neoliberalism create. This is easy to do if we look to the way people oppressed by those systems of domination think about and use sound. Looking to both theories of sound and resonance in black studies and musical practices by black women artists, I show that it's possible to use sound to think about political ontology, vibratory resonance, subjectivity, and even math without appealing to the sonic episteme and the neoliberalism and biopolitics that come with it. Building on Alexander Weheliye's use of the term, I call these practices "phonographies." As I show in chapters 2–5, phonographies study patterns of living that model what Weheliye calls "habeas viscus," Devonya Havis calls "sounding," Katherine McKittrick calls "demonic calculus," Ashon Crawley calls "choreosonics," and Christina Sharpe calls "wake." These all refer to phenomena that behave like acoustic resonance (e.g., they're rhythmic, oscillatory patterns) and/or the math it models, but they are calibrated to the epistemic, ontological, aesthetic, and political practices black people have used to build alternative realities amid white supremacist patriarchal domination.

The sonic episteme upgrades qualitative phenomena to work more efficiently under neoliberalism and biopolitics, and phonographies do the opposite of that. Whereas the sonic episteme takes what Western modernity traditionally disposes of—resonance—and uses it to reinvest and revive white Western culture so it can succeed in neoliberal, biopolitical institutions, phonographies do not reappropriate that discarded material. Phonographies articulate ideas, aesthetics, and relationships that exist in the frequencies perceptually coded out of the sonic episteme's spectrum because the cost of laboring to domesticate them into something that contributes to elite status isn't worth the benefit. To use Tricia Rose's term, phonographies work "in the red."[24] Rose coins this phrase to describe the ways "rap producers . . . pus[h] on established boundaries of music engineering" to create sounds that align with "Afrodiasporic musical priorities."[25] These established boundaries reflected white Western aesthetic priorities (e.g., about pitch or the correct level of bass), which are coded into music technologies like mixers and speakers. Because Afrodiasporic sonic priorities were coded out of these technologies, hip-hop artists had to misuse them and break the boundaries coded into them to achieve the sounds they wanted. "In the red" refers to the way music technologies represent one such broken boundary: the threshold at which increasing a mix's volume or gain distorts the frequencies in the mix. The gain or volume meter on mixing equipment uses green lights to indicate when the mix is below that threshold and red lights to indicate when that threshold is crossed. In-the-red frequencies are outside the spectrum of frequencies that accurately reproduce and transmit white aesthetic values. Focusing our attention on dimensions of verbal, visual, and musical practices that conventional methods of abstraction dispose of, phonographies are "nondisciplinary"[26] or "undisciplined"[27] practices that avoid reinvesting in white supremacist patriarchal models for transmitting knowledge, privilege, personhood, and property, such as the academic discipline. To use sound as a tool for theorizing and realizing a more just world, we can't just reform Western (post)modernity but must do something else entirely. Phonography is one model for this something else; certainly there are others.

II. Basic Concepts and Method

Acoustic resonance, neoliberalism, and biopolitics are the main concepts that run through every chapter, so before I get into the thick of that analysis, I will define what I mean by these terms, explain how they are connected, and identify some of their component parts. Following the conceptual discussion, I'll present my method.

1. Acoustic Resonance

The sonic episteme adopts a sociohistorically specific concept of what sound is, physically, and how it works, mechanically. That concept is what I call acoustic resonance.[28] "Resonance" generally means "vibratory motion"[29]; that's how Hermann von Helmholtz defined it in 1863. Helmholtz thought vibrating bodies transferred their vibratory motion to their surrounding environment, thus generating what he called sympathetic resonances. Whereas sympathetic resonance refers to contagious patterns of vibratory back-and-forth motion, acoustic resonance refers to patterns of high and low pressure, intensity, or energy. From the perspective of acoustics, "a sound wave consist[s] of a condensation or high-pressure pulse followed by rarefaction or low-pressure pulse."[30] This pattern of higher and lower intensity is generally visualized as a waveform, with the upper peak describing that highest intensity and the lower valley describing the lowest intensity. This visualization commonly misleads people into thinking sound waves work like vibrating strings, moving up and down or back and forth; but that's incorrect: sound waves are alternating patterns of pressure, intensity, or energy.[31] These patterns are described as ratios: for example, mHz for pitch or frequency is the ratio of cycles per second. In contemporary physics, acoustic resonance refers to interaction of these kinds of patterns: resonance occurs when frequency patterns align and amplify one another rather than clash and dampen or mask one another.[32]

Resonance, in other words, is a phase relationship. When patterns are in phase, they align at regular intervals; an example of this would be a song sung in "in the round." Composer Steve Reich describes these type of phase relationships as "rational": they align at intervals we are habituated to recognizing, like 1/2, 1/4, 1/3, 2/3, 180 degrees, 90 degrees, etc.[33] Patterns that do not align at regular intervals are "irrational" and out of phase. In Western music theory, overtones that are integer (whole-number) multiples of the fundamental frequency (the main pitch we hear) are called "harmonics," whereas overtones that are noninteger (i.e., fractions) multiples of the fundamental frequency are called "inharmonics" because harmonic frequencies fall in phase with the fundamental frequency and inharmonic ones don't.[34] In this sense, "rational" relationships among patterns are rational when they are proportional and thus expressible as ratios; such relationships are "irrational" when they aren't consistently proportional enough to be expressible as a ratio.

The sonic episteme thinks sound *is* acoustic resonance — the patterned intensity of a flow, expressed as a rate or a frequency ratio. And it's this ratio that makes acoustic resonance a qualitative corollary for the math behind neoliberalism and biopolitics.

8

2. Neoliberalism and Biopolitics
a. As Practices of Quantification

In general, "biopolitics" refers to a style of governing focused on life: life is the object of governance and site of power's investment (or divestment), and killing off internal threats is a common and justifiable way of fostering that life (e.g., eugenics). Neoliberalism is a more contested term, but scholars of neoliberalism agree that it is "the general idea that society works best when people and the institutions within it are shaped to work according to market principles."[35] There are different varieties of both biopolitics and neoliberalism.[36] In this book, I focus on the neoliberalisms and biopolitics that reduce everything to probabilities (such as cost/benefit calculus) and normalized distributions (like Gaussian models).[37]

For example, in a 1983 interview, economist and social theorist Jacques Attali describes neoliberalism as "a more properly statistical vision of reality, a macrostatistical and global, aleatory view, in terms of probabilities and statistical groups."[38] Taking its idea of the market as a model for reality itself, probabilistic statistics are the lenses through which this variety of neoliberalism views the world. Similarly, Foucauldian theories of biopolitics study "aleatory events that occur within a population that exists over a period of time"[39] and use statistics to identify patterns among these aleatory events, thus making them relatively predictable and manageable. Though these are not the newest iterations of either neoliberalism or biopolitics, they are still commonly practiced varieties. Michelle Murphy has shown that over the course of the late twentieth and early twenty-first centuries, the very concept of "population" has been remade in primarily economic terms—first national GDP, then human capital. Modeling population on human capital, this type of neoliberal biopolitics uses the same probabilistic models to imagine life and the market (human capital is the microcosm of the macrocosmic market). These probabilistic models are grounded in the same fundamental mathematical relationship: the frequency ratio. As Shannon Winnubst explains, "the statistic exemplifies the ratio-calculative normativity that Foucault locates in neoliberal theorists," which in turn treats "the norm as number, and especially as ratio."[40] As neoliberalism and biopolitics quantify everything, they treat the frequency ratio as the basic unit of reality.

Because these practices of quantification do not govern relations among people, words/laws, or God but relations among numbers, neoliberalism and biopolitics operate at a different ontological register than other technologies of government (like disciplinary normation, sovereign law, etc.).[41] As Mary Beth Mader explains, "when expressed as ratios, the actual social relations between groups of people are masked in these figural expressions that employ the specific features of mathematical objects to characterize people and groups of people . . . endogenous mathematical traits that are superimposed on the social objects studied, rather than discovered in them."[42]

There are two parts to her claim: (1) social relations—both the concrete relations among people and the abstractions about how we do and should relate—are conceived and remade in terms of mathematical relations among numbers; and (2) because statistics are the mathematical instrument used to measure, manage, and enforce those relations, society is made to embody the specific kind of mathematical relationship statistical norms express—a frequency ratio (i.e., ratios expressing the frequency of a given variable in a population). Mader clarifies: "with the spread of the statistics of population and their role in the constitution of subjects, then, social relations literally become rationalized, or more precisely, *ratio-ized*."[43]

But Plato's *Republic* also rationalizes social relations: the organization of the ideally just city reflects the same proportions or ratios found in Plato's divided line. "A line divided into two unequal sections . . . as an expression of the ratio of their comparative clearness and obscurity," the divided line expresses the relative reality of ideas and physical things: ideas are more real than physical things, so the part of the line that represents ideas is bigger than the

9

part that represents physical things.[44] So the issue here isn't just the transformation of social relations into ratios but the specific way those ratios are calculated. Plato's ratios are geometric; they compare relative size or reality (e.g., the length of segments on the divided line is proportional to the "reality" of what that line represents: thoughts, Forms, images, etc.). The biopolitical ratios Mader describes above are frequential: they compare the relative frequency of a phenomenon in a group. For example, the normal curve (the "bell curve") "is a graphic representation of the distribution of frequencies of values for a given measured property, with the most frequent values being those in the distribution that cluster around a mean or average in a single peak."[45] Normal curves measure a property's pattern of intensity within a given population — this is what infant height/weight charts do, as do percentile scores on standardized tests. Statistical norms are ratios of ratios: they take individual measurements of the rate at which a given property x appears in a population (this is the first set of ratios) and then aggregates these and finds the most common or "normal" rate, the average rate y at which x rate occurs — again, this is measuring a pattern of intensity. "The ratio" is one of "the basic conceptual components of the notion of the normal curve"[46] and of normalization as a technique or technology. It is also the same basic conceptual component behind the notion of acoustic resonance. So, though they may express this DNA slightly differently, both acoustic resonance and neoliberal biopolitics share a common gene or element: the frequency ratio.

Neoliberalism and biopolitics organize this DNA to create mathematical relations that reflect and support their underlying values and commitments (e.g., to white supremacy). Normalization is the mode of governmentality Foucault attributes to biopolitics: it's not the juridical punishment of offenders (i.e., taking something away from those who transgress), nor is it the disciplinary normation of subjects (compelling adherence to a prescribed archetype, rendering docile); rather, it's the *normalization of frequencies* (remember: the object of this kind of power isn't people or groups but numbers). Normalization involves (1) determining the range of "normal" distribution of x, and then (2) bringing frequencies outside that normal distribution back in line with it. As Mader explains, citing Foucault's *Security, Territory, Population*, "the various normal curves are collected and compared. Then, 'certain distributions' are 'considered *more normal than others* or in any case more advantageous than the others. It is these distributions that will serve as norms.' ... The technique then will be to attempt to reduce all of the most deviant of these normal curves to the level of the general normal distribution."[47] Normalized statistical distributions determine both the range of frequencies of variable x

10

that a population must exhibit in order to optimize specific values and commitments and a range of tolerable and intolerable deviance.

As a technique or a technology, this type of normalization is analogous to the technique audio engineers use to compress audio signal.[48] Compression brings the distribution of amplitudes within a "normalized" (in Foucault's sense) range. "Compressors . . . reduce dynamic range—the span between the softest and loudest sounds."[49] In the twenty-first century, compression is generally an automated process performed within a DAW (digital audio workstation). Users decide what the upper limit of gain (i.e., volume) should be, and "a compressor 'turns down' the audio when the level exceeds a threshold set by the user. The amount by which the gain is turned down depends on the ratio of the compressor—for example, if a ratio of 5:1 is set, an input signal exceeding the threshold by 5dB will be output with a level of only 1dB over the threshold. Once the signal falls back below the threshold level, the gain returns to normal."[50]

Compressors bring deviant signal back within, or at least proportionally closer to, "normal" gain range. The primary unit or tool here is the ratio: signals aren't just brought in line with the norm but are brought in *relative proportion* to the normal range. Similarly, in biopolitical normalization, the cases that can't be brought into adequately relative proportion to the normal range get quarantined to preserve the health of those in the normal range and, more importantly, to preserve a specific range of the spectrum *as* normal. Robert Kerr explains the connection between these audio compression and statistical normalization: "If something decides to cross the set threshold . . . it is forced to back down in order to fit within the general wall of sound. If such singular entities are not complicit with this process then they are edited out as nondesirables."[51]

Designed to optimize the enclosure of signal bandwidth, perceptual coding is a kind of compression that uses normalization for explicitly capitalist purposes and highlights the role of white supremacist patriarchal property relations in determining the range of what counts as normal. According to Jonathan Sterne, perceptual coding "descends from Bell [Lab]'s initial quest to squeeze more profit out of its infrastructure."[52] In order to eliminate frequencies that impede the efficiency of signal transmission, perceptual coding "use[s] a mathematical model of human hearing to actively remove sound in the audible part of the spectrum under the assumption that it will not be heard."[53] Editing out superfluous frequencies allows you to transmit more signals over the same bandwidth, thus making this bandwidth capital more profitable. Biopolitical normalization uses a mathematical model of human

11

life to actively remove abnormal people from the spectrum of humanity on the assumption that their dysgenic rates or frequencies ought not be "heard." Because these abnormal frequencies impede the efficient transmission and reproduction of "normal" signals, they are perceptually coded out of hegemonic institutions and the population whose lives those institutions are designed to foster. This process of producing and quarantining abnormals is how this configuration of neoliberalism and biopolitics upgrades classically liberal forms of social exclusion so that they can work without explicitly relying on social identities, so that they can be, in other words, post-identity.

b. As Practices of Domination

What makes statistical normalization suited to the way neoliberalism and biopolitics manage social inequity?

Neoliberalism manages identity-based difference differently than classical, contractarian liberalism does. Classical liberalism asserts that we're all equal because we're universally human, abstract individuals without relevant differences (because differences are only relevant in the private sphere). Neoliberalism asserts that we're all equal because all (formerly private) differences are included and valued.[54] Instead of strictly regulating purity (which takes a lot of resources), laws and institutions include deregulated differences, often under the banner of "diversity." I call this move *the domestication of noise* because it turns what was formerly a problem (in the Du Boisian "how does it feel to be a problem?" sense) into a resource. Just as statistical distributions can reveal predictable patterns in what otherwise appear like chance occurrences, the domestication of noise finds order in what traditionally seems like irrational or unruly behavior.

By including formerly excluded unruliness, neoliberalism purports to be post-identity. Post-identity is an umbrella term that describes views like "post-feminism" or "postracial." These views assert that classically liberal identity-based social exclusion (sexism, racism) no longer exist: such exclusion certainly happened in the past, but we have overcome it today. For example, as Angela McRobbie explains, "post-feminism positively draws on and invokes feminism as that which can be taken into account, to suggest that equality is achieved, in order to install a whole repertoire of new meanings which emphasise that it is no longer needed, it is a spent force."[55] This isn't the "backlash" of the 1990s, but the idea that people and institutions *already* value and practice diversity so that white women and people of color really can and do have equal access to political participation and economic success.

The ontology of statistical measurement lets the claim that we've over-

12

come sexism and racism and everyone is equal now seem plausible. Unlike the classical social contract, which posits an ontological divide between "humans" and "sub-" or "nonhumans,"[56] biopolitical normalization posits a flat social ontology, in particular, the flat ontology of mathematics in which everything is a number and thus commutable. As Mader argues, "it is the continuity of number itself that renders both the individuals counted and the ratio of group to group comparable objects to which basic and sophisticated mathematical operations can be applied. . . . Social discontinuities are homogenized in the continuity of quantum."[57]

For example, the discontinuities produced by patriarchy as a political system are re-aggregated as gender becomes one variable in a multifactor statistical model. As variables, gender and race are disarticulated from the power relationships (patriarchy and white supremacy) that produce social discontinuities. As Mader puts it, "a gradational ontology replaces one of opposition."[58] The continuity among statistical variables or groups is what lets post-identity thinking happen: there are no different social orders for humans and subhumans; we're all on the same human spectrum. This continuum from normal to abnormal *does* in fact put everyone on the same playing field. It's the neoliberal version of classically liberal notions of formal equality before the law or "political emancipation": treating everyone as though they're on the same continuum obscures the fact that we still recognize a difference between good abnormal—"disruptors," geniuses—and bad abnormal—terrorists, thugs. Structural barriers haven't gone away; they've just been remade with different tools and layered on top of the old ones. These new structural barriers are what I call a politics of exception.

The politics of exception is the outcome of neoliberal/biopolitical applications of the ontology of statistical normalization to worlds deeply shaped by centuries of material inequality and domination. This ontology reworks modernity's inclusion/exclusion binary into a spectrum of flexibility and dynamism.[59] In the former case, domination contracts create social identities (races, genders) as tools to disaggregate and purify society by excluding white women and nonwhites from political, moral, and legal personhood. This model excludes by creating discontinuities, such as the discontinuity between noise and signal. However, over the course of the twentieth and twenty-first centuries, it's not just audio engineers that domesticate noise, "using and manipulating noise (rather than eliminating it)."[60] Neoliberalism and biopolitics domesticate noise, excluding people from personhood by using and manipulating them via statistical and ideological *continuities* that incorporate their noise into the big social spectrum. When everyone is on the same statistical

13

continuum or spectrum, everyone seems to have the chance to be or become normal; so, if you're deficiently normal, it must be due to your lack of effort or inherent pathology. This is where the hidden structural barriers factor in: individuals' placement on the normal curve isn't the outcome of just their choices and behaviors but also of the way structural barriers foreclose or facilitate the kinds of choices available to them and the opportunity costs of those choices. Neoliberalism and biopolitics cook the books (the background conditions) so that foreground equity always produces differential levels of success. This process of production is what I call, following Lester Spence's use of the term, the politics of exception.

According to Spence, "neoliberalism relies on three populations, institutions, and spaces: those perfectly formed according to market logic, those able to be re-formed according to that logic, and the exceptions unable to be re-formed."[61] These populations are all situated on the same spectrum — the market — but ongoing structural barriers (like, say, rape culture and the criminalization of blackness) make it more difficult and costly for oppressed people to successfully adapt to neoliberal market logic and inhabit "normal" parts of that spectrum. (And even when they do adapt to these norms, biases prevent them from being seen as successful.)[62] Some traditionally oppressed groups can, with adequate investment, be brought into a relatively normal range of conformity to neoliberal market logics; this is the idea behind campaigns like "black girls code" or Sheryl Sandberg's infamous "Lean In" feminism. Other groups, however, don't bring adequate returns on that investment; they cannot efficiently be reformed to neoliberal market logics. They thus appear static, recalcitrant, and inflexible. These are the exception.

The early twenty-first-century U.S. education program No Child Left Behind is another example of the politics of exception. Instead of segregating public schools explicitly on the basis of race and policing the purity of white schools, NCLB uses nominally inclusive performance-based measures like test scores to dole out both resources and penalties on what are effectively racial lines.[63] Including everyone on the same quantitative, statistically measured spectrum kills two birds with one stone: (1) it serves as evidence that identity-based social exclusion is over, obsolete, a thing we "neo-"s are "post-" because we're all on the same playing field, and (2) it provides the mechanism for producing white supremacist patriarchy without relying explicitly on identity-based social exclusion.

Similarly, the editorial choices in the Hollaback! Project's 2014 video "10 Hours of Walking in NYC as a Woman" render black and Latino men exceptions to postfeminist society. The video claims to document the extensive but mundane nature of misogynist street harassment that (white) women face. However, as many critics noted, the video does not depict any white men as perpetrators.[64] Building on the increasingly prominent trope where "black identity appears as an antiquated state of confinement from which the 'multiracial imagined community' must be delivered,"[65] the video presents men of color as solely responsible for (white) women's street harassment, as embodying a "backwards" masculinity that is out of sync with postfeminist society. The same logic informs the production on Usher featuring Juicy J's 2014 single "I Don't Mind." Playing up Juicy J's association with strip club anthems like his 2012 hit "Bandz a Make Her Dance," the song contrasts R&B-singing Usher's respectable, nominally feminist black masculinity with rapping Juicy J's seemingly pre-feminist objectification of sex workers. Like a good woke boyfriend, Usher sings that he "doesn't mind" that his girlfriend is a stripper because she remains monogamous with him and, perhaps more importantly, makes a lot of money. Juicy J, on the other hand, likes the fact that other men look at, admire, and objectify his stripper girlfriend and has no qualms about being in it for the sex, not the love or long-term relationship. Though the lyrics give space to both styles of black masculinity, the production endorses Usher's performance over Juicy J's. The "booty clap" synth is common in hip-hop of that time; it is a handclap synth sound that mimics the "booty clap" move in hip-hop dance. Like many other trap songs of this era, Juicy J's "Bandz" features this synth on every beat (i.e., quarter notes at 4/4). "I Don't Mind," however, puts these synths only on 2 and 4, transforming trap ratchetness into a more traditional and respectable R&B sound. In this way, the song's sounds exhibit the nominally feminist reform expected of neoliberal subjects and present Juicy J, both in his vocal performance on this track and in his other songs, as an exception incapable of such reform. Unlike the Hollaback! video, which holds men of color in general responsible for all ongoing sexism, the sounds on "I Don't Mind" mark a break in the spectrum of black masculinities between Usher (who, like the booty clap rhythms, is reformed) and unreformed, incorrigibly sexist Juicy J. This break redraws old class- and sexuality-based hierarchies among African Americans in terms that aren't, at least on the surface, about class or sexuality.[66] Confirming Spence's claim that "African Americans constitute the exception,"[67] these examples illustrate how the politics of exception mobilizes the claim that identity-based exclusion has been or should be overcome to mark the same status differences that identities did.

Creating exceptional cases and classes is one component of the politics of exception. Quarantining exceptions is the other key component. From a biopolitical perspective, signals or voices that don't resonate harmoniously,

15

that don't embody the predictable, probabilistic ratios of the neoliberal market (i.e., as I discuss in chapter 4, that don't exhibit sophrosyne), may be legitimately muted, masked, or silenced. The politics of exception don't purify the social body so much as compress it in order to manage away frequency ratios that reduce society's overall efficiency. Compression helps signals circulate efficiently and profitably by "discard[ing] the parts of the audio signal that are unlikely to be audible."[68] Neoliberalism and biopolitics help white supremacist patriarchy operate most efficiently by discarding parts of the population that are least likely to register a positive impact on dominant metrics of social and economic value, like profitability or health. In this way, it resembles Sterne's perceptual coding; I discuss this comparison in chapters 2–5.

In sum, the kinds of neoliberalism and biopolitics I study in this book rewrite social relations as specific kinds of mathematical relations: frequency ratios and normalized statistical distributions. This ontological shift from people to numbers also restructures systematic relations of domination and subordination, remaking formal equality before the law into statistical continuities and the politics of exception. Because acoustic resonance is a qualitative version of the same basic mathematical principles behind this type of neoliberal biopolitics (i.e., frequency ratios), taking it as a normative model (a model for how things *ought* to be) for the economy, ontology, society, personhood, or anything else brings whatever you are modeling in accord with the tools and techniques neoliberalism and biopolitics use to maintain structures of domination and subordination. Each of this book's chapters shows how different constituents of the sonic episteme use acoustic resonance to do just that.

There is a growing literature on sound, music, and biopolitics. Naomi Waltham-Smith's *The Sound of Biopolitics* and Jeffrey Nealon's *I'm Not Like Everybody Else: Biopolitics, Neoliberalism, and American Popular Music* are two recent examples. Nealon is concerned with the impact of biopolitics on Anglophone popular music listening practices; Waltham-Smith pays attention to the role of sound in Nancy, Derrida, and Agamben to think about the sonic dimensions of biopolitics as defined by the latter (which is less focused on the role of math and statistics than Foucault's account). *The Sonic Episteme* contributes to this growing body of literature by showing how sonic discourses are marshaled to produce qualitative versions of the same relationships that neoliberalism and biopolitics produce quantitatively. Because those relationships are designed to intensify white supremacist capitalist patriarchy, this book clarifies how sound and resonance contribute to the gendered, sexualized, and racial project at the heart of biopolitics — marking the line between who must live and who is let to die. And finally, studying phonographic approaches to sound in black studies and African American philosophy, the book points to existing alternatives to the sonic episteme's white supremacist capitalist patriarchal project.

3. Method

The method I use to make this argument is just as important as what my argument is. As I argue throughout this book, the sonic episteme is a type of ideal theory. According to Charles Mills, ideal theory is defined by its approach to its object of study: it begins from how things *ought* to work in ideal (i.e., perfect) conditions, not from how things work in manifestly nonideal and imperfect daily existence.[69] The problem with ideal theory is that it naturalizes those existing imperfections and reinforces them rather than fixes them. Liberal approaches to equality are a classic example of this: treating everyone as already equal — because in the end everyone *should* be equal — reinforces existing inequalities rather than ameliorating them. Similarly, the sonic episteme uses an idealized concept of "sound" to pass off reinvestments in dominant institutions (the academy, white supremacy, etc.) as revolutions that overcome them. By situating my analysis of both scholarly and pop culture texts in the context of a nonideal and imperfect world structured by ongoing relations of domination and subordination, I use *a nonideal approach to theorizing sound and music.*

I am also indebted to the "phonographic" method of "thinking sound/sound thinking" Alexander Weheliye thematizes in his work on sonic Afromodernity. I discuss this method extensively in chapters 2–5, so I will briefly define it here. Just as DJs mix and crossfade between two tracks, phonographic analysis mixes and crossfades between disciplines, genres, and media. For example, Weheliye describes his project as "establish[ing] a dialogue between literary texts and popular culture . . . [that] eschews a strict opposition between popular culture and canonical forms of cultural expression . . . [and] involves using the insights of each field to critically reconfigure the other."[70] Like Weheliye, I use popular music studies and sound studies *as* methods for doing theory or philosophy. Beyoncé's and Rihanna's work aren't just examples of some theory or another; their works are theoretical texts, texts that let us theorize in ways that traditionally "philosophical" texts do not accommodate.[71] As someone trained in philosophy and speaking at least partially to philosophers, I aim in part to model a theoretical practice that is in genuine dialogue with popular music, popular music studies, and sound studies — fields with which philosophy has had little interaction as of this writing. Theoretical work

17

on sound and music must be nonideal and phonographic if it is to have any positive effect on social justice. I use this phonographic method in *The Sonic Episteme* because it allows me to theorize with and through specific sounds situated in sociohistorically local contexts and avoid idealized models of both sound and society.

My method is also grounded in Foucault's concept of epistemes, which I explained earlier. To argue that the sonic episteme exists, I need to show that widely differing theories, concepts, and objects of study manifest, embody, or otherwise exhibit common rules of formation, and that these rules have something to do with sound as acoustic resonance. Each of the chapters traces work by philosophers, economists, literary theorists, astrophysicists, data scientists, journalists, and others to prove that the objects of their study, the concepts they create, and the theories they build are unified by a common set of un-thematized rules or principles, and that these rules or principles can be accurately thematized under the rubric of acoustic resonance.

Overall, I aim for a method that is "undisciplined" in Christina Sharpe's sense.[72] My study spans philosophy, feminist theory, critical race theory, black studies, popular music studies, and sound studies in order to build a project that speaks to audiences from all these fields but ultimately avoids discussions of "how is this paper philosophy?" I'll address why that avoidance is important in chapter 3.

III. Overview of Chapters

I cannot give a comprehensive account of the sonic episteme in this book — that would make a very unwieldy volume. I have chosen to focus on constituents of the sonic episteme that both use acoustic resonance to model a central aspect of social or natural/material existence and have had significant impact across various academic disciplines or popular culture. Each of *The Sonic Episteme*'s chapters studies a different object to which acoustic resonance is applied: the market, political reality, material reality, subjectivity and personhood, and social and theoretical physics. All five chapters also examine alternatives to the chapter's respective dimension of the sonic episteme; the last four focus on phonographic approaches that model political reality, material reality, subjectivity and personhood, and the math behind social and theoretical physics on a concept of sound rooted in black feminist theory. These phonographic alternatives to the sonic episteme both prove that and suggest how people can theorize with and through sound without running into all the problems I identify with the sonic episteme.

The first chapter argues that Jacques Attali's 1977 book *Noise* uses acous-

18

tic resonance to model the math behind both the neoliberal market and the biopolitical concept of life in qualitative terms.[73] I unpack Attali's claim that the "laws of acoustics"[74] have the same underlying principle as neoliberal theories of the market and explain how this informs his book's (in)famous premise that music heralds the future. I then use Attali's theories of repetition and competition to explain the sonic episteme's characteristic methods of social exclusion: the domestication of noise and the politics of exception. Finally, I argue that Attali's concept of composition is an instance of the "the biopolitics of cool"[75] and consider "uncool" as a possible method of resistance to it. Taking Spandau Ballet's 1983 hit "True" and Taylor Swift's 2014 single "Shake It Off" as instances of "uncool," I show that biopolitical uncoolness is a form of inflexibility and nonadaptability. Though this inflexibility and nonadaptability read as uncool when white people perform them, they can also read as toxic and pathological attributes of nonwhite populations or non-liberal-democratic societies. I call these populations "exceptional" populations.

Moving from neoliberal political economy to neoliberal political ontology, chapter 2 studies theories and practices that adopt acoustic resonance as the basic unit of social reality and that use the purported difference between sound and text to mark their departure from classically liberal political ontologies. I focus on Jacques Rancière's account of postdemocratic consensus and Adriana Cavarero's and Fred Evans's theories of "vocal" politics because they all illustrate how notions of voice and universal envoicement can be used to create qualitative versions of the same relations of domination that neoliberalism creates quantitatively. According to Rancière, "postdemocratic" regimes use probabilistic statistics to model society and then translate that math into nonquantitative terms through ideas of harmony or moderation. Cavarero's and Evans's phenomenological approaches directly model society on acoustic resonance. Though all of these projects claim to overcome liberalism's use of social identities to exclude people from full personhood and give everyone equal access to "voice," they use the fact of (supposedly) universal inclusion as the foundation of a different kind of exclusion: the politics of exception. Building on Jonathan Sterne's theory of perceptual coding, I argue that political ontologies modeled on acoustic resonance adopt a type of perceptual coding:[76] they compress away frequencies that impede the efficient transmission of white supremacist capitalist patriarchy into the future. Rancière makes a similar claim in his critique of postdemocracy; I argue that his critique applies to all constituents of the sonic episteme. The second part of the chapter studies political ontologies that tune in to some of the frequencies the sonic episteme codes out of philosophers' "listening ears."[77] Building on philoso-

19

pher Devonya Havis's concept of "sounding," I identify a common move in black feminist thought: a code-switch that opens up possibilities masked by the original, hegemonic code.[78] Reading Rihanna's 2015 single "BBHMM" as an instance of sounding, I argue that sounding models dimensions of existence perceptually coded out of both classical and neoliberal concepts of personhood due to their association with black femininity. Sounding thus exhibits two key features of phonographic approaches to sound: the code-switch and the attunement to in-the-red frequencies.

Shifting focus from political ontology to new materialist ontologies, the third chapter considers cases where theorists in this tradition appeal to concepts of music, sound, and vibration to explain what matter is and how bits of matter interact. The work of Elizabeth Grosz, Jane Bennett, and Karen Barad is foundational to feminist new materialism.[79] Each of their projects uses acoustic resonance—framed as music (Grosz), vibration (Bennett), or diffraction (Barad)—as both a model for the basic unit of material reality (like an atom or subatomic particle) and a method of abstracting from that reality to philosophical concepts. Though they think these resonant abstractions liberate us from the problems baked into Western philosophy's traditional representationalist abstractions, such as identity-based social hierarchies, I will show that they use resonance to create qualitative versions of the same relations of domination and subordination that neoliberalism creates quantitatively. Building on Sara Ahmed's critique of new materialism's "founding gesture"[80] and critiques by women of color feminists such as Diana Leong and Zakkiyah Iman Jackson, I show how new materialism creates the same relations among philosophers and their theories that neoliberalism and biopolitics create in society—a politics of exception in which black people are the exceptional class. The last section of this chapter focuses on phonographic approaches to vibratory resonance. Cristiana Sharpe's theory of the wake, Ashon Crawley's notion of choreosonics, and the choreosonic sounds in Beyoncé's 2016 single "Hold Up" all develop ideas similar to new materialist concepts of vibratory resonance. For example, wake, like resonance or diffraction, is a pattern of pressure in a fluid. However, these phonographic approaches to vibratory resonance model a specific kind of materiality: the kinds that can't be efficiently transformed into private property that can legibly be "owned" by the discipline of philosophy. These are the same in-the-red frequencies that sounding's code-switch tunes into. Whereas new materialism uses acoustic resonance to hide the relations of domination that structure philosophy as a discipline behind claims of reform, these phonographic approaches to vibratory resonance, like Havis's concept of sounding, identify methods of abstraction

20

that are and will continue to be perceptually coded out of capital-P Philosophy because they don't efficiently reproduce those relations of domination.

Chapter 4 studies the sonic episteme's theory of selfhood and personhood.[81] Plato's concept of sophrosyne uses a music-math analogy to translate the geometric structure of the True[82] into nonquantitative terms people could put into practice in their everyday lives. In the twenty-first century, both academic and popular authors use an updated version of the ancient Greek concept of sophrosyne to translate statistical normalization into a qualitative concept of selfhood and personhood. And just as Plato's sophrosyne expresses a relation of subordination, neoliberal sophrosyne also enforces a relation of subordination: it grants personhood only to people whose contributions are consonant with and amplify overall distributions of personhood, property, and privilege. This is especially clear in attitudes about women's feminist voices. Updating Ann Carson's account of feminine sophrosyne in classical Greek literature, I argue that postfeminist patriarchy uses this updated concept of sophrosyne to police women. Women are expected to be loud and noisy, because this proves that patriarchy isn't silencing them anymore. However, voices that don't subordinate themselves to the myth of postfeminist inclusion (e.g., by pointing out ongoing sexism and racism) are condemned as immoderate and attributed the same flaws audio engineers attribute to overcompressed music. The final part of the chapter argues that Katherine McKittrick's concept of "demonic calculus" uses a music-math analogy grounded in a numeracy that doesn't subordinate itself to white supremacist patriarchal concepts of personhood and thus tunes in to the frequencies that neoliberal sophrosyne perceptually codes into the red. Identifying instances of demonic calculus in Beyoncé's 2016 visual album *Lemonade*, I explain how the music part of demonic calculus's music-math analogy works and show how *Lemonade* uses that music to articulate a concept of personhood that doesn't hinge on black women's subordination.

21

For Plato, sophrosyne didn't just apply to individuals; it also governed the city and the cosmos. Chapter 5 examines these aspects of the sonic episteme. Popular science accounts of social and cosmic harmony use updated versions of Plato's music-math analogy to translate the math data scientists use to model society and theoretical physicists use to model the universe into layperson terms. For example, when data scientist Alex Pentland says that the tools of big data can help governments and corporations "design for harmony,"[83] he's using concepts of acoustic resonance to translate the math data scientists use to measure and manipulate people's behaviors — the "rhythm[s] of [people's] daily habits" or "the rhythms of a city" — into nonquantitative terms.[84] Pop science accounts of string theory use the same music-math analogy. String theory blends macrocosmic theories of general relativity with microcosmic theories of quantum mechanics; it's a comprehensive cosmology, a "theory of everything" in the universe. It claims that the fundamental unit of existence is a one-dimensional, looped, vibrating string. Scientists use probabilistic equations to describe strings' vibrations. In order to translate that math into terms a lay audience can understand, writers such as Brian Greene and Stephon Alexander turn to musical analogies. However, because they explicitly refer to Pythagorean accounts of cosmic harmony, their central analogy is actually a *dis*analogy between two different kinds of mathematical relationships—Pythagorean ratios and probabilities. These pop science accounts of social and cosmic harmony adopt acoustic resonance as an analogy for the math neoliberalism and biopolitics use to create social inequalities. Whereas Pentland is explicit that he's using that math to manipulate people so their behaviors fit within the norms established by corporations or states, string theory seems entirely apolitical. However, it presents the mathematical relationships neoliberal biopolitics uses to structure society as facts about the fundamental structure of the universe, thus naturalizing the tools and techniques Pentland and others use to create unequal social relations. The final section of the chapter addresses a phonographic approach to this same music-math analogy. Building on earlier analyses of McKittrick and Weheliye, I show that their coauthored analysis of the TR-808 uses the choreosonic dimensions of twentieth- and twenty-first-century hip-hop and R&B as models for maths that count the mathematical relationships in Pentlandian idea flow (and neoliberal biopolitics more generally) out differently. Their work is evidence that the problem with the sonic episteme isn't that it uses sound to translate math into qualitative terms but rather with the specific kind of mathematical relationships acoustic resonance translates.

In the end, this book is about better and worse ways of using sound as the kind of rule or principle that organizes an episteme. At its worst, it's a misapprehension or sleight that underwrites the functioning of a particular mode of systemic social inequity; at its best it centers the modes of abstraction people have developed as practices for living under and in response to systemic oppression. The sonic episteme is an instance of the former; the phonographies I track from chapters 2–5 are instances of the latter.

1

Neoliberal *Noise* and the Biopolitics of (Un)Cool

Acoustic Resonance as Political Economy

Built on samples of English minimalist composer Michael Nyman's 1983 "Chasing Sheep Is Best Left to Shepherds,"[1] the (also English) Pet Shop Boys' 2013 single "Love Is a Bourgeois Construct" is about Englishness as much as it is about the sonic similarities between seventeenth-century music and contemporary EDM (hint: the similarity is in those arpeggios).[2] It uses early twenty-first-century EDM-pop clichés to comment on the similarly clichéd attitudes of the neoliberal English bourgeoisie. Like the lyrics, which skewer the overeducated middle classes' failed attempts at avant-garde posturing (such as adopting vaguely Marxist critiques of marriage as a property relation), the song's music snarks that then-recent trends toward noisy sonic maximalism are also instances of the mainstream trying and failing to pull off an avant-garde stance. More precisely, the music argues that what was formerly avant-garde is now at the center of neoliberal capitalism.

This is most clearly stated in the song's main climax, which is a twelve-bar soar starting around the 5:15 mark. Soars build tension with a Zeno's-paradox-like intensification of rhythmic events (like drum hits or handclaps) that push the number of events per second either to or implicitly past the threshold of human hearing; maximizing damage makes the return to order on the next downbeat all the more pleasurable.[3] Soars thus mimic neoliberal capitalism's technique of recycling noise and damage into profit and pleasure, which David Harvey calls "creative destruction."[4] The soar for "Love" has three four-bar sections. The first section begins with some stuttered and distorted treble synths, and then in the last two beats of the fourth measure, we hear some lyrics, a stuttered "bourgeoi-bourgeoi→," which carries us over to the "sssssie" on the downbeat of the next section. In this second four-bar chunk, "bourgeois-bourgeoisssssie" happens on each measure, and there is a snare beating out quarter notes throughout this section; this makes the second section's vocals and percussion more rhythmically intense than the first sections. This intensity builds in the third four-bar section, which is subdivided into two two-bar parts. The first subsection double-times the snare, putting it on eighth notes, and shortens the lyrics to "-sssie," which is further stuttered, fragmented, and glitched. The second subsection continues to distort the lyrics but turns up the snare to sixteenth notes. Then, on the last two beats of the final measure, we get a "bourgeoi-bourgeoi-" as a drop that lands us hard on the "-ssssie" on the downbeat of bridge reprise. All the soar's noisy sonic damage both occurs to and is accompanied by vocals that say "bourgeoisie."

Pet Shop Boys use the correlation between noisy damage and "bourgeoisie" to snarkily comment on the status of aesthetic noise and sonic damage in the early twenty-first century: though this sort of distortion was the heart of twentieth-century avant-garde aesthetics, and though contemporary middlebrow audiences might still like to feel like that sort of noise is challenging and oppositional, that noise is what fuels neoliberal modes of aesthetic and economic production.[5] Nowadays, noisy sonic distortion is the most bourgeois thing ever.

———

French economist Jacques Attali made this point thirty-six years earlier in his 1977 book *Noise: The Political Economy of Music*. In a 1983 interview about the book with Fredric Jameson and Brian Massumi, Attali points out the fact that both economists and composers have figured out how to transform statistical and sonic noise from an impediment into a resource.[6] He explains:

> A system of representation closely linked to a harmonizing conception of the "invisible hand," a conception of the ensemble of social life as a kind of harmony (and also a certain notion of value as stable and identifiable) — these older notions now begin to recede behind a more properly statistical vision of reality, a macrostatistical and global, aleatory

view, in terms of probabilities and statistical groups. This last seems to me organically related to that whole dimension of non-harmonic music (I don't know what else to call this) which involves the introduction of new rules and in particular those of chance; and that in turn relates back to the new conceptions of macrophysics (Boltzmann is after all a rough contemporary of Schoenberg, give or take a few years), and that is in its turn the same kind of theorizing one finds in macroeconomics — namely, statistical and global conceptions of the movement of masses and of mass production.[7]

These two long sentences argue that postwar macroeconomics and avant-garde composition both adopt a "statistical vision of reality" that has something to do with chance ("aleatory") and probabilities. In this vision, noise or error isn't an impediment to be eliminated (e.g., harmonized away by some sort of invisible hand or perfect authentic cadence) but something that can be accounted for and rendered productive. From Schaeffer's musique concrète to Reich's gradual processes, lots of midcentury compositions incorporate literal sonic noise and chance processes. But so does statistics, which uses the Gaussian normal curve, more commonly called a bell curve, to find regular patterns among noisy data. In 1801, astronomer and mathematician Carl Friedrich Gauss developed the mathematical function we now know as the normal curve. Gauss was trying to predict where in the sky a newly discovered planet would return into view.[8] Building on Galileo's 1632 observation that all measurements have errors, but that "small errors occur more frequently than large errors,"[9] Gauss developed a formula for calculating the normal distribution of errors. From this normal distribution, he could then infer that the most "normal" measurement was the one whose accuracy was most probable. So error didn't impede his knowledge but facilitated it — averaging out errors is what helped Gauss guess where the supposed planet would reappear from behind the sun. In 1935, mathematician Adolphe Quetelet demonstrated that the error distributions physicists used to measure astronomical relationships could also be used to measure the presence of a particular variable across a population, thus creating the idea of "social physics."[10] In the 1870s, the Gaussian curve came to be known as the "normal" curve when people like C. S. Peirce and, notably, eugenicist Francis Galton began using this language.[11] Normal curves turned error and imprecise measurement into something knowable and controllable. Attali's point in the long quote above is that in the late twentieth century, both statistics-based sciences like macroeconomics and avant-garde composition turn noise into a feature rather than a bug.

25

In *Noise* Attali takes this claim about the commonality between macro-economic statistics and avant-garde composition further. There, he argues that their similar approaches to noise result from a shared underlying principle or protocol: "non-harmonic music"[12] makes "the laws of acoustics . . . the mode of production of a new sound matter" and, in so doing, "displays all of the characteristics of the technocracy managing the great machines of the repetitive [i.e., neoliberal] economy."[13] The basic unit of this technocracy is the normalized statistical distribution, which is a mathematical tool that turns chance occurrences into probabilistic forecasts (e.g., Gauss's forecast of where the planet would appear in the sky). Attali's claim here is that *the mathematical principles behind neoliberal models of the market are the same as the basic principles of the physics of sound,* which he calls "the laws of acoustics."

Writing in 2016, N. Adriana Knouf makes a similar claim about the relationship between the math behind music and the math behind neoliberal markets. According to Knouf, twenty-first-century musicians and sound artists use algorithmic tools to create pieces "via processes that are similar to those of [neoliberal economist Friedrich] Hayek's market."[14] Benefiting from more than thirty years of advancements in computing and data analytics, post-millennial composers use updated versions of the same math Attali identified as the common root of both acoustics and neoliberal models of the market. This is why Knouf can hear resemblances between generative compositions and one of the foundational theories of neoliberal market logics. And those resemblances, she argues, help sound and music translate those complex quantitative relationships into sensory and affective terms.[15] Knouf is not the only theorist to use sound as a metaphor for the math behind neoliberal political economy. For example, security studies scholar Robert Keohane argues that the ideal of a "harmony of interests" is key to neoliberal approaches to international diplomacy,[16] and the idea of harmony appears throughout Katharyne Mitchell's book *Crossing the Neoliberal Line.* Drawing analogies between the way sounds work and the way neoliberal markets work, these theories participate in the sonic episteme.

Though Attali is not the only person to compare sounds to neoliberal markets, his account is both the most well-developed and the most well-known.[17] Thus, I use *Noise* to explain how the sonic episteme manifests in theories of political economy. Attali doesn't use the language of neoliberalism, so the first part of the chapter makes the case that *Noise*—in particular, the chapter on "repetition"—is about neoliberalism. Though he claims that "repetition appears at the end of the nineteenth century with the advent of recording . . . as the herald of a new stage in the organization of capitalism, that of the repetitive mass production of all social relations,"[18] I will show that his concept of repetition also accounts for many key features of neoliberalism Michel Foucault identifies in *The Birth of Biopolitics*, such as deregulation, the systematization of aleatory events through statistical forecasting, human capital, and financialization (M-M1 intensification), and at the same time it connects this political economy to the biopolitical management of life. The political economy of repetition is the political economy of neoliberalism, so Attali's aforementioned claim that repetition takes the "laws of acoustics" as its organizing logic means that neoliberal political economy and acoustic resonant sound behave identically—because they're following the same fundamental principle(s). *Noise* uses acoustic resonance to translate that math into nonquantitative terms. That makes it a constituent of the sonic episteme.

The sonic episteme claims that acoustic resonance fixes the conceptual and political problems with traditional methods of philosophical abstraction. However, applying these mathematical principles to a society already organized by centuries of systemic domination doesn't fix that domination; it updates and intensifies it. *Noise* illustrates how the sonic episteme doubles down on the problems it claims to solve. In the second part of this chapter, I show that Attali's proposed solution to everything that's wrong with "repetition"— which he calls "composition"—actually makes these problems worse. Attali's notion of composition is an instance of what philosopher Shannon Winnubst calls the biopolitics of cool.[19] A "claim to nonconformity as highly valued, preferred social posture,"[20] "cool" makes the avant-garde the new normal where everyone in the bourgeois mainstream (not just elites) is expected to cut a new leading edge. Instead of disrupting hegemonic social structures, noisy transgression feeds them. Neoliberalism domesticates noise and makes it profitable.

In the final part of the chapter, I consider alternatives to composition and the biopolitics of cool. If "cool" is no longer subversive, might blandly regularized averageness be a way to undermine neoliberal imperatives to cultivate and exploit excess? Or is uncool available only to subjects whose inflexibility and nonadaptability will be seen as an individual choice, not a group-based pathology? Is "uncool" a viable option only for white people—and thus not really a counter-hegemonic practice at all? To address these questions, I consider two musical performances of white "uncool": Spandau Ballet's "True" and Taylor Swift's "Shake It Off."[21] Each song performs that uncool in a distinct fashion: "True" via faux-critical inflexibility, and "Shake It Off" through resiliently authentic personal unbranding. Even though both of these practices appear to reject imperatives to entrepreneurial optimization and self-investment, they are both investments in whiteness and white supremacy—producing white-

27

ness maybe not as "property" per se but as financialized capital. The biopolitics of cool turns what would otherwise be bad investments into mechanisms for building whiteness as a kind of human capital. As in the book's subsequent chapters, the last section of this chapter looks to pop music for potential alternatives to the aspects of the sonic episteme elaborated in the first part of the chapter. Whereas those alternatives tune in to what the sonic episteme perceptually codes out of circulation and into the red, these "uncool" practices amplify the relations of domination and subordination that neoliberal biopolitics uses normalized statistical distributions to create and maintain. That's why "True" and "Shake It Off" ultimately fail as alternatives to the sonic episteme.

I. Attali, Foucault, and Acoustic Resonance as Neoliberal Market Logic

Neoliberalism's definitive feature is its assumption that everything, even and especially noneconomic activities like love or parenting, is a private market. Attali also identifies this as a signature feature of the political economy of repetition: "the few aspects of life that still remain noncommercialized now [in 1977] (nationality, love, life, death) will in the future become trapped in exchange."[22] So, what he calls repetition shares this key feature of neoliberalism: the transformation of everything into a private market. However, his use of the word "exchange" here reveals that though the economists Michel Foucault identifies as the primary theorists of neoliberalism are careful to distinguish between industrial mass production and neoliberal financialization, Attali is less careful and uses the term "repetition" to refer to both.[23] Perhaps this is because he understands statistical models of the market as the result of other mathematical models' inability to keep pace with ever-intensifying mass production. According to Attali, the ever-expanding mass production of commodities creates so much stuff that capitalism finally exhausts additive and multiplicative models of expansion. To grow the economy (i.e., extract further surplus value), it must shift to algorithmic models of intensification. "Combinatorics" (his term for modernity's multiplicative model of expansion), Attali argues, "gives way to *statistics* . . . and *probability*" (*Noise* 65) or, as Foucault puts it, to "analytics."[24] Because Attali compares the laws of acoustics to the math behind these statistics and probabilities, my analysis here focuses on the instances where Attali uses "repetition" to theorize entrepreneurial markets, forecasting, and financialization. From this perspective, Attali's concept of repetition exhibits the key features Foucault attributes to neoliberal biopolitics: the shift from exchange to competition (or, in Attali's terms, from representation to repetition), a foundation in probabilistic statistics, a concept of

28

life modeled on neoliberal market logic, deregulation, financialization, and human capital.[25]

1. From Exchange to Competition

In *The Birth of Biopolitics*, Foucault argues that the difference between classical liberalism and neoliberalism is marked by a change in the way markets are understood, namely, "a shift from exchange to competition in the principle of the market."[26] Exchange measures the equivalence among objects that are traded. For example, Marx argues that the exchange value of an object is expressed in money, which is the medium in which equivalences among materially incomparable things can be expressed.[27] Instead of equivalences, competition "measure[s] economic magnitudes":[28] financialization *compounds* the value of money, making money itself more intensely valuable.[29] Arguing that late twentieth-century "science would no longer be the study of conflicts between representations, but rather the analysis of processes of repetition," Attali notes a similar shift (*Noise* 89). Equivalence is a conflict between representations — the commodity form, for example, is a representation of exchange value, just as "money" is "a supposedly stable sign of equivalence" (*Noise* 101). At issue in such conflicts is whether or not representations accurately correspond to one another and to the things they represent. Processes of repetition, on the other hand, are measured by instruments like record charts or the Dow or NASDAQ indices or birth rates — they express relative magnitudes and frequencies, not correspondences. Whether framed as a shift from exchange to competition or from representation to repetition, the underlying idea is the same: the difference between classical and neoliberalism comes down to a difference in the basic mathematical principle one uses to model the market: equivalence or magnitude. Both Attali and Foucault agree that neoliberalism/repetition takes magnitude or frequency as the basic unit of reality. And to calculate relationships among these basic units, you need a specific kind of math: probabilistic statistics.

2. Probabilistic Statistics

Both Foucault's account of neoliberalism and Attali's account of repetition identify the statistically calculated probability ratio that expresses the *frequency* of one phenomenon with respect to another phenomenon as the thing that is distinctive to and definitive of neoliberalism/repetition. For example, Foucault argues that "the mechanisms introduced by biopolitics include forecasts, statistical estimates, and overall measures";[30] similarly, Attali describes repetition as a "macrostatistical and global, aleatory view, in terms of probabilities and statistical groups."[31] (As I will discuss later in this chapter, the frequency ratio is the thing Attali thinks the neoliberal market has in common with acoustically resonant sound.) Attali's repetition and Foucault's neoliberal biopolitics use the same mathematical tool to measure and manage society; at the level of technique, they are analogous if not identical.

Tracking patterns of chance occurrences across large samples, these statistical tools transform what appears aleatory at the micro level into relatively consistent and predictable macro-level rates. As Foucault explains, "the field of biopolitics also includes accidents, infirmities, and various anomalies," phenomena "that are aleatory and unpredictable when taken in themselves or individually, but which, at the collective level, display constants that are easy, or at least possible, to establish."[32] Or, as Attali explains, the individual actor, "whatever he does, he is no more than an aleatory element in a statistical law. Even if in appearance everything is a possibility for him, on the average his behavior obeys specifiable, abstract, ineluctable functional laws."[33] Whereas individual decisions can always deviate from expectations, these individual deviations can be normalized when taken in aggregate; comparing all individuals, it's possible to establish a normal or regular rate of deviation. Instead of policing individual deviations, repetition/neoliberal biopolitics tries to maintain a consistent rate of deviation across society. Because it allows noise and deviation to exist, repetition *appears* less oppressive than law or discipline when actually it's just oppressive in a different way.

The so-called "look-ahead" limiter (a digital audio processing tool) is a good metaphor here: designed to limit the gain or amplitude of sound frequencies in the mixing of an audio track, these limiters don't actually look ahead to compensate for future frequency deviations. Rather, they split the track in two, subordinating the part with the higher amplitudes to the part with the lower amplitudes, "limiting" the gain by toning the most unruly frequencies down to the level or norm set by the limiting part of the track. Just as a look-ahead limiter doesn't look ahead but instead creates a relationship of subordination, statistical models of the neoliberal market don't predict irregularities to compensate for them ahead of time so much as they create relationships of subordination that always produce the same outcomes, no matter what irregularities occur. In both the look-ahead limiter and in neoliberalism's statistical forecasts, relationships of subordination "compensate for variations within this general population and its aleatory field."[34] Instead of eliminating or preventing deviations from happening, they use relationships of subordination to funnel resources to the most highly probable — that is, normal —

events, thus creating a feedback loop in which the norm reproduces itself as normal (and this is a constant throughout the sonic episteme).

Attali points to this feedback loop in his discussion of record charts. He argues that "hit parades" are taken as "a prediction of future success" of the records they list (*Noise* 107). But they only seem predictive because they're rigged to produce the success they claim to predict. A record "has 'value' in the eyes of the listeners, then, by virtue of the ranking to which they think they contributed. When, as usually happens, they buy in quantities proportional to the rankings, they justify them, bringing the process full circle" (*Noise* 107).[35] Rankings influence consumer behavior, shaping purchasing patterns to reflect the rankings. Communications studies scholar and pop music critic Eric Harvey has made a similar observation. He calls the Top 40 chart "a primitive music recommendation algorithm" targeted not at individual listeners but at radio program directors, who use it to decide what to play.[36] Because it influences the programming on media it claims to merely track, the Top 40 record chart is a feedback loop that reproduces the rank ordering it claims to merely describe. Like the Top 40, the statistical forecasts behind Attali's repetition and Foucault's neoliberal biopolitics don't predict the future so much as remake the present in the image of the norm.[37] Though this math may seem more accommodating of chance, noise, and individual deviance than traditional models of social organization, it actually creates new variations on the same relations of subordination conventionally maintained by policing those things. As I mentioned earlier in this chapter, Attali identifies that math as the common foundation of both the laws of acoustics and the neoliberal idea of the market. It is also the foundation of a biopolitical concept of life.

3. Life

According to Foucault, "American neo-liberalism seeks . . . to extend the rationality of the market . . . to domains which are not exclusively or not primarily economic: the family and the birth rate, for example."[38] *Neoliberal* biopolitics (as opposed to mass biopolitics) treats life itself as a market.[39] Centering biological life as a privileged field of "repetitive" knowledge and regulation, Attali's analysis of repetition does just this. "After music," he argues, "the biological sciences were the first to tackle this problem" of understanding everything as a deregulated market (*Noise* 89). The shift from representation to repetition appears, in the life sciences, when "biology replaces mechanics" (*Noise* 89). The latter approach focuses on the regulated, mechanistic functioning of individual bodies (anatomy); the former focuses on the deregulated health and flourishing of populations (epidemiology, genetics). Like biopolitics, which is "a technology in which bodies are replaced by general biological processes,"[40] Attali's biology doesn't study lives but "the *conditions* of the *replication of life*" (i.e., health).[41]

Even though its aim is to maximize life, the discourse of health will require, as both Foucault and Attali claim, "killing others to protect oneself."[42] This isn't about eliminating external contaminants but about managing what Foucault calls "threats born of and in its own body."[43] This manifests not only in Nazi racism, which is Foucault's example, but also avant-garde art music, in which, as Attali explains, "*the musical ideal then almost becomes an ideal of health*: quality, purity, the elimination of noises."[44] According to Attali, this ideal of musical health eliminates noise by recycling "the innocuous chatter of recuperable cries" into signal (*Noise* 124). Echoing David Harvey's description of neoliberalism as "creative destruction," he argues that "noise is life, and the *destruction* of the old codes in the commodity is perhaps the necessary condition for real *creativity*" (*Noise* 122; emphasis added). This ideal of health is neoliberal because it understands noise not as a threat to be excluded or prevented but as a type of "recuperable" abnormality that induces society itself to adapt and evolve for greater efficiency and success (*Noise* 124). For example, Attali argues that "when Cage opens the door to the concert hall to let the noise of street in, he is *regenerating* all of music."[45] The deregulated noisiness of Cage's 4'33" didn't kill music, it made it stronger. Repetition transforms otherwise destructive noises into opportunities for growth and success.

Attali's examples of musical and economic repetition share biopolitical liberalism's ideas of life and health, ideas that are modeled on neoliberal markets. Neoliberal markets are distinguished not only by their privileging of entrepreneurial competition over exchange but also by their emphasis on deregulation and financialization, which I discuss in the next two subsections.

4. Deregulation

Arguing that "the present state of music theory in the West is tied, through its discourse, to the ideological reorganization necessitated by the emplacement of repetition," Attali points to their shared approach to authority: they deregulate foreground activity but use well-controlled background conditions to limit the kinds of activities that can emerge in that foreground, thus creating a "simulacrum of nonpower" (*Noise* 112, 114).

In music, this appears in the form of the open work. Instead of specifying the precise sounds to be performed, open works are recipes or programs for sound-generating practices or "creative emergence" (*Noise* 114). Citing John Cage, Attali argues that such works "'facilitate the process so that anything can happen'" (*Noise* 114). Cage's *Imaginary Landscape No. 4*, for example, is a set of instructions for generating a musical work from radios. The surface-level sounds appear to be randomly generated — what we actually hear depends on the programming schedules of the specific stations available in a particular location, how the individual performers interpret the instructions, the idiosyncrasies of the radios with which they are performing, and so on. None of those factors are *explicitly* controlled for in the composition itself. But this doesn't mean they are totally random and free from control. The composition regulates the *background conditions* for sound production, so that "the most formal order, the most precise and rigorous directing, are masked behind a system evocative of autonomy and chance."[46] The aleatory process is limited by the parameters set out by the background conditions in and on which the process runs. As in neoliberal political economy, where "governmental intervention" addresses "the conditions of the existence of the market,"[47] composers of open works intervene in the condition of existence of sounds. Hiding tight control behind surface-level deregulation, open works thus create the illusion of a complete free-for-all.

Attali uses the metaphor of an audio synthesizer to explain the illusory character of this freedom. In the "free market, the only freedom left is that of the *synthesizer*: to combine preestablished programs" (*Noise* 114). Though a synthesizer is able to generate a much larger range of sounds than an analog instrument, this range extends only as far as the limitations of the hardware and software one uses. Patches, cables, speakers, and so on — these background conditions regulate the process of sound production itself. Or, as Attali puts it, "power is incorporated into the very process of the selection of repeatable molds" (*Noise* 90). Repetition, like neoliberalism, deregulates individual choices while constantly and carefully controlling the conditions within which people make those decisions. Deregulation actually doubles down on coercion and control.

Attali uses these musical examples as metaphors for repetition's political economy. So, to the extent they exhibit deregulation, so does repetition. Deregulation is one definitive feature of neoliberal markets, so this is further evidence Attali uses "repetition" to refer to what we now generally call "neoliberalism." Financialization is another definitive feature of neoliberal markets that Attali discusses in *Noise*, though with a very different vocabulary than contemporary scholarship on neoliberalism. As I will show in the next section, his discussions of financialized intensification and entrepreneurial investment foreground the mathematical relationship he claims is common to both neoliberal economics and the laws of acoustics.

33

5. Recorded Music: Financialization and Human Capital

Arguing that "repetition appears at the end of the nineteenth century with the advent of recording," Attali thinks the record industry is "the herald of a new stage in the organization of capitalism" (*Noise* 32) defined by "stockpiling" (124). Analyzing Attali's discussions of both record charts and record collecting, I will prove that "stockpiling" is Attali's term for what contemporary scholarship on neoliberalism generally refers to as financialization. First, I'll argue that his claim that "hit parades" illustrate how "the commodity could also disappear," to be replaced by the "stockpile" of money (*Noise* 106, 130), marks the shift from an economy based on the *exchange* of commodities (M-C-M1, or money-commodity-money) to one based on the direct *intensification* of money (M-M1, or money-money) through financialized speculation.[48] Second, I will show that his account of recordings as stockpiles of "use-time" reimagines labor-time as a form of human capital.

a. Financialization

Neoliberalism upgrades classical political economy's concept of the market: it makes it both more efficient and more well-suited to a material context where expansion is exhausted (there's nowhere else to expand to) and investment is the most efficient way to generate surplus value. Foucault describes it as the shift from commodity exchange to entrepreneurial competition; in more Marxist language, it's the shift from M-C-M exchange to M-M1 financialization. Commodification invests time and value in exchangeable objects; financialization invests in time and value themselves. As Jeffrey Nealon explains,

> Finance and credit capital skips a step, and its formula might be written as M-M1. In other words, an increase in finance capital requires no direct or overt mediation by a commodity or service: no actual goods or services are required to represent or serve as a placeholder for the abstract value invested in money; and no labour power is required to account for the transformation or generation of surplus value as profit.[49]

Financialization generates surplus value by speculating on value itself (for example, bets on whether the price of bundled subprime mortgages will rise or fall, going into debt for postsecondary education on the assumption that it will increase your human capital). Investment, not exchange or labor, is its main technique. With the commodity out of the value-generating equation, value feeds back or compounds upon itself.

As "the prime movers of the repetitive economy," "hit parades" are instruments that financialize the value of records (*Noise* 106). Tracking both the time invested in a track (the human capital spent in listening) and the rate of its circulation on the market, they measure the intensity of audience investment in a track. Value doesn't express useful qualities or compare quantities but measures the *intensity and velocity* of investment. In this way, record charts aren't that different from the DOW, CAC 40, or FTSE: "the hit parade system" is a "public display of the *velocity of exchange*."[50] This is why Attali thinks that "the hit parade is not unique to music" (*Noise* 108) but applies as well to the general logic of repetitive political economy.

b. Human Capital

Though musical recordings can be and are commodified, Attali argues that record collections exhibit a different relation to time and value than commodities do. Commodities translate the *labor*-time deposited in them into exchange value. Recordings, on the other hand, "transfor[m] *use*-time," the time it takes to listen to a record, "into a stockpileable object" (*Noise* 126). Commodities materialize labor; record collections stockpile capital. "People buy more records than they can listen to. They stockpile what they want to find the time to hear" (101). The point of stockpiling is that you don't have to actually *listen* to the record to benefit from its value; stockpiling compounds use-time on its own, with no listening labor necessary. The payoff from curating a record collection isn't managing the fetish-value of the records, their "object-related differences," as Attali puts it;[51] rather, the point is to increase the amount of use-time at your disposal, augmenting the time you've invested in cultivating yourself. In this way, stockpiles of use-time are analogous to investments in human capital: they're repositories of all the time you might have to do something, to labor on yourself, to cultivate an appropriately branded self through work that superficially looks like leisure. Piles of use-time etched in vinyl, record collections are ways to hoard the time you'd spend cultivating your cultural and intellectual human capital by listening, say, to the canonical Slits album *Cut*, or the newest Record Store Day exclusive release from your favorite band nobody's heard of yet.

Attali's theory of stockpiled use-time strongly echoes contemporary theories of human capital. For example, Rob Horning argues that the neoliberal "self is reconceived as a stock of capital," and that the value of this stock "manifests qualitatively as "cool."[52] Though Horning doesn't explicitly use the term "use-time" in his account of cool, he describes something quite like it: This "stock . . . measured in terms of 'attention,'" manifests affectively as "the

35

amorphous quality called 'cool.'" Thus, "we must view it [cool] . . . as something countable in media-exposure minutes . . . [or] standardized units, that our significance to society could be measured in."[53] A measure of the relative amount and intensity of time people spend paying attention to you (or, for example, your social media profile), "cool" is a qualitative metric for the use-time other people invest in your capital. I will return to this concept of cool later in the chapter; for now I'll just note that Attali's claim that record collections stockpile use-time refers to the same aspect of human capital accumulation as Horning's theory of "cool."

Attali uses "repetition" to describe many definitive features of neoliberal biopolitics: competition, probabilistic statistics, a marketized concept of life, deregulation, financialization, and human capital. Even though he doesn't understand his own project in quite these terms, Attali's repetition is nevertheless a quasi-Foucauldian notion of neoliberal biopolitics. Thus, his claim that the repetitive economy and the "laws of acoustics" are grounded in the same underlying mathematical principle is also a claim about neoliberalism. This makes *Noise* an example of the sonic episteme: it models neoliberal markets and biopolitical life on acoustically resonant sound. Though there are a lot of overstated or overly speculative claims in *Noise*, this isn't one of them. The basic mathematical components of both sound waves and neoliberal markets are, in fact, the same. As Shannon Winnubst explains, "the ratio-calculative normativity that Foucault locates in neoliberal theorists," treats "the norm as number, and especially as ratio."[54] As I discussed in the introduction, statistical normalization and acoustic resonance both rely on the same fundamental mathematical principle: the frequency ratio. Neoliberal political economy treats that mathematical principle as the elemental unit of the market. That common principle is what Attali is pointing to when he compares the laws of acoustics to neoliberal economic theory. Like many of the constituents of the sonic episteme, Attali uses acoustic resonance to translate the math behind neoliberal biopolitics into nonquantitative terms.

That music-math analogy is what makes *Noise* a constituent of the sonic episteme. It is also the crux of the book's main argument about the predictive power of music. Situating *Noise* in the sonic episteme clarifies what exactly this puzzling claim actually means. For as influential as *Noise* has been, most scholars have sidestepped its central claim, that "music is prophecy" and "our music foretells our future" (11). And they've done so for a good reason. The claim feels rather undersupported and overreaching; Attali asserts that music anticipates or foreshadows social change, but he doesn't seem to provide anything more solid than correlations as evidence. For example, Eric Drott thinks "the book never fully spells out the mechanisms by which music performs its prophetic function."[55] Drott is not entirely correct. Attali does spell out this mechanism, though in a somewhat circular argument. *Noise*'s opening premise—that music is predictive—assumes the conclusion of the "repetition" chapter: if the laws of acoustics are analogs of the probabilistic forecasts that neoliberal economists use to model the market, then sounds are also probabilistic models. Attali thinks music is a probabilistic forecast.[56]

For Attali, music is an algorithm that predicts where society will go next: like big data number crunching, "explores, much faster than material reality can, the entire range of possibilities in a given code" and figures out which is most probable (*Noise* 11). Writing in 2014, Attali further explains that this ability to crunch variables and determine the most probable outcome is what makes music similar to finance: "We could also explore the reason why music could be seen as predictive: as an immaterial activity, it explores more rapidly than any other the realm of potentials. In that sense, it is not far from another quasi immaterial activity, finance, which is also very often an excellent predictive tool."[57] He directly connects music's predictive ability to the probabilistic statistics used in contemporary finance. In a 2014 lecture titled "Music as a Predictive Science," Attali repeatedly refers to his project in *Noise* as "forecasting." Forecasting is the same term Nate Silver uses to describe what big data analytics does. In a sense, Attali scooped Silver by more than thirty years; *Noise* uses music in the same way that Silver's *The Signal and the Noise* uses data. Attali thinks both music and statistical forecasts like the ones used in twenty-first-century finance and big data are made of the same stuff, so music is *predictive* in the sense that Amazon's recommendation bot is predictive.[58] To be clear: *I'm* not arguing that music really is predictive—Attali is, but I'm not. What I am arguing is that Attali *believes* that music is predictive, and he grounds that belief in the music-math analogy he draws in *Noise*. This is widely and rightly taken to be the point where *Noise* jumps the shark into pseudo-rationality: music is no better suited to predict the future than astrology is. Forecasting is necessarily pseudo-rational (for example, because historical moments aren't repeatable, you can't repeat a forecast to confirm the accuracy of results).[59] Attali's method seems obviously outlandish because it, unlike big data forecasting, can't hide behind the mantle of scientific objectivity.

Finance capitalism, statistical forecasts, and acoustically resonant sound—according to Attali, they are all variations on the same underlying mathematical principle: frequency ratios. *Noise* is a constituent of the sonic episteme because it uses acoustic resonance to translate that math into non-quantitative terms. And, like the other constituents of the sonic episteme I study in this book, *Noise*'s proposed solution to the philosophical and political problems it inherits from European modernity doesn't fix those problems so much as remake them for better compatibility with the tools and techniques neoliberal biopolitics uses to manage and police social inequities.

II. The Biopolitics of (Un)Cool

Noise concludes with a chapter that proposes to fix all the problems Attali identifies with repetition, like alienation. This supposed alternative to repetition, which Attali calls "composition," actually shares repetition's commitment to the basic principles of neoliberalism. This section argues that Attali's "competition" is an instance of what Shannon Winnubst calls "the biopolitics of cool" and considers two sound-based alternatives to it: Spandau Ballet's critical inflexibility (strict regulation as opposed to deregulation) and Taylor Swift's personal unbranding (intentionally devaluing one's human capital). In each case, I will show that these supposed alternatives actually intensify the very things from which they superficially liberate its practitioners, namely, reliance on neoliberal market logics on the one hand and biopolitical white supremacy on the other.

1. Attali's Composition and the Biopolitics of Cool

In the last chapter of *Noise*, Attali develops the concept of "composition" as a potential solution to the problems of alienated labor and repressed desire. For example, Attali argues that composition is "labor to be enjoyed in its own right, its time experienced, rather than labor performed for the sake of using or exchanging its outcome."[60] The catch is that alienation and repression are the very problems the original theorists of neoliberalism like Gary Becker and Theodore Schultz thought they fixed by reframing labor as human capital. As Foucault summarizes, human capital theory was an attempt to understand labor as a "human activity" and to "ensure that the worker is not present in the economic analysis as an object . . . but as an active economic subject."[61] This supposedly empowers the worker—they are no longer objectified via commodification; they are instead capitalists (owners of their own self as capital). All activity is a form of self-investment, not labor that one alienates for a wage. "Open[ing] the way for the worker's reappropriation of his work . . . not the recuperation of the product of his labor, but of his labor itself,"[62] composition also releases us from the need to alienate our labor. Like Foucault's entrepreneurial subject, "composition belongs to a political economy" in which "production melds with consumption," and activity "is not channeled into an object [i.e., alienated], but *invested*" in one's self and one's pleasure.[63] The entrepreneurial subject "produces his own satisfaction,"[64] just as Attali's composer produces *"one's own enjoyment."*[65] Attali's composition is basically a theory of human capital.

Just as human capital supposedly liberated labor from alienation, deregulation supposedly frees us from repression. Occurring amid "the disappearance of codes,"[66] composition is also deregulatory. The enjoyment it produces for self-reinvestment is not governed by some Marcusean performance principle; composition releases us from prohibitions, taboos, and the "repressive channeling of desire" that characterizes "the standardized products of today's variety shows, hit parades, and show businesses."[67] You produce your own idiosyncratic enjoyment unconstrained by norms or prohibitions. Like unalienated labor, unrepressed enjoyment sounds like a good thing until we think about how capitalism itself has evolved so that leisure and enjoyment themselves are not opposed to, but part of, surplus-value extraction. As Steven Shaviro explains,

> In Hardt and Negri's expanded redefinition of "subsumption," it isn't just labor that is subsumed by capital, but all aspects of personal and social life. This means that everything in life must now be seen as a kind of labor: we are still working, even when we consume, and even when we are asleep. Affects and feelings, linguistic abilities, modes of cooperation, forms of know-how and of explicit knowledge, expressions of desire: all these are appropriated and turned into sources of surplus value.[68]

Neoliberalism transforms leisure into something that is both an investment in individuals' human capital and a source of surplus value for others. Even though Attali thinks compositional self-investment is "noncommercial" (*Noise* 32), it mimics human capital's logic of entrepreneurial self-investment via real subsumption; it's commercial in a specifically neoliberal way.

Composition isn't an alternative to repetition/neoliberalism, just a different manifestation of the same underlying ideas and values. Like repetition, composition domesticates noise: it is modeled on musical practices that bring sonic noise and chance (statistical noise) into the compositional process, and it co-opts aesthetic transgression. For example, Attali argues that composition is possible because repetition ultimately turns everything into meaningless noise. "Now that the codes have been destroyed, including even the code of exchange in repetition . . . we are all condemned to silence unless we create our own relation with the world and try to tie other people into the meaning we thus create. That is what composing is" (*Noise* 134). Because there is no code

39

to tell us what to tune into as signal and what to tune out as noise, it's all just noise. Composing is the collective attempt to tune into and give voice to the signals that can emerge from all that noise.

To do this, composition uses the same deregulatory processes Attali attributes to neoliberal free-marketism and midcentury avant-garde composition. For example, it involves "inventing new codes, inventing the message at the same time as the language" and "creat[ing] its own *code* at the same time as the work" (*Noise* 143, 135; emphasis added). Attali's account echoes Steve Reich's idea that "musical processes . . . determine all the note-to-note (sound-to-sound) details and the over all form simultaneously."[69] In both accounts, the macro-level code emerges from generative, micro-level processes. These generative processes *appear* to be random because the composer is not *directly* choosing each individual musical event—the process is, as Reich puts it, "impersonal."[70] However, in this style of deregulated composition, "musical processes can give one a direct contact with the impersonal and also a kind of complete control. . . . By running this material through the process I completely control all that results."[71] Reich's musical processes—like swinging a microphone over a speaker to generate feedback, or setting two identical tape players to play the same looped recording in and out of phase—articulate the *background conditions* within which individual sonic events arise. As "program producers" (*Noise* 40), Reichean and Attalian composers are de/regulators; what they compose or arrange is the "code within which" sounds are generated. "Composition, nourished on the death of codes" (*Noise* 36), does not subvert neoliberal deregulation. "The permanent affirmation of the right to be different . . . the right to make *noise*, in other words, to create one's own code and work" and "the conquest of the right to make noise" (*Noise* 132), epitomizes neoliberal market logic by subsuming noisy transgression into the means of production.

Shannon Winnubst calls this "neoliberal aestheticization of difference" the "biopolitics of cool."[72] The biopolitics of cool is the deregulated cultivation of difference *as surplus value*.[73] In modernist aesthetics and politics, power compels conformity and rule-following; difference is transgressive, and transgression is the critical, oppositional, counter-hegemonic practice par excellence. In neoliberal aesthetics and politics, power is deregulatory; it requires people to transgress limits and assume risk. As Attali puts it, "statistical scientism results in the elimination of style and at the same time the demand for its impossible recovery, the search for an inimitable specificity" (*Noise* 115). Putting everyone on the same statistical continuity flattens difference, but it also incentivizes otherwise "normal" individuals to be as quirky, bizarre, unruly, and noisy as possible. What Jack Halberstam calls "gaga feminism" is an example of this. As Halberstam argues, gaga feminists

> celebrate variation, mutation, cooperation, transformation, deviance, perversion, and diversion. These modes of change, many of which carry negative connotations, actually name the way that people take the risks that are necessary to shove our inert social structures rudely into the path of the oncoming gagapocalypse. Making change means stepping off the beaten path, making detours around the usual, and distorting the everyday ideologies that go by the name of "truth" or "common sense."[74]

Treating gender trouble as the new normal, gaga feminism superficially "disrupts" patriarchy, allowing entrepreneurial postfeminist subjects to emerge from a milieu that is still, nevertheless, patriarchal. As with Lady Gaga herself, wild transgression — noisy, deregulated risk-taking as personal branding — increases one's cool human capital. Attali's composition is just another type of "cool" self-capitalization. Its deregulated, disruptive noises don't resist or avoid neoliberal market logics but feed them.

2. This Is the Sound of Uncool

How do you fight a power that feeds on anticonformism and noisemaking? Not by prosuming (i.e., consuming in a way that also produces surplus value), edgy self-expression, and not by continually reinvesting in your own coolness. In their "Youth Mode" manifesto, art collective K-Hole claim that resolute averageness — which they call "normcore" — is a viable alternative to "the neoliberal aestheticizing of difference"[75] and its imperative to push boundaries and test limits.

If massive corporations like Apple want employees and customers to "Think Different" because that's what maximizes profits, one refuses this mandate by being merely average. Normcore feels like the refusal of capitalism's mandate that we all be increasingly hardcore, just as chill is too low-key to be properly cool. Conformity (that is, the mastery of sameness) puts you on the fringes of a society focused on the deregulated production of "cool." Uncool is a way to opt out of the biopolitics of cool.[76]

J. Temperance builds a theory of aesthetic "uncoolness" from yacht rock, which is a late-1970s, early-1980s easy listening genre characterized by "intentionally trite lyrical themes and an almost nonchalant instrumental virtuosity or 'smoothness.'"[77] This aesthetic avoids all musical transgression — no indecent lyrics, no noisy, dissonant, or otherwise offensive sounds — and

If the rule is Think Different, being seen as normal is the scariest thing. (It means being returned to your boring suburban roots, being turned back into a pumpkin, exposed as unexceptional.) Which paradoxically makes normalcy ripe for the Mass Indie überelites to adopt as their own, confirming their status by showing how disposable the trappings of uniqueness are. The most different thing to do is to reject being different all together. When the fringes get more and more crowded, Mass Indie turns toward the middle. Having mastered difference, the truly cool attempt to master sameness.

smooths rock's edginess into noise-free, risk-free, "soft" or "lite" versions. From a modernist perspective, uncool is conservative: because it "open[s] up a space in which the popular was not subservient to the status games of cool-hunting and the disciplinary function of novelty[, . . .] yacht rock was counter-revolutionary."[78] Uncool music is popular without being edgy; its mainstream success and ubiquity is the opposite of avant-garde coolness. From a neoliberal perspective, minding limits is a way to deflect the imperative to push limits. Normal, middle-of-the-road, mainstream taste may be an antidote to cool's prescribed transgression. Mainstream success deflates "cool" cultural capital. Abandoning the avant-garde for the mainstream, the politics of uncool *seems* to have found alternatives to the biopolitics of cool.

Frequently included in the yacht rock canon, Spandau Ballet's "True" is a particularly revealing example of musical uncool.[79] Instead of sharpening punk and postpunk's cutting edge, Spandau Ballet blunted it; rather than provoke, oppose, and negate mainstream pop tastes, they seem to have reworked their aesthetic to accommodate these norms. And they accommodated them quite well — "True" was and is a massive hit, even though the song and the band are critically panned. Their work is commonly considered conformist music for yuppies. For example, their "nostalgic evocation of aristocratic elegance coupled with their smooth, almost un-expressive music"[80] and their "rejection of the truculent politics of negation and social realism evidenced by the Sex Pistols and the Clash" leads people to accuse them of "kitsch foppery"[81] and "soft romanticism."[82] "Un-expressive" detachment is the failure

42

to invest and intensify, and smoothness is the failure to accelerate and push limits. The gendered and sexualized character of these critics' disapprobation is significant. They interpret the lack of intense emotive investment as a failure in masculinity. The band's whole aesthetic rejects the neoliberal imperative to cool-hunt, to be uniquely noisy (like the Pistols), to perform the behaviors that grant access to patriarchal privilege (such as capital, wealth in the well-invested self, etc.).

While all yacht rock is performatively uncool, "True" is *sonically* uncool, and this sonic uncoolness clarifies the relationship between uncool and neoliberal market logics. As Tomas et al.'s 2007 audio engineering study suggests, this song's original mix is so precisely and carefully executed that it cannot be dynamically processed for maximal loudness. Dynamic processing is an automated system for constantly monitoring and rebalancing audio signals (like an FM radio signal). In the late 1990s and early twenty-first century, it has been common practice to use dynamic processing techniques to "push the loudness envelope as far as it goes"[83] — to maximize the ratio between a carrier signal's frequency deviation (how much the signal speeds up or slows down as it is broadcast) and its amplitude (how much power it has, its voltage). "In many markets, broadcasters believe that being louder than the competing stations will make listeners stop on their station when tuning across the dial."[84] Maximally loud signals are supposedly more competitive — they exhibit the most successful and profitable ratio.

In their study of the limits of loudness, specifically music listeners' tolerance of distortion and "potentially fatiguing sound," Tomas et al. chose to use a thirty-second sample from "True" as the audio track for the control and, in remixed form, the variables.[85] They chose "True" for their study because "it is difficult to process dynamically," because the original is so "spectrally sparse" that generating a sufficiently loud imbalance between frequency and amplitude introduces obvious glitches and distortions into the mix.[86] Pushing "True" to its loudest limit actually creates diminishing returns: it won't sound attractively loud, just odd or damaged (i.e., distastefully overcompressed). Insofar as this taste for sonic loudness is a version of cool-hunting (pushing audio signals to their limit), "True" is uncool because it can't be profitably loudened. *The cost of achieving this aesthetic ideal of loudness outweighs the benefits.* In other words, "True" is uncool because it can't profitably leverage noise. Because "True" can't be profitably compressed or loudened, it appears inflexible and unadaptable.

Working in the early 1980s, neither the band nor the record's producers could have anticipated postmillennial audio engineering technologies and conventions. They wouldn't have known this specific type of loudness would be "cool" (i.e., a profitable transgression), so sonic uncoolness of "True" isn't an intentional result of an explicit, subjective choice. However, the song's immunity to distortion anticipates later, more explicitly critical uses of uncool. Writing in 2004, Jace Clayton notes shifts away from distortion in various musical subcultures including crunk and grime: "Think about Lil Jon's clean synth lines, squeaky clean, narcotically clean, as clean as synthetic drugs in a plastic pill case — crunk is HEAVY, but without distortion. . . . The new hardcore embraces cleanliness like never before."[87] Here Clayton argues that underground music aesthetics use "cleanliness" as a way to distinguish themselves from a mainstream aesthetic that emphasizes distortion. The Los Angeles EBM (Electronic Body Music) band Youth Code's "Strict BPM" catchphrase is another example of this "new hardcore" — normcore — aesthetic of cleanliness and inflexibility.

Inflexibility and nonadaptability read as uncool when Spandau Ballet and Youth Code perform them, but they can also read as toxic and pathological attributes of supposedly "backward" populations like urban black and Latino men, non-liberal-democratic societies, or "social justice warriors" on the internet — that's why Lil John sounds defective ("crunk" or "*narcotically clean*") rather than boring when he does it. After political theorist Lester Spence, I call these populations "exceptional" populations. According to Spence, "neoliberalism relies on three populations, institutions, and spaces: those perfectly formed according to that logic, those able to be re-formed according to that logic, and the exceptions unable to be re-formed. African Americans constitute the exception."[88] "Exceptional" populations are the ones filtered out of a biopolitically healthy society because they cannot be "br[ought] . . . in line with this normal, general curve" of acceptable risk.[89] Seen as individually and collectively incapable of reform or adaptation, of currently or potentially embodying the dynamism and flexibility that are thought to characterize neoliberalism's healthy, successful subjects, exceptional populations are subjected to various techniques — like surveillance, quarantine (e.g., in the prison-industrial complex [PIC]), debt — that *produce* the material, social immobility these techniques claim to manage.

So, what makes uncool read as individual resistance and not group-based pathology? Whiteness. Uncool always manifests as whiteness: just as normcore fashion references middle-class white brands and aesthetics, Spandau Ballet's and yacht rock's nontransgressiveness read *as* white. It's the whiteness of this nontransgression, this otherwise unprofitable and "toxic" behavior, that makes it a profitable risk. A bet against oneself, one's capacity to entrepreneurially self-capitalize, uncool performance compounds whiteness, makes it (apparently) extra risky and thus extra profitable. Uncool human capital is like a bundle of securitized mortgages that can't perform well on the market. But this bet against oneself is a gamble on whiteness, an *investment in whiteness, financialized whiteness*. The surplus value produced by uncool "labor" or self-capitalization is paid in whiteness and white privilege—namely, the appearance of transcending markets and the imperative to self-capitalization, and/or the ability to reap the benefits of one's own labor, to maintain if not the "property" in one's person then the capital invested in it. Whiteness is what makes inflexibility and nonadaptability appear benignly uncool and not pathologically regressive.

Inflexibility—or rather, the extreme flexibility of being, even, inflexible—is one mode of white "uncool." Normcore personal unbranding is another method that uses uncool performance to leverage whiteness.

3. Betting against Coolness

Uncool is a way that elites opt out of the imperative to build "cool" human capital, a "cool" personal brand. Just as mid-twentieth-century white hipsters appropriated black culture as a way to disidentify with mainstream whiteness and establish their elite status among whites, uncool neoliberals disidentify with the economic rationality of the market. Their safe, generic, choices appear to lack the risk or noise necessary to turn a profit, but in fact they demonstrate their ability to transcend the imperatives of self-capitalization.

Taylor Swift's 2014 single and video "Shake It Off" is about uncool personal and artistic unbranding. "Shake It Off" is the lead single on Swift's 2014 album *1989*, which was explicitly intended to move her from country crossover squarely into pop territory. So, in part, the song is about her musical transcendence of the genre-based narrowness of country and conquest of the limitless possibilities of the pop mainstream and all its tributaries. We hear this in the song's instrumentation.[90] As *Billboard*'s Jason Lipshutz remarks, her previous album's hit singles "paired their fizzy melodies with slick guitar strums, but 'Shake It Off' disregards the instrument altogether, instead coiling its verses around a subtle saxophone line. . . . Swift and company clearly have been paying attention to radio trends."[91] She shakes off the guitar and its country connotations, grooving instead to some staccato bari sax beats and a horn line. The sax reads as "pop" not only because it has been a prominent feature of some then-recent pop hits (Macklemore's "Thrift Shop" and Meghan Trainor's "Lips Are Moving," for example), it also, and perhaps more importantly, isn't immediately associated with any contemporary pop subgenre, like hip-hop or EDM, with their powerful, synthesized bass lines, or indie rock, with its bass guitar. Because the bari sax doesn't have any immediately obvious sonic baggage, it can represent a generic, unbranded sonic space. "Musically speaking," Fallon argues, "with the blandly perfect pop-ness of 'Shake It Off,' she sort of becomes . . . boring." The song is certainly catchy, but it is at the same time totally "non-descript."[92] "Shake It Off" makes no attempt to be recognizably different than anything else we might hear in the pop charts.

Just as Swift the musician shakes off the narrowness of genre for the abstract universality of pop, Swift the persona shakes off the limitations of narrow gendered stereotypes, like being a dumb blonde, or boy crazy, or fickle and irresponsible. The video makes this clear: she tries on and rejects a variety of racialized femininities, most of which are tied to musical genres (classical, R&B, rap, etc.). This move isn't just in the video—it's in the song itself. Throughout the song, there is a pattern of quarter-note handclaps on beats 2, 3, 4. The pattern appears on the final three beats of the measure leading into each chorus. It also appears on the final three beats of the chorus—the 2, 3, 4 of the measure that begins by landing on "off." Its position in the song's climax indicates that this pattern of handclaps is the music that Swift's character should groove to if she's to shake off all the identity and genre baggage she wants to overcome. At the end of the bridge, leading up to what is effectively the song's drop, she has followed the three quarter-note shake pattern enough to loosen this three-beat pattern into an extended "shake, shake, shake," which she recites across four beats. After shaking up the song's rhythms, Swift belts out a wild vocal flourish where an "off" usually goes (which is also the place in a drop where the bass wobble usually goes). Those three shakes actually shook off the song's imposed constraints, so Swift's character can appear to offer a purely authentic expression unconstrained by external determinants—the embodiment of the music in her mind.

This vocal flourish is an example of Attalian composition, the sonic equivalent of the improvisatory rule-breaking the lyrics describe. However, musically, it's not "composed"—it's not an emergent process, nor is it a proper sonic parallel to the apparently unstructured dancing we see at this point in the video. She *belts* that lick in an uncharacteristically Swiftian pop-diva-like move. To pull off that vocal flourish, Swift has to be a really good, practiced singer. This may actually be the most properly, traditionally "musical" moment in the whole song. And it comes at a very compositionally savvy moment— a drop that is climactic precisely because it is so demure compared to other pop drops. We may find it fun to watch apparently unchoreographed dancing, but would we really want to listen to an untrained singer or fifth-grade band students play this song? Or is this song musically pleasurable—catchy—only because Swift is a skilled musician working with a very smart team of collaborators?

This tension between the advice the song professes—shake off the rules—and the compositional and performance practices it follows—no, actually, please follow some rules—is reflected in what Kevin Fallon identifies as the "odd hypocrisy to the song and video as a package. The music video and the song's lyrics are all about breaking the rules unapologetically.... How confusing, then, that 'Shake It Off' musically represents . . . Taylor Swift's arrival as a run-of-the-mill, straight-and-narrow pop artist."[93] It cheers for individual distinctness in the most generic voice possible. But this tension isn't a bug; it's a feature. It articulates a paradox central to white identity in a white supremacist society: for whites, the generic and the individual coincide because the generic is nothing but a false generalization of/from white existence and experience. In "Shake It Off," *what appears to be uncontrived expression is really the contrivances of whiteness as they materialize in Swift's body and musical performance.* She can simultaneously follow no explicit rules and yet perform in accordance with those rules because those rules are embodied in her supposedly authentic, natural self anyway, as her white, cis/heteronormative, feminine, "able" body. Here we run up against both Kant's theory of genius working "as if" he followed no rules and neoliberal deregulation: the carefully manicured background conditions, here in the form of Swift's normalized body, ensure that no matter what emerges, it's safe. That body also determines how her supposedly unruly expression is interpreted: it's not toxic unruliness in need of quarantine (such as Mike Huckabee's description of Beyoncé as "mental poison")[94] but relatable, accessible, and so unthreatening and nontransgressive as to feel boring.

"Shake It Off" isn't failed cool. It's an elite disidentification with coolness. It feels boring because it's generic and nondescript. Katy Perry's 2015 Super Bowl halftime performance was also accused of being boring, but because it tried too hard and failed. In an article titled "Katy Perry's Boring Super Bowl Performance," Erin Vargo writes that Perry's family-friendly show with dancing sharks and bright colors "was, frankly, super boring. It felt a little like watching Sesame Street Live. . . . Perry's performance seemed inauthentic. . . . It appears that she just wanted people to like her. I don't think I'm isolated in feeling slightly underwhelmed as a result."[95] Vargo isn't alone in her assessment; plenty of tweets echo this view.[96] People thought Perry was boring because she gave an inauthentically spectacular performance: too many gimmicks, not enough heart. With insta-meme dancing sharks and an entrance on

47

a shooting star descending from the sky, Perry seemed to be trying too hard to craft a hashtag-able, ready-to-go-viral, *cool* show. Rather than follow her own creative muse, she appeared to be gaming audience taste. Though both Perry and Swift performed straight-up pop tunes and made aesthetic choices based on marketing strategies, Perry's performance reads as crassly calculated in a way that Swift's does not. With her wacky spectacle, Perry appears subservient to (and unsuccessful at realizing) neoliberal coolness, whereas Swift, with her normcore dance party, appears to transcend it.

Betting against her coolness (that's the disidentification), Swift actually wins. She appears to be breaking the rule of self-entrepreneurship, but in fact she's found a way to make even better investments in the specific self she embodies. Her performance of pop genericness is an investment in her whiteness — acting and sounding uncool, Swift risks an uncompetitive performance, of failing to be exciting and buzzworthy enough to perform well on the record charts (and in social media metrics). There are no dancing sharks here, after all. However, because she is white, her nonbrandedness reads as uncool rather than as pathology: she doesn't fail to meet the imperative to be cool, she *transcends* it. Swift shakes off both gendered and genre stereotypes and the external judgment of others: she doesn't need to concern herself with the market value others place on her, with her reputation. She's free to be *boring* and vanilla because that's what she *is*. This *freedom* — the ability to succeed while being resolutely average (think George W. Bush) — *that's* the whiteness Swift's hedged bet returns in abundance.

Swift's unbranding financializes her whiteness. Think of it this way: if traditional white hipness passes through a performance of blackness and/or femininity, it's the M-C-M equivalent to uncool's M-M1 intensification of whiteness. Blackness and femininity still play a role here: instead of occupying the role of the commodity in the M-C-M transaction, they are the exception. Rehearsing racialized, gendered genres and stereotypes as that which Swift overcomes, "Shake It Off" calls them up not as value or human capital that can be intensified as such, but as risk that must be ventured by others in service of compounding the value of Swift's own self-investment, risk that she shakes off as she closes the M-M1 circuit. And that's what the performance of uncool does here: it intensifies the value and power of whiteness by rendering unprofitable risk as exception. This closed M-M1 circuit is, more or less, the aim of Attlian composition. This type of uncool labor isn't just an unsuccessful alternative to composition/the biopolitics of cool — it realizes their aims. As "True" and "Shake It Off" indicate, even when white people deviate from proper market logic — when they make apparently irrational cost/benefit calculations, when they embody abnormal ratios — their choices read as benign uncoolness. These choices seem merely uncool and not hazardous because those deviations actually *compound* white supremacy.

Philip Gunderson takes Danger Mouse's *The Grey Album* (which mashed the Beatles' *White* with Jay-Z's *Black* album) as grounds "to speculate that late capitalist society is on the cusp of the 'composition' stage of musical development, as described in Jacques Attali's Noise."[97] The reading of *Noise* I've offered in this chapter shows that Gunderson's speculation has proven accurate: "composition" does exist, now, in the twenty-first century, as the stage of late capitalism we call "neoliberalism." "Laden with risk, disquieting, an unstable challenging, an anarchic and ominous festival,"[98] the practice of composition is more or less a practice of deregulated entrepreneurial self-investment. Composition domesticates noise — the noisy "disagreement" of Rancièrian politics, the "black noise" Tricia Rose identifies as central to hip-hop aesthetics, the statistical and sonic noise in frequency ratios. As such, it is not an alternative to neoliberal governmentality but its quintessence. Attali recognized this possibility. He suggested that composition could lead to "automanipulation . . . the trap of false liberation through the distribution to each individual of the instruments of his own alienation" (*Noise* 141). All the technologies that "empower" us to become entrepreneurs, disruptors, and the like — these might not be the instruments of our own alienation per se, but they are definitely the instruments that falsely liberate us. They "liberate" us to become more efficient producers of surplus value and, as I will discuss in the next chapter, of relations of privilege and domination.

49

———

I began my analysis of the sonic episteme with *Noise* because it clearly exhibits several of the sonic episteme's key features. First, Attali's music: society analogy points out the kind of relationship or structure that acoustic resonance models. He explicitly connects acoustics to the statistical tools the neoliberal political economy uses to model the market. The "laws of acoustics" and probabilistic statistics are analogs in the strict sense of the term: they share a common logos. The sonic episteme uses acoustic resonance to translate the math behind neoliberal markets and biopolitical norms into nonquantitative terms. Second, *Noise* uses the difference between (implicitly verbal and visual) "representation" (Attali's term for the era before repetition) and sound/resonance to mark repetition's departure from European modernity and its characteristic methods of philosophical abstraction. Third, it uses this claim that it has overcome the limitations of European modernity to remake those limitations in new formats; in particular, it uses the claim of universal inclusion (the domestication of noise) to craft relations of domination and subordination that frame phenomena (theories, populations, etc.) that have not overcome European modernity's limitations as insufficiently adaptive, flexible, or evolved. Though this chapter has focused primarily on the domestication of noise, the next chapter examines the sonic episteme's politics of exception in more detail. Shifting from political economy to political ontology, chapter 2 studies various theories of neoliberalism and post-identity politics that argue "resonance" is the basic unit of society and/or personhood.

2

Universal Envoicement

Acoustic Resonance as Political Ontology

I. Neoliberal Biopolitics and Its (Counter)Rhythms

Attali argued that both postwar avant-garde art music and economic theory used the "laws of acoustics" to transform chance and indeterminacy into features rather than bugs. Both practices identified background patterns or parameters behind foreground noise, thus subsuming or domesticating noise into the means of artistic and economic production. Writing in 1905, W. E. B. Du Bois develops a similar approach to sociological noise. He defines sociology as "the Science that seeks the limits of Chance in human conduct."[1] Here, chance means "the scientific side of inexplicable Will" or "undetermined choices."[2] According to Du Bois, sociologists can't study chance directly: you can't plan to find unpredictable phenomena. But you can observe the *rate* at which unpredictable things happen. So Du Bois argues that "the duty of science, then, is to measure carefully *the limits of this Chance* in human conduct."[3] Tracking chance occurrences across a defined set of phenomena, you can determine the parameters within which these chance occurrences operate, that is, their normal range or rate.

Like Attali, who uses patterned intensities and frequency ratios to describe how composers and statisticians harness chance, Du Bois also uses the concept of rhythmic patterning to explain how chance becomes an object of sociological observation. If sociologists measure the rate of chance events, he says we can observe this in "the rhythm of birth and death rates" or the "lines of rhythm" that organize complex human interactions like, say, "the operation of a woman's club."[4] This rhythm is what makes "Chance . . . as explicable as Law";[5] we can't explain the why or wherefore behind chance events (i.e., their causes), but we can identify patterns in their frequency. Vital statistics and the daily operations of an organization fall into regular patterns or "uniformities," and those patterns are sometimes interrupted by irregularities like a "more or less sudden rise at a given tune."[6] Tracking and measuring the regular and irregular rhythms of daily existence, sociologists find the limits of chance in human life.[7]

Du Bois uses rhythm and melody as metaphors for statistics that measure the average rate of aleatory events. He uses rhythmic metaphors to translate the math behind statistically normalized distributions like birth and death rates into nonquantitative terms. Because neoliberalism and biopolitics use this mathematical relationship to shape and govern relations among people, we can extend Du Bois's metaphor to it: neoliberalism and biopolitics govern rhythms and frequencies. They establishes a normal range of rates, paces, or frequencies and renders rates, paces, and frequencies that can't profitably be brought within that normal range as exception. Perceptual coding is a good metaphor for how they govern those rhythms and frequencies because it foregrounds the role (racialized, gendered) private property relations play in frequency normalization (again, in Foucault's sense, not the audio engineering sense) — the whole point is to optimize the reproduction of white supremacist patriarchal private property relations.

If rhythmically patterned sound and audio compression are good metaphors for Gaussian neoliberal biopolitics, then they're not the best foundation for a just and nonoppressive political ontology. But this is precisely what a collection of contemporary philosophers claim: that acoustically resonant "voice" is a more inclusive social model than the ones we've inherited from classical liberalism, such as speech or deliberation. This chapter studies these political ontologies to demonstrate that this claim is false. As constituents of the sonic episteme, these vocal political ontologies hide a politics of exception behind that claim of universal inclusion, thus creating qualitative versions of the same relationships that neoliberalism and biopolitics create quantitatively.

However, the frequencies that these political ontologies perceptually code out of existence are productive models for more just and nonoppressive political ontologies. The second half of the chapter studies black feminist political ontologies that use sound to model the dimensions of existence that white supremacist patriarchal political ontologies perceptually code out of circulation because they impede the efficient transmission and accumulation of (racialized, gendered) private property. These political ontologies tune in to the "in-the-red"[8] dimensions of existence where black women have developed ways of being, knowing, and relating that affirm their personhood while tuning out white supremacist patriarchal frequencies on the assumption that they don't *always* need to be heard as the loudest part of the mix. They acknowledge the structuring reality of white supremacist patriarchy while also pointing to other realities below its radar, realities where people build entire ways of being in parts of the spectrum neoliberalism and biopolitics think we don't need to hear.

But before I get to the theory, I want to illustrate the claims I've just made: that Gaussian neoliberal biopolitics works as a kind of perceptual coding, and that oppressed people turn to in-the-red frequencies to develop strategies for coping with this specific form of domination. To do that, I use Lauren Berlant's discussion of slow death and Kemi Adeyemi's analysis of lean aesthetics in hip-hop. First, Berlant describes how neoliberalism and biopolitics establish norms governing the rate or pace of people's daily habits. Following these norms involves "coordinating one's pacing with the working day, including times of preparation and recovery from it" (*Cruel Optimism* 116). When we do this, the rhythms of our habits sync with and amplify the rhythms of large-scale social institutions. However, as Berlant points out, some people are positioned so that working enough to meet their bills and other obligations (like parenting) gives them insufficient time and disposable income to maintain the sort of institutionally mandated self-care and health routines demanded of us by things like health insurance policies (which charge more for individuals they classify as obese). For example, working several jobs at once gives you little time to cook from scratch or exercise. These are cases "where life building and the attrition of human life are indistinguishable" (*Cruel Optimism* 96). Performing the activities required for full social inclusion — work — puts you out of sync with "normal" patterns of self-care and diminishes your capacity to meet another criterion for full social inclusion — health and cost-effectiveness. These populations' investments in themselves diminish their human capital because they are incorrect estimates of "what kinds of sacrifices best serve the reproduction of labor power and the consumer economy" (108); instead of amplifying "'productivity' at work, business profits, insurance, health care providers, and the state" (109), they supposedly diminish it. Because these populations are defined by their abnormal rates — of self-care, of productivity — Berlant calls the type of social exclusion they experience "slow death" (97). Their slowness impedes the efficient accumulation of capital and human capital, so these dissonant rhythms are perceptually coded out of social circulation.

Berlant presents the fact of obesity (in the sense of "facticity" as lived experience) as a contemporary example of slow death (*Cruel Optimism* 102). However, for all the negative consequences of being obese, Berlant thinks these dissonant, coded-out rhythms are a source of pleasure for people whose low social status prevents them from successfully adopting "normal" life rhythms. From the perspective of capital and the biopolitical state, the routines and rhythms that lead to obesity are economically irrational: their rhythms and patterns appear to cost more than they nourish and benefit, burning people out and diminishing their viability. But from the perspective of people living in this way, the benefits actually outweigh the costs. For someone who can never get out of literal and metaphorical debt, all short-term benefits are worth it. "A relief, a reprieve, not a repair," the sensuous and social pleasures of these life rhythms "are often consciously and unconsciously not toward imagining the long haul" (117). In this case, going deeper into the red isn't a problem because there's nothing you could ever do to get into the black. So, for exceptional populations, populations that neoliberalism and biopolitics perceptually code out of the "living" whose lives must be fostered, these abnormal frequency patterns actually sustain their existence.[9]

Kemi Adeyemi observes a similar strategy in hip-hop's lean aesthetics. Lean is basically a mix of prescription cough syrup (promethazine and codeine) and some flavoring ingredients. Adeyemi argues that hip-hop artists and fans use both the drug and music written to mimic its effects as a "coping mechanism" that transforms black people's pathologized patterns of living into sources of pleasure.[10] In other words, this style of hip-hop *aestheticizes* frequencies that white supremacist institutions perceptually code out of legibility. For example, rapper Mac Miller describes lean's high as a "slowed down" feeling that "put me out of the fast-paced industry."[11] Artists try to translate that feeling into sounds. For example, rappers use serial repetitions of a lyric to create an effect similar to slow-motion film, which doesn't actually record events at a decelerated pace but takes more frames per second. Capturing many more repetitions of the same image than you would at twenty-four frames per second, slo-mo turns an otherwise imperceptible moment into a series of iterations, a series rather than an instant. Rappers apply a similar technique to their delivery, serially repeating a single lyric three or more times in a row. A$AP Rocky's "Purple Swag," Future's "Codeine Crazy," Drake and Future's "Jumpman," Desiigner's "Panda," and Beyoncé's "Formation" and

54

"Sorry" all do this. This overblown serial iteration of a lyric does in music what slow-motion photography does in film: it captures a hugely long series of iterations of the phenomenon, creating the effect of slowed-down time and intensified sensory impact, carving out space *within* the ongoing hustle and bustle of everyday life that continues apace. Lean immerses users in dimensions of experience that are inessential if not counterproductive to cultivating human capital and bringing oneself in sync with social norms, and rappers and producers have translated this into an aesthetic that creators and audiences find pleasurable. Marking out patterns of experience in the frequencies that neoliberal biopolitics and its listening ear[12] perceptually code out of legibility, lean aesthetics create an alternate reality, a parallel universe, within hegemonic reality.

Taking frequency as the primary unit of political reality, you are faced with which frequencies you abstract or compress away as you build your overall political ontology: Do you eliminate frequencies that impede the efficient reproduction of existing and totally oppressive social relations, or do you tune into the frequencies the hegemonic listening ear is trained to un-hear? In the rest of this chapter, I'll argue that political ontologies that take acoustic resonance as the fundamental unit of reality do the former, and I will identify phonographic approaches to sound or sounding that do the latter.

II. A Society That Includes All Voices: The Sonic Episteme as Political Ontology

Philosophers regularly present sound, voice, and resonance as rescuing Western liberal democratic theory from the errors that speech- and vision-centrism have supposedly baked into its foundation. This chapter addresses the variation of this move that understands sound, voice, and resonance as acoustic resonance. I show that these ontologies are constituents of the sonic episteme because they take acoustic resonance as the basic unit of society and create the same relations of domination and subordination in that society that neoliberalism and biopolitics use statistics to create and maintain.[13] In this section, I closely read Jacques Rancière's account of neoliberal "postdemocracy" and Adriana Cavarero's and Fred Evans's use of "voice" in order to establish that these postdemocratic and vocal political ontologies are constituents of the sonic episteme. Later, I will show that despite their claims to solve identity-based social inequality, these political ontologies modeled on acoustic resonance don't solve white supremacist patriarchy, they just rework it into post-identity biopolitics, which in turn uses the politics of exception to mark the cutoff between eugenic and dysgenic signal.

1. The Phusis of Sound as Community Nomos: Rancièrian Postdemocracy

As I discussed in the previous chapter, Attali thinks the "laws of acoustics" and the statistical probabilities that neoliberal economists use to model the market are instances of the same underlying method of abstraction. In his 1999 book *Disagreement*, French political philosopher Jacques Rancière argues that these same statistics have fundamentally changed the way "democracy" is practiced, creating a "postdemocratic" society that takes "the *phusis* [nature] of enterprising, desiring man . . . as community *nomos* [law or principle]."[14] If the "nature" of enterprising man is a microcosm of the broader neoliberal market and the "nature" of acoustically resonant sound is an analog for that market, then Rancièrian postdemocracy takes the laws of acoustics as a model for how society ought to work. As I will show below, Rancière points to this fact, but that point is made in philosophical jargon that requires some deep knowledge of the role of sound in Plato's work to fully appreciate. Rancière is not endorsing postdemocracy: he's identifying it to critique it. Nevertheless, the concepts he uses to define it situate it in the sonic episteme.

a. Democratic Disagreement

The first step in explaining what Rancière means by "postdemocracy" is to figure out what he means by "democracy." In the United States, "democracy" usually refers to a system of government or a set of political commitments and moral values, "a regime or a social way of life"[15] that usually has something to do with representative government. This is not Rancière's understanding; he thinks "democracy is *not* a regime or a social way of life. It is the institution of politics itself" (*Disagreement* 101; emphasis added). Politics, another term he uses in an idiosyncratically technical way, is the interruption and re-organization of an "'ethical' harmony of doing, being, and saying" (101). So, for Rancière, democracy is not a style of government but a specific method of disrupting governing institutions, such as "democracy" in the American vernacular sense.

This vernacular sense of "democracy" overlaps with Rancière's concept of democracy: the former, vernacular "democracy" is a structure or order that has both theoretically and historically allowed for "political" or democratic-in-the-narrow-sense disruption. This structure "distribut[es] bodies into functions corresponding to their 'nature' and places corresponding to their functions" (*Disagreement* 101). Social identities (gender and race) are indices of a body's nature or phusis: gender indicates sex, race indicates phenotype. Gender role and racial status determine your place in society. Bodies whose function allows them to be rational, independent, and active — they participate in public life as fully enfranchised citizens; bodies whose function allows them to be only appetitive, caring, and passive — they are prohibited from full political enfranchisement and generally made to occupy spaces of undercompensated servitude in private enterprise and domestic life. This structure is the harmonious status quo that democracy-in-the-narrow-sense disrupts.

Politics happens when some body performs a function supposedly inconsistent with its "nature" — when it utters or practices a *logos* its phusis was thought to be incapable of producing. For example, white women or people of color might say something rational. This performance is evidence that the current organization of bodies into positions or statuses is not necessary but "continge[nt]"[16] and open to reorganization. This reorganization is a meta-level process that challenges and reworks the very concept of harmony itself — definitions of what counts as noise, what counts as signal, how consonance and dissonance are measured, how hearing and speaking happen, and who can hear and be heard. As Rancière puts it (with a not-so-thinly-veiled jab at Habermas), democracy "is not a discussion between partners but an interlocution that undermines the very situation of interlocution" (*Disagreement* 100). When the "situation of interlocution" is undermined, we have to reassess what a voice is, what it means to speak and to listen, the presumed harmony of existing social structures — this is what Rancière means by "disagreement." Democracy in his narrow sense is disagreement brought about when the "demos" — the most severely excluded part of society — performs a disruption that leads to a case of disagreement.

b. Postdemocratic Consensus

"Postdemocracy," then, is the situation where disagreement/politics is impossible because there is no harmonious order of inequity to disrupt (*Disagreement* 95). That's why Rancière also refers to postdemocracy as "consensus" — the opposite of disagreement. Disagreement happens when the excluded demonstrate they meet the conditions for inclusion. "Consensus," on the other hand, is "the presupposition of inclusion of all parties and their problems. . . . Everyone is included in advance" (116). Instead of assigning each different phenotype or sex its definitive vocal pitch or pattern and policing overly noisy voices, consensus wants everybody, no matter what their phusis is like, to emit sounds. To achieve overall social consensus, "the individual," he writes, is "called on to be the microcosm of the great *noisy howl* of the circulation and uninterrupted exchange of rights and capabilities, goods and the Good" (114).

57

Just as the population is a "noisy howl" of diverse voices, each individual voice is a signal emerging from undisciplined phusis.

With its undisciplined deregulation of noise, consensus renders the relationship between phusis and logos contingent: any body is capable of producing any sound. Speaking up and making noise, "a multiplicity of local rationalities and ethnic, sexual, religious, cultural, or aesthetic minorities affir[m] their identity on the basis of the acknowledged contingency of all identity" (*Disagreement* 104). The more different types of sound we hear a body emit, the more convinced we are that the relationship between body and voice is contingent (or "socially constructed," to use an old 1990s term) and emergent, not essential(ist). Postdemocratic noisiness naturalizes the contingency that disagreement points out, thus neutralizing the disruptive and revolutionary power disagreement once offered. In other words, consensus domesticates noise. It is a post-identity discourse that claims to overcome conventional practices of social exclusion.

c. Postdemocracy and the Sonic Episteme

Rancière's descriptions of postdemocratic political ontology refer to two central features of acoustic resonance as I define it in this book. First, he argues that postdemocracy takes probabilistic statistics — in the form of both neoliberal market logics and statistical forecasts — as a model for society. Aligned with and attuned to neoliberal market logics, neoliberalism's *Homo economicus* is defined by his cost/benefit calculus and probabilistic rationality. If consensus takes "the *phusis* of enterprising, desiring man as community *nomos*" (*Disagreement* 96) then it takes those mathematical relationships as the community's organizing principle.[17] In practice, this manifests as the "scientific modeling and forecasting operating on an empirical population carved up exactly into its parts" (*Disagreement* 105). Writing in 1995, Rancière sees this forecasting primarily in opinion polls (such as Bill Clinton's much-remarked on and then-innovative use of opinion polls during his administration), which predict how entire demographic groups will act (e.g., at the voting booth) based on samples from that group. Fifteen years later, this type of forecasting has become a whole new industry: big data (which I discuss in chapter 5). Both in principle and in practice, postdemocracy models society, both as a whole and in its segments, as a statistical forecast and probabilistic distribution. These are the same quantitative relationships that the sonic episteme uses acoustic resonance to translate into nonquantitative terms. And Rancière does that translation for us, though somewhat indirectly.

Arguing that postdemocratic consensus is "the perfect realization of the empty virtue Plato called *sophrosune*," Rancière describes postdemocracy's organizing principle with a term that, for Plato, has explicitly sonic and musical connotations.[18] Often translated as "moderation" or "self-mastery," sophrosyne is the practice of living that brings your physical and mental parts into alignment with the hierarchical ratios that organize the parts of the True/Beautiful/Good. Think of the divided line and its proportions: it is a "line divided into two unequal sections and cut each section again in the same ratio (the section, that is, of the visible and that of the intelligible order), and then as an expression of the ratio of their comparative clearness and obscurity."[19] The line expresses the metaphysical relationship between visible and intelligible as a *geometric* ratio — the soul is more real than the body, so it takes up a longer segment of the line. The "beautiful order and continence of certain pleasures and appetites, as they say, using the phrase 'master of himself'" (*Republic* 430e), sophrosyne is the True put in practice, a *rational* practice of subordinating the visible to the intelligible in proper geometric proportion.

As I explain more fully in the next chapter, Plato models his concept of sophrosyne on contemporary-to-him notions of musical harmony, which calculated consonance and dissonance in terms of geometric proportion. For Plato, sophrosyne was the practice of embodying the same kinds of mathematical relationships — i.e., geometrically calculated ratios — that harmonious sounds exhibited. For example, *Republic* 410c describes a "harmoniously adjusted" or "attuned" soul as "moderate." Or, as Judith Peraino puts it, the ancient Greeks thought moderation "tunes the soul to the cosmic scale,"[20] which, as Plato says in *Timaeus* 32c, "was harmonized by proportion." Harmonic proportions didn't express a relationship among sound waves or frequencies but among both (a) the parts of the instrument that made sounds and (b) the physical construction of the instrument and the sounds it produced. The assumption — or ideal — was that geometrically proportional instruments should produce acoustically proportionate sounds, because the same mathematical proportions ought to govern both the geometry of the instrument and the vibrations it emits. As Rancière explains, Platonic "sophrosyne was that paradoxical virtue that achieved the law of interiority of the community in exteriority, in terms of the sheer distribution of bodies, times, and spaces" (*Disagreement* 106). That law distributes bodies, times, and spaces in the same geometric proportions that Plato attributes to harmonious sounds. Musical harmony wasn't a metaphor for sophrosyne — they were both applications of the same mathematical principle.

Postdemocratic consensus follows the same general premise behind Plato's concept of sophrosyne, but it updates the math from what he used to

59

calculate musical harmony to what we in the twentieth and twenty-first centuries use to do the same thing. If, as Milton and Rose Friedman argue, the neoliberal market is a system of "proportional representation,"[21] and postdemocratic consensus takes that market as its organizing principle, then consensus, like Platonic sophrosyne, is the practice of bringing something into harmonious proportion—except it calculates those proportions statistically rather than geometrically.[22] As I argued in the introduction to this chapter, these probabilistic statistics—the statistics that express things like birth and death rates or the rhythms of complex organizations like women's clubs—are built out of the same mathematical element physicists use to measure acoustic resonance: the frequency ratio. Postdemocratic sophrosyne is still modeled on musical harmony; it just updates the math used to calculate relative consonance and dissonance to fit with twenty-first-century practice. Taking statistically measured sophrosyne as its organizing principle, postdemocratic consensus ontologizes acoustic resonance. That's why Rancière can call consensus a "happy harmony" (*Disagreement* 108).

With a little unpacking, Rancière's account of neoliberal political ontology reveals evidence that this type of political ontology is a constituent of the sonic episteme. All this unpacking is worth it because Rancière explicitly ties consensus to post-identity white supremacy. Combining his text's implicit argument (that neoliberal political ontology takes acoustic resonance as community nomos) with its explicit argument (that this type of political ontology creates and supports a vaguely biopolitical post-identity racism) gives me one of this book's central claims: political ontologies that use acoustic resonance as the principle or quasi-natural "law" that orders society adopt a qualitative version of the same logics that neoliberalism and biopolitics frame quantitatively. When you apply these logics to twentieth- and twenty-first-century Western liberal democratic societies, the result is a political ontology that hides post-identity biopolitics behind apparently neutral and benign discourses of envoicement. But because this is a general claim about political ontologies modeled on acoustic resonance, before I get to arguing it in detail I'd like to identify a few more of these political ontologies so I have a bigger sample on which to ground the claim. In the next section, I turn to two generally phenomenological approaches that take vocal resonance as the basic unit of society.

2. Vocal Resonance as Political Ontology

Adriana Cavarero's "politics of vocal resonance" and Fred Evans's theory of the "multivoiced body" both use the resonance of the human voice as model for the subject and for social cooperation. Cavarero replaces European philosophy's traditional "videocentric" ontology with a vocal one.[23] Evans also argues that "'voices,' not individuals, the State, or social structures, are the primary participants in society."[24] They define "voice" both negatively, as what traditional methods of philosophical abstraction exclude, and positively, as a kind of acoustic resonance.[25]

a. What Voice Isn't

Cavarero and Evans present the phusis of acoustically resonant sound as a replacement for both the structure of modern subjectivity and the various community nomoi that go with it—speech, reason, deliberation. So their definition of resonance is in large part negative: resonance is whatever speech isn't. For Cavarero, "the vocal" is not so much a sonic or physiological phenomenon as it is the constitutive outside of the philosophical tradition that Nietzsche calls "metaphysics" and Derrideans call "the metaphysics of presence."[26] Arguably beginning with Plato's theory of the divided line, which holds that the sphere of ideas is more real than material life on Earth is, the metaphysics of presence privileges conceptual abstraction over material specificity, phallogocentrism over feminized irrationality, mind over body, stasis over dynamism, inside/outside binaries over bottom-up emergence—the metaphysical over and above the physical. From Nietzsche to Derrida to Irigaray to Sarah Kofman, plenty of philosophers have critiqued and deconstructed these binaries. Unlike these others, Cavarero argues that privileging vision over sound is the foundation of the metaphysics of presence.[27] "The visual metaphor," she argues, "is not simply an illustration; rather, it constitutes the entire metaphysical system."[28] The problem with this videocentric metaphysics is that it "legitimates the reduction of whatever is seen to an object"[29] and cannot "anticipate" or "confirm the uniqueness" of each individual.[30] In other words, it objectifies and abstracts, and that's bad. If vision is the foundation of the metaphysics of presence, one way to fix its problems is to replace the foundation with something else. Cavarero thinks vocal resonance avoids the objectifying and abstracting tendencies that vision supposedly lends to philosophy.

While Cavarero is correct that philosophical modernity does rely on a 2D metaphysics that makes it easy to objectify and abstract, she is incorrect in ascribing these limitations to vision *as such*. These limitations are features of vision as it works within the metaphysics of presence. As Alia Al-Saji argues via a reading of Merleau-Ponty, this "objectifying vision" is just one model of visuality—albeit the model that has dominated much of European philosophy since the Enlightenment. "Objectifying vision" takes seeing as "merely

61

a matter of re-cognition, the objectivation and categorization of the visible into clear-cut solids, into objects with definite contours and uses."[31] Because it operates in a two-dimensional metaphysical plane, it can only see in binary terms (same/other). "Objectifying vision is thus reductive of lateral difference as relationality."[32] Up to this point, Al-Saji's account mainly agrees with Cavarero's. However, unlike Cavarero, Al-Saji recognizes that objectifying vision arises from specific philosophical commitments, not from the nature of light or human sight. For example, she argues that Merleau-Ponty's theory of painting develops an account of vision that is "nonobjectifying" and relational.[33] In this account, we do not see paintings as already-constituted objects but as visualizations, the emergence of vision from a particular set of conditions. Such seeing allows us "to glimpse the intercorporeal, social and historical institution of my own vision, to remember my affective dependence on an alterity whose invisibility my [objectifying] vision takes for granted."[34] Emergent, bodily, relational, this model of vision exhibits the same ontological features that Cavarero attributes exclusively to the vocal, so much so that Al-Saji herself turns to sonic language: "more than mere looking, this is seeing that *listens*."[35] This Merleau-Pontian vision not only departs from traditional European Enlightenment accounts of vision; it gestures toward traditional European accounts of hearing. Comparing Cavarero's critique of "videocentrism" to Al-Saji's critique of objectifying vision clarifies that "metaphysics" is not, as Cavarero claims, the effect of videocentrism, but rather that objectifying vision is the practice of seeing that "metaphysics" makes possible. Seeing and listening have no essential or inherent structures; rather, there are multiple regimes of seeing and hearing, each attuned to specific epistemological and ontological discourses.

Abstracting away from the "social and historical institution" of the concepts of vision and voice she uses, Cavarero adopts a version of what Jonathan Sterne calls "the audiovisual litany."[36] This litany misrepresents the differences between two philosophical systems as the "differences between the senses."[37] Cavarero uses the litany to present the difference between her political ontology and classical liberalism's as equally natural, inherent, and radical as the purported difference between voice and vision. As I will show a bit later, this litany lets Cavarero hide a specific set of philosophical and political commitments behind an apparently neutral and objective concept of vocal resonance.

Evans avoids the audiovisual litany, but he still defines voice negatively against the false opposition between modernist commitments to purity and universality—"univocal[ity]" (*Multivoiced Body* 75)—and postmodernist commitments to unconstrained heterogeneity—a completely noisy "Babel, where equal audibility becomes radical inaudibility" (271), which he calls the "dilemma of diversity" (2). Voice is whatever modernity and postmodernity are not. "Voices are intrinsically hybrid or 'impure'" (15) in a way that both "push[es] the rigid ideas of purity and univocity to the edge of the political map that they have dominated for so long" (14) and "evokes a 'unity composed of differences'" (2) that combats postmodernism's tendency to see turtles all the way down. As what "valorize[s] the unity that 'postmodernists' shun in their penchant for heterogeneity and, on the other, endorse[s] the heterogeneity that 'modernists' efface in their embrace of the universal" (2), Evans's account of voice resembles what sociologists Richard A. Peterson and Roger Kern call "omnivorous consumption." Omnivorous consumption is "an openness to appreciating everything. In this sense it is antithetical to snobbishness, which is based fundamentally on rigid rules of exclusion."[38] Omnivores think they have both overcome obsolete snobbish investments in purity and retained some sense of elite or highbrow status in their preference for pleasing, respectable, rational hybrids over noisy, chaotic messiness (think of the "I listen to everything but country and/or hip-hop" music fans). Evans similarly treats voice as overcoming obsolete investments in purity yet retaining some sense of status or value that avoids complete relativism.

Both Cavarero and Evans use these litanies to negatively define voice against the obsolete and problematic foundations of Western political philosophy. They think that because the problems of inequity, injustice, and oppression that continue to plague Western liberal democracies can be traced back to underlying principles modeled on sight, speech, and/or language, these new resonant foundations will fix those problems. But because they define voice in relation to *that* history instead of the history of music, music theory, or aesthetics, they mistake a sociohistorically specific concept of voice for the nature of voice as such. That concept is, as I show in the next section, acoustic resonance.

b. What Voice Is: Acoustic Resonance

Cavarero and Evans both define "voice" as a type of acoustic resonance. To briefly recap, acoustic resonance is, for the purposes of this book, a specific type of vibratory movement: rhythmically oscillating patterns of intensity, such as the condensation and rarefaction of air pressure. These patterns interact in rational or irrational phase relationships. Resonance thus describes either the consonant, rational interaction of phase patterns or the dissonant, irrational interaction of such patterns.

Cavarero directly labels acoustics as the basis of her concept of sound,

63

and she uses the term in a way that is consistent with my definition of acoustic resonance. According to Cavarero, the voice "obeys the natural laws of sound" (*For More Than One Voice* 80); these laws are "rules [that] are not semantic but acoustic" (171). Acoustic rules take the form of "rhythmical" patterns (80). For example, the "rhythmical" patterns of organs' and cells' cyclical functions are a kind of acoustics "inscribed in the internal body" (80). As far as corporeal rhythms go, cardiovascular rhythms, including the inhale-and-exhale patterns involved in vocalizing, are most closely analogous to the rhythmical oscillation of air pressure. Cavarero thinks voice sonifies these internal patterns and turns them into a soundprint of the body's unique constitution. She argues that the individual's voice is the signal that "emerges" from the interaction of rhythmically patterned body parts "against a background of sheer noise" (7), like the gurgling of a stomach or the flow of blood in our veins and vessels (which we can hear in the absence of all other sounds). These emergent patterns don't communicate a content but rather information about the conditions of their production, such as the relative size of one's vocal chords, or the relative consistency of sexual object choice or dietary choice. This is what Cavarero means by the claim "the human condition of uniqueness *resounds* in the register of the voice."[39] The rhythmic patterns of one's voice communicate the individual uniqueness and "concrete reality of differences" due to aleatory aspects of the environment and individual choice, such as the size of your vocal chords or whether you smoke tobacco. Voice's rhythmic patterns thus communicate the same sorts of information about individual variability that Du Bois thinks sociological statistics communicate: the indeterminacy of life.[40] Cavarero's concept of voice and vocal resonance is a type of acoustic resonance.

Evans doesn't directly use the term "acoustics," but he uses "voice" as a metaphor for a Deleuzo-Guattarian metaphysics that works the same way acoustic resonance does. Evans calls that metaphysics "chaosmos" or "composed chaos" (*Multivoiced Body* 86). Chaosmos has an "open texture" that, like an "open work"–style musical composition, builds the note-to-note details and overall form simultaneously: voices "have a pattern, but this pattern is progressively determined by the interplay [of parts] rather than being imposed . . . from the outside" (150–51). Rational patterns emerge from noisy interaction like—and here Evans is citing Bakhtin—"echoes and reverberations" (150). These patterns incorporate and adapt to aleatory occurrences, which Evans calls the voice's "anexact form" or "indeterminacy" (150). Chaosmos is patterned chance, the relatively consistent order that emerges from more or less deregulated social interaction. Voices, then, are the patterns that emerge from chaosmotic interaction. And just as the composer of an open work has "impersonal" but "complete control,"[41] voices have "an agency that is both us and not us, anonymous and personal at once."[42] So, even though Evans doesn't use the term "acoustics," he attributes to voice and chaosmos the same organizational principles that physics attributes to acoustic frequencies and, as I discussed in chapter 1, that Attali thinks the "laws of acoustics" impart to Reichian-style open works.[43] Because he models his idea of voice on acoustic resonance, his theory of vocal resonance is a constituent of the sonic episteme.

Both Cavarero and Evans define vocal resonance as rhythmic patterns of emergent, chance occurrences. Like the rest of the constituents of the sonic episteme, Cavarero's and Evans's theories of voice translate the mathematical relationships behind neoliberal biopolitics into nonquantitative terms. For example, they use resonance to describe frequencies distributed across a spectrum of (ir)rationality.[44] Cavarero's "plurality of voices that are already linked to one another in resonance" situates every voice in a continuity (*For More Than One Voice* 200). Evans finds a microcosmic version of this continuity within each individual voice. Arguing that there are many "voices resounding within one's own," Evans models the internal heterogeneity of the individual's voice on sonic overtones.[45] Every pitch contains a fundamental frequency — a "dominant or lead voice" — and a series of overtones or "others that resound within it."[46] Overtones are co-sounding frequencies whose phase patterns — i.e., the frequency or pattern of peaks and valleys in a wave — fall into rational relationships (fractions with integers as numerator and denominator, like $2/3$) with the fundamental tone. When we hear two or more sounds together, we hear not just the interaction of the primary tones but all their overtones too. All these concurrent vibrations nest together in more or less consonant ways, forming larger-scale patterns, like the death rate or the rhythms in the yearly operations of a women's club.

Cavarero and Evans treat this universally inclusive spectrum of voices as an alternative to and improvement on metaphysical hierarchies. They argue that resonance is "politically subversive" because it replaces the "impersonal, objective hierarchical order" of most political philosophy since Plato with "the horizontal reciprocity of resonance"[47] and the "clamor of all in all."[48] With all voices on the same, continuous spectrum, there's no more domination and subordination. Thus, Cavarero argues that the turn to vocal resonance eliminates political sovereignty altogether: "the simple truth of the vocal makes the crown fall without anyone ever hearing the crash."[49] However, while cutting off the head of the king[50] might abolish relations of sovereignty, it leaves plenty of room open for other kinds of power relations—like neoliberalism and biopolitics.

Cavarero's and Evans's voice-based political ontologies are instances of the sonic episteme because they use the concept of acoustic resonance to overcome the conceptual and practical limitations of post/modernity, particularly the limitations of classically liberal identity-based politics they call "identity myths of community"[51] and the "dilemma of diversity."[52] Like all constituents of the sonic episteme, their appeal to voice naturalizes post-identity biopolitics behind a dehistoricized concept of acoustic resonance. In the next section, I show how these political ontologies leverage the supposed difference between voice and more traditional methods of philosophical abstraction to enact a politics of exception. So, even though they claim to overcome identity-based social exclusion, these political ontologies merely adopt a different method for creating and maintaining the relations of domination and subordination traditionally produced via such exclusion.

3. Consensus and the Politics of Exception

To recap a bit, the politics of exception is what happens when neoliberal market logics are used to maintain white supremacist patriarchy. As Lester Spence argues, these logics divide society into three main groups: those who have already adapted to neoliberal ideas of success (in Rancière's terms, those who already embody the phusis of enterprising man), those who haven't yet but are nevertheless capable of adapting to such ideas, and those who can't or won't adapt. Social status is not overtly attributed on the basis of bodily difference but instead on the basis of performance. So, for example, the status of feminization is not limited to feminine phenomena (like chick lit), and not all feminine phenomena occupy a feminized status (e.g., *Lean In*–style corporate white feminism exempts women from the low status that comes with feminization). However, because the background conditions are deeply shaped by centuries of identity-based white supremacist capitalist heteropatriarchy, intersectional identities significantly affect both one's performance and others' perceptions of one's performance. Identities still determine the distribution of both opportunities and resources, on the one hand, and evaluative bias and credibility, on the other. Thus, the social position of feminization will still, in general, be occupied mostly by women, especially black, queer, disabled, and undocumented women. Because it doesn't directly appeal to identity-based differences, the politics of exception hides white supremacist patriarchy behind the claim to have adapted and progressed past it.

This section argues that political ontologies modeled on acoustic resonance use a politics of exception to remake traditional identity-based status differences in new terms. Because acoustic resonance translates the same mathematical relations embodied in neoliberal markets and biopolitical statistical distributions into nonquantitative terms, adopting resonance as the fundamental unity of society demonstrates your theory's conformity with neoliberal market logics and its membership in the politics of exception's first, highest-status group. At the same time, this casts theories that don't frame themselves as surpassing classical liberalism's ontological commitments and the style of identity politics that follows from them as insufficiently adaptive — i.e., as exception. Both Rancièrian postdemocracy and Cavarero's and Evans's vocal politics do exactly this.

a. Postdemocratic Consensus and the Politics of Exception

According to Rancière, postdemocratic consensus claims to eliminate the old hierarchy between rational speech and irrational cries, as well as the essentialist metaphysics that ties rationality and irrationality to specific kinds of bodies. But the point isn't to reform social injustice; rather, postdemocratic consensus uses the performance of these reforms to enact a politics of exception.

67

First, postdemocratic consensus claims to overcome old social divisions by putting everyone on the same "continuum of positions" (*Disagreement* 116), often through the same use of statistics I described, via Mader, in the book's introduction. Erasing the "dividing line separat[ing] the private world of noise, of darkness and inequality, on the one side, from the public world of the logos, of equality and shared meaning, on the other" (116), postdemocratic consensus puts everyone on the same spectrum of noisiness. Instead of constitutively excluding animal noise from human speech (as, say, Aristotle does), consensus gets rid of the difference between them. Likewise, instead of constituting itself as a space of communicative deliberation by excluding noise from the realm of speech, consensus democracy encourages as much noisy interactivity as possible. This "unconditional requirement of mobilization" (117) is the neoliberal demand that everyone demonstrate adaptability and the capacity to reform — to speak up where formerly they were silenced. Disavowed histories of white supremacist patriarchy continue to shape background conditions within which individuals speak and act, so that there will be groups "who are not able to be those inventive alliance-forming individuals" who can "internalize and reflect the great collective achievement" (116–17) of overcoming social injustice by speaking up and contributing to the noise spectrum. By "giv[ing] back to each person excluded the identity of a mobilized capability and responsibility" to speak and participate in conversation (117), postdemocratic consensus hides structural inequity behind claims of liberation. Eliminating the explicit dividing line between social inclusion and exclusion, postdemocratic consensus frames the people who continue to experience the effects of systemic social domination as incapable of exercising the new mobility, responsibility, and liberty they've been so generously granted—i.e., as exception. I have given many examples of this move in *Resilience and Melancholy*, so I won't rehash them here.

Second, postdemocratic consensus claims to deregulate the traditionally essentialist relationship between bodies and capacities. Traditionally, in both Plato and liberal identity politics, a body's nature was thought to be directly related to the kind of logos it could follow and/or express. For example, the kind of body you had determined whether you were capable of rational deliberation or just uttering cries of pleasure or pain. Postdemocratic political ontology claims to sever that link between phusis and logos: the connection between the kind of body you have and the logics you can follow and express is contingent and emergent, not predetermined by some law or principle (nomos). The "*phusis* of enterprising, desiring man"[53] is tied not to the kind of body he has but to his patterns of choices. Postdemocracy appears to deregulate identity: instead of tying it to essentialist top-down categories, it grounds it in individual performance.

However, "separating phusis, conceived as the power of whatever flourishes, from . . . antinature, conceived as the power of the proliferating multiple," postdemocratic consensus distinguishes between eugenic and dysgenic patterns of behavior (*Disagreement* 121). Unlike the phusis of enterprising man, which exhibits a regular, predictable pattern, this "anti-nature" or antiphusis appears to follow no regularizable rate, that is, to be "lawless" (121). These supposedly lawless patterns of choices don't rationally nest into and thus amplify large-scale distributions of power and privilege. In other words, they aren't *consonant* with the phusis of enterprising man and the community nomos built on it. According to Rancière, this lawless dissonance is perceivable only as the "anthropological nakedness of a different race and skin" (118). Your body's racial identity determines whether your patterns of choices read as consonant or dissonant with the community nomos. For example, African American women's self-care routines are criticized as economically irrational by countless memes that chide "welfare moms" for spending too much money on things like manicures and smartphones. So, just as Spence argues that African Americans constitute the exception, Rancière shows how postdemocratic consensus frames nonwhites as lawless exception incapable of adapting to and embodying the community nomos.

Even though postdemocratic consensus claims to overcome traditional models of social exclusion by putting everyone on the same spectrum of noisiness, it nevertheless marks out populations who make noise at an insufficient or incorrect frequency. People who either don't demonstrate their ability to overcome systematic silencing or whose racial identity leads their patterns of choices to feel dissonant with white supremacy appear as exceptions—i.e., as undeserving of full political membership and the protections that come with it. So, though it claims to include precisely those who used to be excluded as incapable of deliberative democratic speech, "th[is] 'fight against exclusion' is also the paradoxical conceptual place where exclusion emerges" (115). Either as the phusis of enterprising man or as neoliberal sophrosyne, when acoustic resonance is the code that runs society, the output is the politics of exception.[54]

b. Vocal Resonance and the Politics of Exception

This claim is further borne out by Cavarero's and Evans's arguments that voice, as community nomos, overcomes the problems inherent in old nomoi, problems like hierarchical exclusion and the "purity" of conceptual abstraction. Their arguments mark the status differentials that define the politics of exception. Though they identify different things as exception, Cavarero and Evans each mark a break in what they otherwise describe as a universally inclusive continuum of resonance.[55] This break is evidence that their claims to fight exclusion are the conceptual place where newer forms of exclusion emerge.

Both Cavarero and Evans think voice is superior to social identity as a basis for political membership or personhood because voice is a more nuanced abstraction that registers fine-grained differences that social identities abstract away. For example, Cavarero argues that resonant interaction "avoids imposing cultural identities on the unrepeatable uniqueness of every human being" and lets us "stri[p] ourselves of our western, eastern, Christian, Muslim, Jew, gay, straight, poor, rich, ignorant, learned, cynical, sad, happy—even guilty or innocent—being" (*For More Than One Voice* 205). Grounding personhood in individuals' nongeneralizable idiosyncrasies, voice supposedly liberates people from compulsory conformity to ill-fitting and blunt stereotypes. Likewise, "the voice . . . dethrones the 'subject' of traditional metaphysics" (30)—i.e., the abstract individual who does not bring his "private" differences to bear on public life. Evans makes a similar claim, but with one crucial difference from Cavarero. Whereas Cavarero thinks identities abstract away from individual difference, Evans thinks identities don't capture the full range of individual differences. "The multivoiced body view of society speaks of voices rather than cultural identities" because identities are just a subset of the many, many voices that resound both in the individual and in society (*Multivoiced Body* 266). Because the multivoiced body contains lots of different components, taking it as the basic unit of society "militates against the tendency of our more particular identity to provide a basis for a politics of exclusion" (263). So both Evans and Cavarero think voice is a better basis of political subjectification than social identity because voices are more accommodating of a range of differences.

For both thinkers, the shift from identity politics to vocal politics fixes the problem of identity-based social exclusion. For example, Evans argues that as a "principle of justice, the interplay of equally audible voices" requires "demarginaliz[ing] excluded voices."[56] All voices are legible as expressions of personhood, including and especially subalterns who have traditionally been denied the capacity for political speech. Cavarero's concept of the "absolute local"[57] comes close to Evans's principle of equal audibility. She thinks that once individual voices are "liberated from the cartography of nations and the individualist ontology"[58] of classical liberalism, then each voice's uniqueness — its absolute locality — will be audible to and have an effect on society. A politics of the absolute local tunes into each and every voice in its uniqueness, demarginalizing excluded voices and allowing for equal audibility. "Voice" is the spectrum or continuity that includes everyone, especially those traditionally excluded from traditional concepts of personhood.

If this sounds a lot like postdemocratic consensus, that's because it is![59] This new "vocal" or "resonant" method of social organization superficially includes all noises and identities while at the same time cutting the same status differences traditionally marked by those identities in new, non-identity-based terms. Vocal politics replace identity-based hierarchies with a politics of exception. Evans and Cavarero identify the exception in different ways. Marking a status difference between theories that can overcome past commitments to exclusivity and embrace hybridity and those that can't or won't, Evans's method sticks more closely to Spence's model of the politics of exception. Marking a distinction between eugenic and dysgenic resonance, Cavarero identifies the exception in a more narrowly biopolitical way.

First, although Cavarero thinks vocal politics replace hierarchal discontinuities with a resonant continuity, she uses an upgraded version of the good old Aristotelian distinction between voices that can enunciate rational patterns and voices that can only utter irrational cries to make a break in that continuity. To participate in society's resonant spectrum, a voice's rhythmic patterns must be ordered in a way that can resonate with other voices to rationally nest within the bigger patterns of political life. And for Cavarero, the most important of those bigger patterns is speech. "Animals and men have a voice—but the destination of the human voice to speech is what distinguishes them. The humanity of human being plays out precisely along the division (which is rooted in the vocalic) of this destination."[60] Human sounds resonate in ways that nonhuman sounds do not. Human voices are rationally divisible into speech, but nonhuman sounds are irrationally related to the patterns of spoken language. The point isn't that human voices actually enunciate speech but that their "unique" patterns are capable—in the future or even just in theory—of aligning with others in the big meta-patterns of spoken language. For example, even humans who are reduced to a state of bare life in which they are capable only of vocalization and not deliberation nevertheless possess "the *quintessence* of the human that the voice destines to speech"[61] because their protolinguistic vocalizations still resonate with "unique" patterns that can be rationalized into legible speech patterns.

Though Cavarero appears to be rejecting the traditional biopolitical distinction between the population proper and bare life, she just shifts this break from the distinction between life and bare life to the distinction between voice and sound. Unlike sound in general, voice resonates with language to form regular patterns interpretable as speech—i.e., as signal rather than noise. As Cavarero explains, speech is "the point of tension between the uniqueness of the voice and the system of language."[62] This point of tension or friction is the point at which resonant frequencies bump up against each other and generate new, distinct signals. The friction/resonance between each individual human voice and the abstract system of a language generates a second-order "uniqueness," an individual variability that renders speech adaptable, flexible, alive.[63] Only frequencies that exhibit "uniqueness" can generate enough friction with the empty abstractions of language to produce resonant vocality. Nonhuman sounds don't rise to the level of "voice" because they don't interact with language to form rational patterns legible as human speech—they just generate noise. Even though all voices are on the same continuity of resonance, Cavarero uses the distinction between voice and sound to mark a break in that continuity: all humans may have vocal resonance, but not all sounds resonate.

In Cavarero's system, resonance is a feature only of sounds whose frequency patterns are legibly human and/or are capable of consonantly interacting with other recognizably "human" frequencies. Nonhuman sounds aren't capable of interacting with language to produce resonant vocality. In

Spence's taxonomy, that makes nonhuman sounds the exception—the group incapable of reforming themselves to accord or be consonant with dominant logics. "The ontological horizon disclosed by the voice"[64] establishes a politics of exception because it both claims to be universally inclusive and marks a break in that inclusive spectrum between eugenic and dysgenic, consonant and dissonant resonance.

Cavarero's political ontology establishes a politics of exception because she directly marks a break in the continuity of voices. This is not a universal feature of the sonic episteme—there are resonant political ontologies that don't mark this sort of break. However, there are also other ways of establishing such breaks. All constituents of the sonic episteme mark a break between their "resonant" projects and some older, more traditional philosophical project with respect to which resonance is "neo-" or "post-." Evans's project illustrates this aspect of the sonic episteme. He presents vocal resonance as superseding and progressing past old-fashioned commitments to purity (either pure unity or pure difference). In this framework, hybridity that is not the result of rejecting and evolving beyond former commitments to purity appear static and incapable of reform—i.e., as exception.

For Evans, the central and definitive feature of voice is its hybridity—and not hybridity as such but hybridity as opposed to or in place of purity: "each voice is a dynamic hybrid and not the purity or univocality so many thinkers thought to be the essence of identity" (*Multivoiced Body* 261). Evans presents purity and univocality as outdated and obsolete remnants of a troublesome past, of which hybridity is the progressive future. Oppression, he argues, is a "penchant for purity" (268), and his concept of voice is intended to "push the rigid ideas of purity and univocity to the edge of the political map that they have dominated for so long" (14). Vocal hybridity supposedly fixes the injustices enforced to maintain the purity of dominant institutions.[65]

Overcoming purity with hybridity, Evans's theory of vocal resonance is part of what sociologists Richard Peterson and Roger Kern identified as a "historical shift from highbrow snob to omnivore."[66] Over the course of the twentieth century, U.S. cultural elites abandoned exclusive taste—especially exclusive taste for fine or "high" art—as a marker of elite status. By the end of the twentieth century (Peterson and Kern published their study in 1996), elites ought to demonstrate a broad range of tastes for both traditionally highbrow and lowbrow things. This does not mean they like "everything indiscriminantly. Rather, it signifies an openness to appreciating everything. In this sense it is antithetical to snobbishness, which is based fundamentally on rigid rules of exclusion."[67] Omnivorousness, as Peterson and Kern define it, is the preference for curated mixes *and* the distaste for snobbish exclusivity. Together, this preference and distaste establish the omnivore's elite status: their preference is refined and not indiscriminate, and this distinguishes them from lowbrow fans who unreflectively like their own culture's vernacular arts;[68] but this preference is also not held back by traditional rules and hierarchies, and that distinguishes them from previous generations of hidebound cultural elites. Omnivorousness is not mere broad taste but the overcoming of "an antecedent practice that laid claim to a certain exclusivity of insight."[69] Diverse practices that don't reference traditional highbrow taste aren't omnivorous because they haven't rejected old-fashioned commitments to purity and exclusivity. In other words, the only people who can be omnivores are those who are or are expected to be highbrow snobs. Diversity is a positive, progressive accomplishment only for people and institutions who did the excluding, not for those who were (and continue to be) excluded. In this way, omnivorousness uses a term that connotes inclusion and diversity to mark the same old status differences among races, genders, and other identity groups that were once marked through exclusion and purity.

So when Evans says things like "hybridity has become respectable against the backdrop of a history that was usually captivated with purity,"[70] he's making the same gesture that omnivorous music fans make. Vocal hybridity is a status available only to those who once embodied or could embody "purity" — the purity of reason, enlightenment, universality, white racial purity, and so on. Arguing that "the multivoiced body is the basis for a *new* form of solidarity that valorizes heterogeneity and creativity,"[71] Evans erases the long-standing practices of code-switching, double consciousness, and "world-travelling" (as María Lugones puts it) that white women, nonwhites, and other minorities have used for millennia.[72] That sort of diversity has not overcome an antecedent claim to exclusivity and thus doesn't count as "hybridity" in Evans's sense. Because they don't fit this definition of hybridity, nonelite traditions may register as their own kinds of exclusivity or purity, a commitment to one's own minority culture because one can't or won't adapt to the language of the global elite. They are the exception. Evans explicitly argues for this exception: "We are justified in limiting the political status of nihilistic voices within a society that valorizes hearing all its interlocutors" because "excluding the excluders" prevents them from "undermining the creative heterogeneity of society" (*Multivoiced Body* 270, 269). And, as Sara Ahmed and other feminists of color have pointed out, it is often people who point out ongoing sexism and racism that get branded as "excluders" in need of silencing. Evans thinks the only way to preserve the vitality of vocal hybridity — to make sure the resonance of the

73

multivoiced body isn't diminished or dampened — is to quarantine the voices that seem wedded to antecedent commitments to exclusivity, which happen to be the same voices excluded by traditional hierarchies. So, even though Evans privileges hybridity over hierarchical exclusivity, he nevertheless creates an exceptional class of voices who must be excluded to preserve the health of that hybrid mix.

Evans's project illustrates a general feature of the sonic episteme. The sonic episteme presents resonance as the inclusive, equitable overcoming of antecedent theories' commitments to purity and hierarchy, and it leverages this very claim of inclusion to exclude the same people that these antecedent practices did. Those who never had or were attributed commitments to highbrow purity and exclusivity — i.e., those excluded as impure — will appear unable to perform or articulate behavioral patterns that align with the large-scale pattern of overcoming snobbish exclusion. In fact, their behavioral patterns may be felt to interfere with that pattern. These irrationally resonant and maladaptive signals constitute an exception. When resonance marks progress past some antecedent practice of stasis, purity, or exclusivity, then resonance becomes the criterion that cuts the line between the biopolitical population and its exception.

This doesn't mean all sound-based political ontologies are doomed to reproduce the same old systems of domination and subordination we've inherited from Western political philosophy. Part of the reason the sonic episteme fails is that it looks for new solutions to those systems in the same old place: they replace one model grounded in Western philosophy's ideas of perception and communication (speech) with another (voice). They're just turning to a different component of a system designed to reproduce white supremacist cisheteropatriarchy, so it's no wonder these superficial reforms don't fix the underlying inequities.

Fortunately, there are plenty of scholars who get their models from different places. The next section considers political ontologies grounded in concepts of sound drawn from black women's epistemic and artistic traditions. Unlike the sonic episteme, which defines sound as acoustic resonance, these theories define it as code- or register-shifting. Specifically, sounding is the shift from hegemonic codes to the registers of existence they perceptually code out of circulation, such as the ontological registers that white supremacist cisheteropatriarchy discard as superfluous and unprofitable. Sounding is an example of both the kind of theory or intellectual practice the sonic episteme renders exception and the kind of theory or intellectual practice that uses sound as the basis of a political ontology that doesn't reproduce the same old systems of domination we've inherited from Western political philosophy.

III. Sounding as Phonographic Political Ontology

In her study of black women's philosophical methods, Devonya Havis identifies a technique named "sounding." It is also called an "oblique pivot," a "spark," or "viscus deviance."[73] These terms describe a particular kind of movement—sounding isn't vibration but a code-switch. As a method of abstraction, sounding both feigns complicity with dominant narratives and also works "in the red," beyond the reach of these narratives' perception. Sounding is a way to tune in to modes of existence that white supremacist patriarchy—and the philosophical tools designed to support it—perceptually code out of transmission and analysis. Sounding, in other words, is a phonographic method of abstraction.

This section studies several theories of sounding and one music video that uses sounding to focus on a concept of personhood grounded not in resonance or voice but in patterns or frequencies that get perceptually coded out of white supremacist patriarchal concepts of personhood as a form of private property. Unlike the sonic episteme, which looks for alternatives to the classically liberal notion of personhood in Western notions of voice and resonance, sounding looks for alternatives to those ideas of personhood in registers that would otherwise be coded out into the red. If these frequencies are coded into the red because they impede the efficient transmission of personhood-as-property among the beneficiaries of white supremacist patriarchy, then political ontologies modeled on them can do what the sonic episteme can't: articulate a mode of existence that interferes with the reproduction of a white supremacist patriarchal social order.

1. Sounding as Oblique Pivot

Devonya Havis uses sound as a way to theorize a set of philosophical practices that emerge from black women's lived experience and thus don't necessarily bump up against, resonate with, and give voice to the names (Rawls, Deleuze) and/or concepts (Gettier problems, determinate negation) that make something recognizable to academic philosophers as capital-P Philosophy—practices that are more phonographic than Philosophical. Her concept of sound comes from a vernacular use she encountered in her father's stories about his childhood in rural Arkansas. One such story features a black Native American woman named Mamma Ola asking Havis's father "now, how do you sound?" to encourage him to think more carefully when he was acting "out of line."[74] It demands self-examination and reflection, but instead of directing that reflection back upon one's self in cogitation to produce justified true beliefs, the question directs reflection to consider the impact and effect you have on others. "'Now, how you sound' functioned as a call to consider not only the final result of one's thinking but also the framework and context from which the actions or choices issued."[75] This question tunes us into the same things that Al-Saji's critical-ethical vision and Cavarero's concept of the vocal bring into focus: context and relationality. Though they appear superficially similar, Havis's "sounding" and the sonic episteme's "resonance" describe two very different methods of abstraction. For example, they are different in scope. The sonic episteme uses the supposedly objective and universal laws of acoustics as a metaphor for a generalized practice of philosophical abstraction, whereas Havis uses "sound" as a metaphor for a practice of abstraction situated in a specific relation to history and to institutionalized relations of domination. Havis models sounding on black women's ways of examining the contexts and relationships opened and foreclosed by ongoing relations of domination (white supremacist patriarchy, coloniality, etc.) in order to "creativ[ely] negotiat[e]" them and "generat[e] possibilities that extend beyond those that have been externally imposed."[76] So sounding is what happens when what Du Bois calls "inexplicable Will" or "undetermined choices"[77] emerge in response to circumstances overdetermined by white supremacist patriarchy.

Because they figure possibilities beyond externally imposed metrics, instances of sounding don't resonate with those large-scale social patterns (as, say, Cavarero thinks human voice resonates with language), either in consonance or in dissonance. Rather, sounding's friction with these large-scale social patterns ignites a spark. Citing Audre Lorde, Havis explains that sounding involves "forms of community that affirm the 'creative function of difference in our lives' using difference 'as a fund of necessary polarities between which our creativity can spark like a dialectic . . . ' (Lorde 1984, 111)."[78] Lorde describes a principle of community organization that transforms the friction caused by the motion or oscillation between two poles into energy: a spark. Unlike a Hegelian *Aufhebung*, which aims to resolve the motion between polarities into a higher-order coherence, a spark is what happens when you "hold the dissonance of conformity and nonconformity"[79] and the polarity between them catalyzes a redirection in the flow or circulation of energy. Where Hegel levels up, Havis and Lorde bend circuits. Havis calls this redirection an "obliqu[e] pivot."[80] Just as an electrical spark might melt the solder on a circuit board and redirect the flow of electricity across the circuits, these oblique pivots bend circuits—patterns—of relation and thought. Like queered pitches/blue notes, syncopated rhythms, going into the red, or sub-bass frequencies, these oblique pivots redirect us to rhythms and rationalities that are perceptually coded out of dominant political ontologies. This spark, then, is what makes sounding a phonographic abstraction: it tunes practitioners in to registers of existence that conventional methods of philosophical abstraction render exception.

Havis homes in on one specific style of pivot that is common in black women's political philosophies. "Feigned complicity," she argues, "is one strategy used to pivot into new possibilities that have not readily been presented."[81] As Michel Foucault argues in *The History of Sexuality*, European political philosophy tends to view power as something that is either accepted or opposed.[82] Feigning complicity means appearing to conform because what you're doing isn't legible, within this standard philosophical framework, as transgression or insubordination. Pivoting away from the polarities of complicity and resistance opens a space for living and experiencing pleasure and protects that space from policing by hiding it in plain sight. In other words, the frequencies and dimensions that dominant political ontologies abstract away have been productive spaces for black women's thought and activism precisely because they allow one to fly under the radar and work with minimal interference from oppressive institutions.

Black women pop musicians often use sound to open this space — that is, they pivot to sound to open out alternatives foreclosed by "controlling images" of black femininity.[83] As Angela Davis has shown, twentieth-century singers like Bessie Smith and Billie Holiday use vocal ornamentation and timbre to bend banal, white patriarchal pop lyrics into something more critically aware and reflective of working-class black women's lived experience.[84] Though the lyrics may be about clichéd heterosexuality or romanticized domestic violence, the sound of the lyrics changes their meaning, bending it away from their conventional propositional content and toward a more sarcastic and critical take. Similarly, Regina Bradley argues that "Beyoncé uses sound to distance her performances from the established ideas of womanhood that she visually satisfies."[85] Though Beyoncé's visual image often feigns conformity to class- and sexuality-based ideas of respectable femininity, her sound — both her vocal performance and the accompanying music — obliquely pivots beyond the poles of respectability and ratchet. For example, the production in "Bow Down/I Been On" literally bends her voice and, in so doing, "obliquely pivots" gendered politics of respectability. As Bradley explains, "her vocalization, reminiscent of Houston's chopped and screwed production style — the extreme slowing down of a track and the resulting slurring and distortion of voice — dismounts Beyoncé from international recognition and makes room to (re)claim space to experiment with the boundaries of her womanhood and its recognizable aspects. The deepness of her voice does not fit within the more recognizable and established feminine context of Beyoncé as an R&B diva."[86]

According to Bradley's analysis, "Bow Down/I Been On" does exactly what Havis describes: it obliquely pivots from the polarities of respectability and ratchet, thus opening up a space for Beyoncé to become something other than what the limited alternatives for black women pop singers prescribe. Shifting from verbal to sonic dimensions, Beyoncé's performance in "Bow Down/I Been On" artistically represents sounding's oblique pivot, much in the same way Plato's diagram of the divided line visually represents his idea of the True. Here, we have an oblique pivot from one sensory register to another. Because of the U.S. Constitution's construction of freedom as either speech or representation, only these dimensions fit American pop fans' and critics' idea of what "politics" is, so they limit their assessment of a song's politics to its lyrics and video.[87] Though sounds and music do tons of political work, that work goes unheard as politics. In this context, the moves from lyrics and images to sound that Davis and Bradley identify constitute a kind of sounding. Pivoting to dimensions perceptually coded out of hegemonic ideas of politics, these performances open out "space to experiment" for "new possibilities . . . not readily presented" by that idea.

This pivot from verbal expression to sound isn't limited to black women's musical performance traditions. Sounding also appears in black feminist theory as a method of phonographic abstraction that pivots from the verbal to the sonic dimensions of a written text. In his study of "the detours, digressions, and shortcuts that . . . lay dormant in bare life and social death,"[88] Alexander G. Weheliye discusses several texts that make this exact pivot, which he calls a "viscus deviance."[89] Because his account foregrounds the role of private property in white supremacist patriarchal concepts of personhood, I use Weheliye's version of sounding to clarify how sounding's pivot or deviance moves from realities perceptually coded for the efficient reproduction of white supremacist patriarchy to those that get coded out into the red.

2. Sounding as Viscus Deviation

In his book *Habeas Viscus*, Weheliye investigates modes of existence that "remain largely imperceptible within man's political and critical idioms" because liberal and biopolitical concepts of personhood perceptually code them out of transmission (135). Following Hortense Spillers, Weheliye calls this kind of being "flesh." Flesh describes "alternative modes of life alongside the violence, subjection, exploitation, and racialization that define the modern human" (2).

According to Weheliye, white supremacist patriarchal concepts of person-hood are organized by a series of intersecting binaries: white/black, masculine/feminine, straight/queer, and so on. The two terms of each binary define the spectrum of humanity and the nonhuman. However, these two terms also act as poles that spark or "kindle" oblique pivots and viscus deviations (97). Flesh is one of those deviations. Weheliye repeatedly refers to flesh as a "humming relay" that is "bracketed" from intellectual and sensuous perception because it is "synchopated" with white supremacist patriarchal distributions of non/personhood (121, 138, 138). Existing alongside but below the radar of white supremacist cisheteropatriarchal concepts of the human and practices of dehumanization, flesh exhibits all of sounding's main features. It feigns complicity with those concepts and practices of de/humanization while also articulating what Ashon Crawley calls, in his review of the book, "otherwise possibilities" and "otherwise worlds"[90] that can be "heard, seen, tasted, felt, and lived"[91] by obliquely pivoting to dimensions perceptually coded out of these concepts and practices.

Perceptual coding compresses signals to eliminate frequencies that impede the efficient transmission of frequencies and their transformation into private property. In his analysis of Spillers's concept of pornotroping, Weheliye clarifies the role of private property and personhood-as-property in defining both the spectrum of in/humanity and what it brackets or codes out. As Jennifer Nash explains, pornotroping is "the pornographic pleasure that is taken in producing race" via "a repeated sadistic white pleasure in black female suffering."[92] Pornotroping establishes racial status differences as and through gendered distributions of personhood-as-property. Private property is classically defined as that which cannot be intruded upon without consent. Because it typically involves the physical and sexual assault of black women by white men, pornotroping shows that black women's bodies can be intruded upon, by certain kinds of people, without those women's consent. According to Nash, "pornotroping hinges on . . . the fundamental availability of black female sexuality — to meaning-making, to co-optation, to violence."[93] It treats black women as sexual property available to white men and white audiences at their will. Framing white men and audiences as entitled to intrude upon the sexual property in black women's bodies without the women's substantive or nominal consent, pornotroping solidifies their relative racial and gender statuses as a distribution of ownership in bodies as sexual property. Human personhood is reserved for whites, whose bodies are sexual private property owned either by themselves or by husbands,[94] whereas sub- or nonpersons are a commons available for anyone's use and appropriation.

As clear-cut as this status difference may be, pornotroping is nevertheless paradoxical. Following Spillers, Weheliye argues that the pleasure it generates relies on the "simultaneous sexualization and brutalization of the (female) slave" (*Habeas Viscus* 90): audiences experience pleasure in her sexualized dehumanization, but sexual desirability is a human attribute tied to gender performance. Accordingly, pornotroping attributes black women a queered femininity, one that's queer because it's not precisely or fully "human."[95] Building on this observation, Weheliye argues that pornotroping produces "queer" or "deviant" sexualities that aren't located on the human-nonhuman spectrum; instead, it attributes them to flesh. Thus, Weheliye argues, "the idea of pornotroping must also be understood as conceptually igniting the im/potential libidinal currents" (108; emphasis added). This "ignition" is a spark in Lorde's and Havis's sense: it obliquely pivots to registers of existence which appear "impotent" because pornotroping's private property relations compressed them out of perception via a process of perceptual coding. However, the currents or frequencies it disposes of have the potential to ground modes of existence that bend the circuits of that private property relation — to ignite or spark in Lorde's and Havis's sense.

To perceive these modes of existence, we have to follow that spark and pivot from the sensory register pornotroping establishes to those patriarchal racial capitalism codes in the red. According to Nash, pornotroping is "a quintessentially visual practice."[96] Alongside the scopophilic pleasure that audiences experience when watching it, as Weheliye explains, "the dysselection of the black subject as not-quite-human requires visible inscriptions on the flesh and in the field of vision" (*Habeas Viscus* 111). In other words, pornotroping compresses our perception so that we reduce black people only to visible markers of racial blackness (think of drawings and cartoons with overexaggerated physical features). Even though pornotroping emphasizes the visual to the apparent exclusion of other sensory registers, Weheliye argues that there's a whole lot "happening . . . off the screen, off the map, off the charts, off the books, which is what renders the symbols etched into and written by the flesh indecipherable" (111). The white supremacist patriarchal private property relations established by pornotroping perceptually code these "off-the-screen" sensory registers into the red. And, like all "in-the-red" frequencies,[97] these coded-out happenings have the potential to distort the screens, charts, and books that compress them out of the frame. This distortion ignites a spark, pivot, or deviation from the frame or ledger drawn up by pornotroping's perceptual coding.

Weheliye identifies several instances of this shift from one perceptual register to another in textual depictions of pornotroping. For example, in the historical accounts of pornotroping Spillers analyzes in her canonic article "Mama's Baby, Papa's Maybe: An American Grammar Book," the violence is present in the literary text as sound. Spillers cites William Goodell's study of the North American slave code; there "Goodell narrates, 'the smack of the whip is all day long in the ears of those who are on the plantation.'"[98] The text turns or deviates from verbal propositions to sounds: "smack," with its hard consonants, onomatopoetically re-creates the whip's strike. Likewise, when the grain of the voice or "regionally accented expression" is the sonic marker of racial difference in a literary text, the rhythm of the prosody "lends quasi-decipherability to the hieroglyphics of the flesh" (*Habeas Viscus* 111). Rhythm flies under the radar of a white supremacist patriarchal listening ear tuned to hear and police the sonic color line as a matter of timbre or accent. Like the oblique pivot Havis theorizes under the term "sounding," Weheliye's deviances all begin from existing practices of white supremacist patriarchal perceptual coding and turn toward the "im/potential . . . currents that slumber in all acts of political domination" (108). These "im/potential" currents are outside the range of "normal" human perception. For example, "bare life" is thought to be absolutely inert, immobile, and nonvibrant. However, Weheliye demonstrates that those relegated to bare life have sensory lives that fall outside the speech/silence poles defining the human/nonhuman spectrum. Though Agamben's example of the most extreme form of bare life, the Muselmänner of the Nazi camps, "may have appeared withdrawn, passive, and lifeless," Weheliye points to archival evidence that reveals they "'retained selective receptivity for . . . olfactory, gustatory, and auditory stimuli.'"[99] Here, Weheliye applies the oblique pivot he notices in Spillers's texts as a method of scholarly analysis, and this method lets him access sensory registers that conventional methods of philosophical abstraction perceptually code out of the archive.

Weheliye's concept of viscus deviances parallels what Alexander Galloway and Jason LaRiviere call the philosophical practice of "lossy compression," which "extends the logic of philosophy and media (data loss), but deploys itself against the spirit of philosophy and media (expression, distinction, representation)."[100] Instead of eliminating superfluous frequencies for greater clarity and efficiency of legible human expression, which is what perceptual coding does, lossy compression eliminates or abstracts away from key factors that contribute to such legibility. The flesh and its currents are perceptually coded out of hearing by white supremacist technologies (like pornotroping); in this context, white supremacy is a mode of compression. The flesh creates existence in the "in the red" zone that white supremacy compresses away, much in the same way Galloway and LaRiviere think lossy compression theorizes in "opaque" zones that traditional "metaphysics" (in the metaphysics-of-presence sense) codes out of our epistemologies.[101] The advantage of Weheliye's account over Galloway and LaRiviere's is its attention to the work of race/gender/sexuality in determining what gets perceptually coded or compressed out of dominant frameworks.

Havis, Lorde, and Weheliye all point to the same basic technique: a pivot or shift in perceptual registers to whatever dominant methods of philosophical abstraction perceptually code out of archives, out of transmission, out of consideration, and into the red. Whereas the sonic episteme builds new political ontologies out of Western ideas of acoustic resonance, sounding is a technique black women use to build ways of existing in the regions perceptually coded out of white supremacist patriarchal political ontologies. These are fundamentally different approaches to identifying alternatives to the philosophical status quo: one looks for new metaphors within Western philosophy, and the other looks to existing intellectual practices whose dismissal as capital-P Philosophy allows capital-P Philosophy to efficiently and profitably transmit itself into the future. The sonic episteme's political ontology is Philosophical; sounding's is phonographic.

The next and final section of this chapter discusses one example of the kind of reality modeled by sounding's phonographic political ontology. Rihanna's 2015 single and video "BBHMM" reworks classical pornotroping narratives to redistribute the narrative's racialized, gendered property relations.[102] This redistribution maps a political reality pornotroping perceptually codes out of transmission, that is, one in which black women are persons and personhood is not grounded in a private property relation.

3. Rihanna's "BBHMM" and Sounding as Political Ontology

Riffing on pornotroping narratives, "BBHMM" depicts both a reality those narratives perceptually code out of circulation and the pivots and register shifts one needs to make to perceive and conceive such a reality. It illustrates sounding as a technique and the kind of political ontology this technique produces. I begin by discussing the way "BBHMM" takes up and inverts pornotroping as a trope. I show how this riff on pornotroping creates an instability that sparks a shift in the meta-coda to a musical register overlooked and deprioritized in the song's main body. Then I argue that this register shift represents, in music, the sort of alternate dimension Havis and Weheliye theorize.

Even though the video begins and ends with shots of Rihanna's blood-drenched, naked body, it isn't an instance of pornotroping, at least in the conventional sense. It is in conversation with pornotroping as a trope, mixing around some of its elements — the spectacular presentation of black women's sexuality through representations of violence, the production of property ownership — to dramatize a process that resembles pornotroping but has a different outcome. The song "BBHMM" articulates a "bizarro" or inverted pornotroping that represents what classical pornotroping codes out into the red.

The narrative premise of "BBHMM" is that Rihanna's character's accountant embezzled the money he was managing for her, and she and her two friends go after him for recompense and revenge. They kidnap the accountant's wife and torture and kill the accountant. The video has five sections, each defined sonically as much as visually. There's the (1) birdsong-filled shot of Rihanna's legs leaning out of the trunk, (2) the shots of the accountant's wife and her home accompanied by schmaltzy classic Hollywood orchestral strings, cut in with cricket-filled shots of Rihanna carrying the trunk with a bound and gagged wife inside back into this home, (3) the song's verse/chorus/verse body, which shows Rihanna and her crew on the run with the accountant's wife as their hostage, and (4) the song's coda, which begins with the cricket-filled shots of Rihanna from (2) and then shows her torturing the accountant. We then return to an extended version of (1), which I'll call (1a); this then fades out into (5) a second coda of shrieking synths punctuated at the end with a piano chord; here we see "BBHMM" in white letters on a red background and then cut to a blood-soaked close-up of Rihanna's steely-eyed face.

Sections (3) and (4) flip the script on the standard pornotroping narrative: Rihanna's protagonist isn't the recipient of the violence but its perpetrator.[103] She directs some of that violence at the accountant's wife, who is kidnapped and stripped, pistol-whipped, and somewhat of an object of the camera's/audience's scopophilic pleasure. But most of it is addressed to the accountant. The video shows him bound to a chair as Rihanna's character selects weapons from a collection of torture instruments labeled according to various ways one may be wronged by a romantic partner.[104] But we never see her character use those weapons; violence is never represented directly on-screen, only implied. Rihanna's character's body is the medium that depicts racialized sexual violence of which she is neither recipient nor object. Though the accountant did the exact thing white men do to black women in classical pornotroping narratives — he intruded upon her private property (her money) without her consent — Rihanna's character is the one executing the violence, not the accountant. That's one significant reason why this isn't clas-

83

sic pornotroping: it is an exact inversion of both the roles (executor/object of violence) and of the content of the visual spectacle (the violence is off-screen). Whereas pornotroping classically presents spectacular violence with a barely implicit sexual charge, the beginning and end of "BBHMM" present a spectacular image of Rihanna's body that is explicitly sexual but implicitly violent — we don't see that violence, only the blood that remains afterward. So "BBHMM" has many of the components of a classic pornotroping narrative, but they're in the opposite order.

Inverting pornotroping's narrative and formal logics, "BBHMM" represents the "im/potential" or "in-the-red" registers those logics ignite but cannot perceive. It does this both narratively and sonically. Narratively, "BBHMM" depicts a reality that inverts pornotroping both as a trope and as a technique for distributing personhood as a private property relation. The narrative presents patterns of spending and accumulation that don't efficiently reproduce hegemonic distributions of personhood as sources of musical and aesthetic pleasure. As Doreen St. Felix notes in her piece on "BBHMM," this song is one of several in Rihanna's catalog that depicts "the image of propertied black women in general, of black women recouping historical debts."[105] The form in which these recouped debts appear is key. According to St. Felix, the "money" Rihanna recoups isn't wealth but cash — a less respectable form of currency marked by its distance from whiteness and from whiteness as a private property interest. So, "BBHMM" recoups what pornotroping takes from black women — personhood as a kind of private property — but alters its underlying form. This alteration is evident, St. Felix argues, in the way Rihanna's "Pour It Up" avoids opulence, which is a spectacle, in favor of cash as something you smell: "liquid like a stack, but also liquid like a perfume."[106] Pornotroping relies on the visual to distribute personhood as private property, but, in St. Felix's interpretation, Rihanna takes back what is denied her not as visual spectacle but as smell. Taken either as cash or as smell (or both), the "money" recouped in the inverted pornotroping narrative of "BBHMM" is a kind of personhood that is perceptually coded out of white supremacist patriarchal distributions of personhood-as-property. To perceive that personhood, one must, as St. Felix does, make a shift in perceptual register to those in-the-red frequencies, be they cash or smell.

Depicting such a register shift in sound, this song's meta-coda gives audiences the interpretive key to the song. The video adds a coda to the song's radio version; that coda is where the torture and murder happen (section 4 above). But "BBHMM" goes even beyond that, supplementing that coda with a further coda, a meta-coda (section 5 above). This meta-coda depicts musical dimen-

84

sions that the composition of the song's main body frames out of the picture. That main body, sections 1–4, is organized as a contrast between rhythmic instability and rhythmic stability. In the verses and choruses (sections 1–3), the meter is very woozy and it's not always easy to find the downbeat. In the intro and the chorus, the music-box-like treble synth forms a two-bar loop that emphasizes the fourth beat of the first bar, drops out on the downbeat of the second bar, and then comes back in on the second beat. This makes it seem like every other fourth and second beat are emphasized. The vocal phrases (including the brraps) begin on the third beat of every measure and emphasize the downbeat. So we have the music-box synth on a 2/4 pattern and the vocals on a 1/3 pattern—which is totally common. What's uncommon about "bbhmm" is that it's really a 4/2 and a 3/1 pattern. It's the reverse of the conventional pattern of rhythmic emphasis, and it sounds off-kilter to ears accustomed to the conventional pattern—it may even sound somewhat off-meter. The bass synth in the choruses comes in on the downbeat, and then again on two offbeats spread over the two-bar loop; their syncopation contributes to the woozy off-kilter feel. The coda (section 4), as codas do, resolves the main body's metric instability into a very unambiguous 4/4. Traditionally codas reinforce the harmonic resolution of a piece—they usually rearticulate a main theme in the tonic, kind of hitting us over the ears with "yes this is the key no really it is." The coda in "bbhmm" produces a sense of closure by emphasizing the song's rhythmic and metric organization, the 4/4 in which "money" always lands on the downbeat. The coda resolves the body's metric instability. So the song uses rhythm to mark out large-scale formal sections and to organize its main tension-release gesture.

The meta-coda abandons rhythm and instead uses harmony to organize its structure and to generate and release tension. This meta-coda has two images, each accompanied by different chords. The first image is "bbhmm" in white on a red background, and the second image is a close-up of Rihanna's bloody face and hair. In the first scene, there's a very dissonant, treble-synth-heavy sustained chord, and then a percussion hit right before we switch to the second scene, which takes that dissonant chord and slowly raises the pitch of some of the higher notes; this builds tension that then would conventionally be resolved by the piano chord at the very end. But that piano chord isn't a root-position tonic chord (which is the gold standard for harmonic resolution), so it doesn't resolve the chord in conventional terms. Nor does the meta-coda emphasize the metric resolution in the first coda. Instead of resolving, this meta-coda sparks, ignites, and pivots away from the logics that organize both the main part of the song and mainstream songwriting conventions. These "in-the-red" sounds in the meta-coda represent the "in-the-red" ontological dimensions that sounding pivots to and opens up. In this way, the song's composition represents in music the kind of deviation or register shift the video's narrative makes in its departure from classical pornotroping tropes.

Rihanna's "BBHMM" illustrates how sounding works as a political ontology: it turns and tunes in to a register of existence that the sonic episteme perceptually codes out of consideration, a register where black women have full political status because personhood takes the form of something that's not private property. Because political ontologies modeled on acoustic resonance code these registers out as exception, sounding conceives of sound as an oblique pivot or queerly charged spark instead of acoustic resonance.

The sonic episteme's political ontology produces a new version of the same relations of domination and subordination that it claims to eliminate by taking resonance as the fundamental unit of social reality. This is a philosophical approach to sound-based political ontology: it looks for alternatives to traditional methods of philosophical abstraction in other parts of Western philosophy. That's why it reproduces the same old relations of domination and subordination in a slightly different shape. Sounding looks for models for the fundamental unit of social reality outside capital-P Philosophy, that is, in phonographic approaches to sound grounded in black intellectual and expressive traditions.

The next chapter traces a similar dynamic between philosophical and phonographic ontologies but focused on materialist rather than political ontology. Strains of the broad, internally heterogeneous, transdisciplinary theoretical approach called feminist new materialism are constituents of the sonic episteme that use acoustic resonance to upgrade philosophy's methods of abstraction so they're compatible with the kinds of methods and abstractions privileged by biopolitics, data analytics, and the neoliberal market. This renders theories of resonant, vibratory materiality that do not present themselves as upgrading European post/modernity exception, thus reproducing among theories the same relations neoliberal biopolitics produces among populations. However, among these theories there are phonographic ontologies modeled on methods of sonic and musical abstraction that tune practitioners in to the frequencies and realities the sonic episteme perceptually codes out of consideration. They are examples of intellectual practices that deliver on the promise the sonic episteme fails to realize: they use sound to remake capital-P Philosophy into something that doesn't reproduce the same relations of domination and subordination that it always has — namely, something that isn't Philosophy.

3

Vibration and Diffraction

Acoustic Resonance as Materialist Ontology

I. The Visual Microphone and Feminist New Materialism: Giving Voice to Silenced, Vibrating "Things"

Researchers at MIT are developing a device that reads video recordings of vibrating objects and reconstructs the sounds that caused and resulted from those visible vibrations. They call it a visual microphone because it sonifies contextually inaudible vibrations. As lead researcher Abe Davis explains, "We're recovering sounds from objects. That gives us a lot of information about the sound that's going on around the object, but it also gives us a lot of information about the object itself, because different objects are going to respond to sound in different ways."[1] The visual microphone (re)sonifies otherwise silent or silenced phenomena, giving "voice" to inanimate things or objects. It can also be used as something loosely akin to a mass spectrometer: because they are fine-tuned models of vibrating bodies, these recovered sounds give researchers information about the material properties (such as composition or structure) of those bodies.

The heart of the visual microphone is a set of "algorithms that amplify minuscule variations in video, making visible previously undetectable motions."[2] Amplifying the visual noise in video images and processing it through a variety of filters, the visual microphone compiles a database of noise, from which it then pulls out the profile of vibrations that would generate the most probable, "common sense" auditory signal.[3] The more visual data it can collect, the more successfully it can predict a legible *audio signal*. Instead of tuning noise out, it amplifies it so that the hidden "harmonics" emerge from all the irrational noise. The noisy data is then statistically normalized to produce a frequency that then gets transduced, through speakers, for us to hear.[4]

The visual microphone is an instrument that uses statistical normalization to reveal the "voice" or the sonic potential of traditionally nonspeaking or nonsonic phenomena. Recovering sounds from objects by attending to their material vibrations, the visual microphone embodies Jane Bennett's description of new materialism as "giving voice to things."[5] To be somewhat overly general, new materialisms argue that the ontologies we've inherited from European modernity are pernicious because they obscure the "true" nature of being behind human and humanist biases, the worst of which are subject-centrism and representational abstraction. In contrast to modernity's static, hierarchical divisions of the world into subjects and objects, humans and non-humans, new materialisms posit relatively flat ontologies of networked assemblages.[6]

Some strands of new materialism claim that material reality is fundamentally a kind of vibratory resonance. For example, defining "vibration" as "the specific relation of 'movement and rest' that obtains between its parts,"[7] Bennett echoes the idea that acoustic waves are patterned rhythms of condensation (when air molecules are under greater pressure and pressed closer together) and rarefaction (when air molecules are under less pressure and farther apart). Similarly, Elizabeth Grosz argues that "'in the beginning' is chaos, the whirling, unpredictable movement of forces, *vibratory oscillations* that constitute the universe."[8] Karen Barad's theory of philosophical diffraction is modeled after the same underlying scientific principles that contemporary physicists attribute to sounds. As I explained in the introduction, I use the term "acoustic resonance" to refer to these principles and the idea of sound that follows from them. In this chapter, I demonstrate that new materialist ontologies such as Grosz's, Bennett's, and Barad's ground their theories in the idea of acoustic resonance—rhythmic patterns that interact via phase relationships[9]—and argue that by using acoustic resonance as a model for philosophical theorizing, they create the same relationships among philosophers and their theories that neoliberalism creates among people.[10] That makes vibratory new materialisms constituents of the sonic episteme. I take Grosz's, Bennett's, and Barad's work as representative of vibratory new materialism both broad scholarly influence and for the clear and central role acoustic resonance plays in their work.

The "new" in "new materialism" refers to its claims to replace Western philosophy's traditional methods and the values associated with them with better alternatives. The new materialisms I study in this chapter treat vibratory resonance as new with respect to philosophy's ocular- and text-centric status quo. They hold these old methods and values responsible for political inequality, so leaving them in the past is supposedly sufficient for eliminating that inequality. Treating social domination as something it leaves behind, the "new" in new materialism abstracts away from ongoing relations of domination. Though new materialism claims to fix what's wrong with conventional philosophical practice by replacing representationalist abstractions with vibratory resonance, it just creates new versions of those same old problems. New materialism theorizes in qualitative terms the same relationships that post-identity biopolitics and neoliberal market logics address quantitatively. It creates the same relationships among intellectual practices that neoliberalism does among populations — i.e., a politics of exception.

To be absolutely clear: I am *not* critiquing the claim that we need to study the physical dimensions of things or that matter is important. I generally agree with that idea, and I think Barad's account of intra-activity is largely correct, but for different reasons than she does, reasons that are beyond the scope of this book.[11] New materialist arguments about anthropocentrism, correlationism, or human-subject-centrism are also outside the focus of my critique because they don't bear on my analysis of the sonic episteme.[12] My argument in this chapter is more narrow: new materialism is a constituent of the sonic episteme to the extent that it uses acoustic resonance as an idealized ontological model that translates the mathematical relationships behind neoliberal market logics and biopolitical governmentality into nonquantitative terms. This is caused by the specific way new materialism orients its concept of vibratory resonance to the world it theorizes and to the Western philosophical canon. It is not inherent in or universal to all theories of sound or resonance.

I begin this chapter by showing that Grosz, Bennett, and Barad use concepts of resonance, vibration, and diffraction that fit my definition of acoustic resonance, and that they use this concept of acoustic resonance to create qualitative versions of the relations of inequality that neoliberalism and biopolitics create quantitatively. Then, using Sara Ahmed's analysis of new materialism's "founding gesture" and Charles Mills's concept of ideal theory, I show how these vibratory new materialisms use a version of the audiovisual litany (the favorable opposition of sound to sight) to both (1) reform white, Western philosophy to function more efficiently in the neoliberal academy and (2) situate theories of sound and resonance outside white Western philosophy as an exceptional class in Spence's sense. As in the last chapter, the final part of

89

this chapter considers black feminist approaches to resonance, vibration, and diffraction as an example of phonographic resonant ontologies. I argue that Christina Sharpe's concept of wake and Ashon Crawley's notions of choreosonic vibration model the same sorts of relations and do the same conceptual work as new materialist notions of resonance, vibration, and diffraction, but they lack the political baggage that comes with the sonic episteme. In fact, Sharpe's and Crawley's analyses clarify the political problems with new materialist methods. Building on Crawley's argument that traditional methods of philosophical abstraction are a type of enclosure that transforms intellectual material into private property and whiteness as property (in Cheryl Harris's sense of that term), I show that new materialist uses of vibratory resonance continue philosophy's practices of enclosure.[13] I conclude by showing how Beyoncé's 2016 visual song "Hold Up" puts ideas of wake and choreosonic vibration in practice and models methods of addressing ideas and intellectual traditions that do not transform them into private property.

II. New Materialisms

1. New Materialism and Acoustic Resonance

90   Although Grosz, Bennett, and Barad all mix literal (i.e., nonfigurative) and metaphorical uses of sonic terminology, their primary claim that vibration is the elementary ontological structure of matter is a factual claim about reality. They make this claim in a variety of ways, but each use of vibration fits my definition of acoustic resonance.

Grosz argues that "vibration is the common thread or rhythm running through the universe."[14] She further explains that "the vibratory structure of matter itself" exhibits "peristaltic movements" like condensation and rarefaction and that these movements generate waves in the material or medium that surrounds them.[15] Similarly, Bennett defines vibration as an "indeterminate wave of energy" like Spinozan "conatus[, which] refers to the effort required to maintain the specific relation of 'movement and rest' that obtains between its parts."[16] Bennett's explanation here resembles contemporary understandings of sound waves as alternating patterns of pressure that are transmitted by the movement and rest of objects as they displace the ambient air. Arguing that both "what philosopher Brian Massumi describes as the 'pressing crowd of incipiencies and tendencies' that is matter"[17] and "life" are "differential[s] of intensities,"[18] Bennett specifies that vibration is a pattern of variable pressures (i.e., condensation and rarefaction).

Barad's concept of diffraction likewise centers on patterned intensities. In Barad's work, diffraction patterns are "the fundamental constituents that make up the world";[19] matter, apparatuses, phenomena — they are all diffraction patterns. She takes this concept of diffraction from physics, where it is used to describe the behavior of waveforms, including sound waves.[20] Diffraction is a pattern of alternating pressure or intensity. In physics, diffraction refers to the way a wave bends as it encounters another thing. When two or more waves interact, they produce "alternating pattern[s] of wave intensity" or "increasing and decreasing intensities,"[21] like ripples in water or alternating light frequencies. All three new materialist theorists define their basic unit of reality as a kind of acoustic resonance.

They use the term "resonance" and concepts of consonance and dissonance, which are subtypes of resonance, to explain how these units interact to form more complex structures and systems. In *Nick of Time* Grosz argues that "emergent patterns . . . resonate and interact with each other" and that the process of evolution incorporates past variations in current patterns with a type of "consonance" (248, 26). In *Chaos, Territory, Art*, it's clear that Grosz understands consonance as a kind of rational phase relationship wherein individual patterns nest rationally within large-scale social and environmental patterns. These large-scale patterns are a "pregiven counterpoint with which the living being must harmonize if it is to survive."[22] Evolution happens when individuals develop "randomly emergent qualities" that "harmonize" or fit within those large-scale patterns (44). Here she uses "counterpoint" and "harmony" in a not entirely technically correct sense to describe the behavior of consonant frequencies, whose phase patterns rationally sync up with one another.[23] This same phenomenon happens at the cosmological scale, where matter's vibrations interact and give rise to regular patterns or, in Deleuzian terms, "refrains"[24] as the "oscillations and vacillations of difference"[25] lock into rational phase relationships. These "rhythm[s]" are "a mode of *resonance* or *harmonious vibration*, an *oscillation* extracted from the fluctuating, self-differentiating structure of the universe itself."[26] Though she doesn't use this term, Grosz is talking here about consonance — frequencies whose phase patterns relate rationally.

Bennett and Barad also use concepts of consonance and dissonance to explain how vibratory and diffractive patterns interact. Bennett defines the kind of harmony produced when everything vibrates together negatively against a variety of different Western concepts of harmony. Claiming that this harmony is "neither a smooth harmony of parts nor a diversity unified by a common spirit,"[27] she specifically rejects classical notions of harmony as geometric proportionality ("a smooth harmony of parts"), as well as Enlightenment notions of (tonal) homophony as assimilation to a general will/underlying

91

tonic. Her positive definitions of harmony and resonance emphasize the idea of phase relationships: when "a chord is struck," she writes, "'effects' resonate with and against their 'causes'" in rational ("with") and irrational ("against") phase patterns (*Vibrant Matter* 120, 52). These patterns form a "complicated web of dissonant connections between bodies" in which "each member-actant maintains an energetic pulse slightly 'off' from that of the assemblage" (4, 24). Dissonance, as Bennett conceives it, is what happens when pulsed or rhythmic patterns interact in not fully rational ways. For Bennett, dissonance is a normal and positive thing, not a deficiency.

Barad frames her description of consonance and dissonance in scientific rather than musical terms. For example, she explains the effect of diffracting light waves around a razor blade as interference rather than harmony: "bright spots appear in places where the waves enhance one another—that is, where there is 'constructive interference'—and dark spots appear where the waves cancel one another—that is, where there is 'destructive interference.'"[28] Constructive interference is consonance: the synced patterns amplify one another; destructive interference is dissonance: the out-of-sync patterns mask each other. Both types of interference are varieties of resonance, a rational or irrational phase relationship among frequencies. For all three new materialist theorists, acoustic resonance—periodic oscillations of condensing and rarefying intensity that interact to form rational and irrational phase relationships—is the basic unit of reality.[29]

Their ontological claims about resonance are literal: reality isn't like a kind of resonance, it *is* resonant. But Grosz, Bennett, and Barad also use sonic metaphors to make epistemological and methodological claims about philosophical practice. Barad often uses the idea of resonance to translate wave behavior into materialist philosophical methods (*Meeting the Universe Halfway* 83). For example, she argues that "diffractively read[ing]" philosophical texts means processing "insights through one another for the *patterns of resonance and dissonance* they coproduce" (195, emphasis added). Similarly, she advises her readers to tune into the "dissonant and harmonic resonances" (43) that emerge when they try "diffracting these insights [from an early chapter in her book] through the grating of the entire set of book chapters" (30). This diffractive methodology studies phenomena for their differential patterns of intensity and the constructive or destructive interferences they produce when brought together with other phenomena.

This resonant methodology is what makes new materialism new. New materialism doesn't study representations or propositions but resonances. For example, announcing that "I will try to give voice to a thing-power," "spea[k] a word for vibrant matter," and "give voice to a vitality intrinsic to materiality,"[30] Bennett identifies "voice" as the object that new materialist theory studies. Importantly, she identifies resonant vocality as something philosophy has silenced, marginalized, and excluded with its focus on "the human semiotics"[31] of propositional speech. New materialism is "new" because it replaces philosophy's traditional methods and objects of study with ones that are supposedly more accurate and more just and inclusive. Later in the chapter I'll explain how new materialism's claims to overcome philosophy's traditional relations of domination and subordination just refashions them to work better in neoliberal and biopolitical institutions.

Grosz, Bennett, and Barad all posit acoustic resonance as the fundamental structure of reality and argue that this structure is a more accurate, more equitable, and just foundation for philosophical practice. They also use this idea of resonance to translate the probabilistic math behind neoliberalism and biopolitics into qualitative terms. Diana Leong argues that new materialist ontology is in general an attempt to account for "the effects of chance, unpredictability, and indeterminacy."[32] She explains: "As the new materialisms emphasize, the virtual field of differential relations is immanent to matter in such a way that it is impossible to anticipate all of the effects a material configuration may have, or the organizational forms it may take. . . . Matter and materiality are 'real' because they actively produce reality in unpredictable ways." New materialist ontology is an attempt to build a theoretical rationality that can incorporate chance, much in the same way Du Boisian statistics thematize and regularize chance. For example, Bennett uses the concept of vibration to explain a probabilistic approach to chance. She emphasizes in *Vibrant Matter* that "vital materiality . . . includes the aleatory" (119) in "an emergent causality . . . [that] may produce patterns of effects, though not in ways that are fully predictable" (42). Grosz explains how vibration systematizes chance occurrences in more detail. "A practice the living perform on chaos to extract some order and predictability," "rhythm [is] the emergence of a periodicity"[33] — that is, a regularized pattern or distribution. Like Du Bois's statistician, Grosz thinks these vibratory rhythms make chance something predictable: "vibrations are oscillations" that reveal "the promise of a future modeled in some ways on the rhythm and regularity of the present."[34] According to Grosz, the future is predictable not because it conforms to a pre-given image or telos but because the rhythm and regularity of chance ought to remain consistent. In *Nick of Time*, Grosz likens vibratory ontologies to probabilistic calculation. There, she describes life as a kind of cost/benefit rationality or bet: as "we act in a world . . . which we cannot fully anticipate or control, that we invent, we make more of ourselves than life makes of us. . . . It is a gamble, like Nietzsche's throw of the dice."[35] Assuming risky ventures, we can turn a profit that we can reinvest in ourselves, thus making more of ourselves than the universe initially made of us. And we do that by thinking probabilistically about risk, chance, and future profit or loss.[36] Contrasting her methods to the mathematical methods used in science, Grosz explicitly states that vibratory resonance is a qualitative version of what scientists do with probabilistic statistics. Unlike "science," which takes "the vibratory structure of the universe" and "makes of it a pattern, and eventually, measurement, ratio, or formula,"[37] Grosz takes the vibratory structure of the universe and makes it into something nonquantitative, that is, "resonance."[38]

Whereas Grosz and Bennett use resonance to talk about normalized distributions of chance occurrences in qualitative terms, Barad's account of diffraction homes in on a more fundamental element of that same math: the frequency ratio. According to Barad, diffraction and traditional methods of philosophical abstraction express different kinds of mathematical relationships: traditional philosophical reflection is "geometric" whereas diffraction is "physical" (*Meeting the Universe Halfway* 80). She argues that geometric relationships are mimetic and draw "homologies and analogies between separate entities" (88). For example, Plato's theory of the divided line is concerned with the accuracy with which things represent the Good/True/Beautiful and identifies homologous relationships among its various parts (e.g., forms : thoughts :: objects : images).[39] Physical relationships, in contrast, account for patterns of variability, like the variability of a waveform's peaks and valleys. They are "alternating patterns" (77) such as "the dynamic relationality between continuity and discontinuity" (182) legible in the alternating colors in the diffractions around the razor blade or in a tree's rings (181). Geometric and physical relationships are expressed as two different kinds of ratios. Drawing homologies and analogies, geometric ratios express likeness or correspondence. Tracking alternating dynamics, physical/topological ratios express a rate or a frequency. Arguing that diffraction is a method of abstraction that reduces phenomena to physical relationships, Barad directly tells us that her concept of diffraction translates frequency ratios into nonquantitative terms.

Grosz, Bennett, and Barad model both existence and philosophical practice on acoustic resonance, and they use resonance to translate the math behind neoliberalism and biopolitics into qualitative terms that can easily be used in philosophy and other humanities scholarship. As I explained in the introduction, this math reshapes the way white supremacist patriarchal relations of domination and subordination are structured. The ontological shift

94

from juridical to calculative rationality replaces law's discontinuities with statistical continuities: instead of excluding specific groups from civil personhood from the start, neoliberal and biopolitical instruments put everyone on the same spectrum or distribution and then deny personhood to groups whose deviance threatens the health or success of everyone else on the spectrum (e.g., bare life). The next section argues that new materialism's shift from representationalist to resonant methods of abstraction is a qualitative version of the neoliberal episteme's upgrade of juridical to calculative rationality. After that, I will show how Grosz, Bennett, and Barad apply qualitative versions of the same quantitative mechanisms neoliberalism and biopolitics use to create white supremacist, patriarchal, capitalist relations of domination and subordination out of statistical continuities to create the same relations among philosophers and their theories that neoliberalism and biopolitics create among people.

2. From Visual Discontinuity to Vibratory Continuity: New Materialism's Audiovisual Litany

As the name suggests, "new" materialism defines itself negatively against philosophy's "old" way of doing things. New materialists' main target are representationalist methods of abstraction that supposedly "reduc[e] 'everything' to language, signification and culture"[40] and constitute "a discursive reductionism that rebuffs the empirical for the ideal, or the material for the symbolic."[41] According to this view, representationalism is bad because it creates discontinuities between disembodied abstractions and concrete reality, and between humanistic and scientific inquiry, and values the former over the latter.[42] Running from Kant through Butler and beyond, representationalism is the status quo against which vibratory resonance appears as "new." In Grosz, Bennett, and Barad, this shift from representational discontinuities to resonant continuities is a qualitative version of the same upgrade to Western modernity that the neoliberal episteme performs in its shift from juridical to calculative rationality. They use a variation on what sound studies scholar Jonathan Sterne calls the "audiovisual litany"[43] to perform this upgrade, while misrepresenting its reform of identity-based social exclusion as the abolition of it.

a. The Audiovisual Litany

The audiovisual litany is a rhetorical device that favorably opposes sound and sonic phenomena to a supposedly ocular-centric status quo. It goes roughly like this: Western culture is ocular-centric, but the gaze is bad, so luckily sound and listening fix all that's bad about it.[44] Though the specifics of seeing and hearing vary with each articulation of the litany, all of them share the common assumption that "sound draws us into the world while vision separates us from it."[45] Vision, in other words, creates discontinuities, whereas sound sutures them or avoids them entirely. According to Sterne, the audiovisual litany is traditionally part of the "metaphysics of presence" that we get from Plato and Christianity: sound and speech offer the fullness and immediacy that vision and words deny.[46] However, new materialism appeals to a different metaphysics. As Marie Thompson explains, new materialism's version of the litany flips the original script: it associates sight and vision with the metaphysics of presence and "the 'staleness' of social theory, discourses of signification and representation, textual analysis and cultural critique" and then associates sound with dynamic, generative, relational processes that refuse such staleness and distancing.[47] In this model, what's missing from words isn't the fullness of some unadulterated metaphysical reality, like the Platonic Forms, but the fullness of material or physical reality in its complex generativity. Grosz's, Bennett's, and Barad's audiovisual litany opposes representationalist discontinuities (above all, the discontinuity between humans and nonhumans) to resonant continuities (all matter vibrates).

For example, Barad repeatedly rehearses the idea that "reflection still holds the world at a distance"[48] and is "untethered from the material world."[49] For Barad, representationalism uses language to address the world in the same way Kant's disinterested spectator addresses artworks: at a physical and intellectual distance. It assumes "the intrinsic separability of knower and known" and treats "theoriz[ing]" as "leav[ing] the material world behind."[50] As the visual side of the audiovisual litany, representation draws us out of the world.[51] As the audio side of that same litany, diffraction connects theorists back to the world and reconnects theorists to all the stuff representationalism distances us from. Treating diffraction rather than words as the model for philosophical abstraction, "it is once again possible," Barad argues, "to acknowledge nature, the body, and materiality in the fullness of their becoming without resorting to the optics of transparency or opacity."[52] This is a textbook audiovisual litany: sight removes philosophers from the world, whereas acoustic resonance in the form of diffraction reconnects us to it.

Bennett and Grosz rehearse similar litanies in which representationalism distances us from the world, whereas vibratory resonance puts us back in touch with it. Bennett argues that traditional philosophical skepticism—like "demystification" and the "hermeneutics of suspicion"—makes us insensitive to nonhuman agency and life.[53] Thus, in order to "enhance *receptivity* to the

96

impersonal life that surrounds and infuses us," "one needs . . . to *suspend suspicion* and adopt a more open-ended comportment" modeled on vibratory resonance.[54] Similarly, Grosz argues that music brings "philosophy" back to health by reconnecting it with matter, embodiment, and affective receptivity. For example, in the epigraph of *Chaos, Territory, Art*'s second chapter, she likens her project to that of Vladimir Jankélévitch, a twentieth-century French philosopher who argued that music, unlike philosophy, is primarily corporeal and affective. Her claim that "music is not just a useful metaphor . . . it is a literal form by which nature can be understood as dynamic, collective, lived rather than just fixed, categorized, or represented"[55] shows that like Jankélévitch, she thinks music draws us back to the world that philosophical representation leaves behind. The audiovisual litany is not just an opposition between sight and sound; it also is an opposition between a technique that creates discontinuities between knower and world and one that re-creates or preserves continuities between them. Grosz, Bennett, and Barad use this latter aspect of the audiovisual litany to upgrade white Western philosophy from a method of marking discontinuities with the material or nonhuman world to one that re-creates and preserves those continuities. In new materialism, the audiovisual litany performs a qualitative version of the neoliberal episteme's shift from juridical to calculative rationality.

As Sterne cautions, the audiovisual litany relies on dehistoricized caricatures of both sight and sound in order to obscure the fact that the difference between the litany's terms is not absolute and natural but contingent and biased. Treating "sight" and "sound" as synecdoches for contrasting sets of normative commitments, the litany thus naturalizes those commitments behind supposedly objective facts about human perception. In Grosz, Bennett, and Barad, the audiovisual litany obscures the stakes of their shift from representationalism to resonance. As I mentioned in the introduction, resonance hasn't had a singular or stable meaning throughout the history of Western thought. In vibratory new materialisms, the representationalist/resonance litany misrepresents a sociohistorically specific concept of resonance as an unbiased, uncontingent fact about sound and vibration, thus deflecting questions about why Grosz, Bennett, and Barad find this particular account of resonance so appealing. To redirect our attention to this question, I will briefly compare new materialism's critique of representationalism to musicologists' critiques of it. If sound, music, and even resonance can be theorized representationally, then Grosz's, Bennett's, and Barad's audiovisual litany doesn't mark an objective difference between two sets of tools (representationalist versus resonant methods) but rather the difference between two sets of normative commitments that produce distinct ways of understanding sight and sound. With this in mind, we can get a better sense of why Grosz, Bennett, and Barad think acoustic resonance is superior to all other ontological and methodological models in philosophy.

b. Musicological Critiques of Representationalism

Whereas Grosz's, Bennett's, and Barad's audiovisual litanies offer music, voice, and resonance as solutions to representationalism's disconnection and discontinuity with biophysical materiality, musicologists have identified representationalist approaches to sound and music that disconnect sound, music, and voice from their lived material reality. For example, in her highly influential 2004 article "Music — Drastic or Gnostic?," musicologist Carolyn Abbate critiques musicology's traditional representationalism and contrasts that to the vibrant immediacy of live, performed music. She argues that musicologists don't study music so much as abstractions about music: "the abstraction . . . [is] the true object of interest and acclaim" (509) because musicology treats music as an object for "reflection" at a "metaphysical distance" (511). Employing the same metaphor Barad does to describe traditional philosophical methods of abstraction, Abbate argues that "to reflect, must one in some sense depart" (511) from the "material and carnal" (527) dimensions of the "immediate aural presence" of "performed music" (502). And like Barad, Abbate connects reflection to linguistic reductionism: "verbally mediated reasoning" (510) produces propositional representations that require hermeneutic decoding. When musicologists translate music into philosophical abstractions, its definitively and distinctively "musical" features get lost because philosophy requires metaphysical distance from its object of study. Abbate contrasts these representationalist approaches to musicology with ones that attend to performed music rather than abstractions about music. As she argues, studying performed music without the middleman of representationalist abstractions "allow[s] actual live performance . . . to become an object of absorption" (506). Absorbed in that performance, musicologists can pay attention to the parts of "actual, live performances . . . [that] remain wild" (509). In Abbate as in Grosz, "real music" is a metaphor for patterned reverberations that incorporate "wildness" and chance.[56] Abbate's definition of music as a material process with a "temporal wake and its physical demands or effects"[57] echoes Barad's concept of diffraction patterns. Although Abbate rehearses the same representationalist vs. resonance litany that new materialists do, she situates it as the contrast between two ideas of sound or music (the "drastic" and the "gnostic"), not as the contrast between sight and sound.

Similarly, musicologist Nina Sun Eidsheim contrasts musicology's conventionally representationalist sonic abstractions, which "thin[k] about sound as an object," with ones that think about sound as vibration.[58] These traditional sonic abstractions are representationalist because they reduce sound to "the realm of the symbolic" and abstract away sound's relationality and dynamism, "reduc[ing it] to something static, inflexible, limited, and monodimensional."[59] In contrast to this approach, Eidsheim redefines sound as acoustic resonance.[60] For example, she cites Lindsay's wheel of acoustics (166) and describes vibration as "fundamental physical acoustics" (167), "oscillatory motion" (167), and "'amplitude and frequency acceleration applied to the body'" (171). Like Grosz, Bennett, and Barad, Eidsheim thinks vibration puts us back in touch with the material reality representationalism abstracts away by transducing sound's materiality into scholarly text. In acoustics, transduction is the transfer of a signal pattern from one medium to another; for example, the ear uses cilia attached to nerve fibers to transduce mechanical sound waves into electrical signals that the brain interprets as sounds. Whereas representationalist approaches to sound require scholars to abstract in ways that distance them from materiality and relationality, transduction maintains the connections severed by those abstractions. Because transduction describes a signal pattern's transformation as it moves from one set of material properties (i.e., medium) to another, it foregrounds "the materiality through which sound is transduced" rather than abstracting it away (148). Thus, according to Eidsheim, when vibration is taken as the object and transduction as the method of musical inquiry, "musical discourse then shifts from the realm of the symbolic to that of the relational" (181). Though she uses different terms than Abbate, Eidsheim likewise rehearses a litany between representationalist and resonant concepts of sound to advocate for the superiority of the latter as a method of musicological abstraction—vibration puts us back in touch with the material reality from which representationalism distances us.

Abbate and Eidsheim accuse musicology of the same flaws that Grosz, Bennett, and Brad identify in philosophy, and propose the same solution. They all argue that traditional methods of abstraction distance us from the materiality of the phenomena we study, but the study and experience of musical vibration puts us back in touch with that materiality. In the context of music scholarship, where music and sound have always been the object of analysis, claims that the difference between two different methods of abstraction can be reduced to the difference between words and sound are hard to credibly defend. Especially in Eidsheim's work, it is clear that the difference between "the figure of sound" and vibratory sound is the result of ontological differences not between sight and sound but between various methods of abstracting from performance-based practices to text-based scholarly practice. And the things that distinguish these methods from one another are their respective normative, ideological, and ontological commitments. In musicology, the representationalist vs. resonance litany contrasts representationalist scholarly methods that assume reality is and ought to be dualist and hierarchical with resonant ones that assume reality is and ought to be flat and emergent. So the real question here is *why the latter set of ontological commitments is increasingly appealing to scholars across the humanities.*

I argue that the representationalism-to-resonance upgrade adapts humanities disciplines to the neoliberal logics and values that now dominate the academy. It is a qualitative version of the same shift the neoliberal episteme performs in its upgrade of classically liberal juridical rationality to neoliberal calculative rationality. The next section explains how this works. I will pay special attention to the way this representationalism-to-resonance upgrade creates the same relations among philosophers and their theories that neoliberalism creates among people (i.e., a politics of exception).

3. New Materialism's "Founding Gesture" and the Politics of Exception

Situating resonance as "new" with respect to traditional philosophical commitments to hierarchy, exclusion, anthropocentrism, and representationalism, new materialist theorists claim to supersede or progress past established norms and practices. Sara Ahmed calls this new/old rhetorical device new materialism's "founding gesture." This gesture "evoke[s] a position that is not held by the speaker . . . as a way of making a counter-claim."[61] According to Ahmed, the gesture treats 1990s feminism as a straw-woman against which it can stake its claim for newness; "new" materialism is everything "old" feminism isn't. Adding to Ahmed's analysis, I argue that the framing of acoustic resonance as *newly* surpassing old epistemological and ontological commitments creates the same status differential among theories and intellectual traditions that neoliberalism and biopolitics create among people, and it is this status differential that motivates the preference for these "new" commitments over the old ones. Grosz, Bennett, and Barad use "resonance" to keep philosophy on the upper side of evolving status and power differentials while continuing to marginalize theories of sound, resonance, and vibration in nonwhite intellectual traditions. *The "new" in new materialism is a rhetorical gesture that enacts a politics of exception.*

But before I get to that argument, I will briefly recap what I mean by the politics of exception. The politics of exception rejects hierarchical exclusion and praises diverse mixes. As Lester Spence argues, the politics of exception breaks this mix down into three types of solute: (1) those who already exhibit the behaviors required for membership, namely, those who have reformed and adapted to new ideals of mixing and diversity; (2) those who are included as in need of reform, or those who do not currently but can potentially exhibit the behaviors required for membership; and (3) those who are excluded as unreformable, or those who are incapable or unwilling to adopt the behaviors required for membership.[62] Group 3 is the "exceptional" group. This group is seen as pathological—i.e., as dangerously inflexible, unchanging, and nonadaptive. Building on and syncing up with historical relations of oppression (e.g., white supremacist anti-blackness), such regulation generally produces the very un-adaptability it claims to quarantine. It's a viciously circular feedback loop. In what follows, I will show that in new materialist theory, the capacity to perform "newness" with respect to hidebound philosophical representationalism situates new materialism in Spence's first class and groups theories that don't perform this gesture into Spence's third class.

Grosz, Bennett, and Barad all describe new materialism's newness as surpassing and progressing past regular old philosophy. For example, Barad claims that taking Niels Bohr's quantum physics as a model for philosophical inquiry allows philosophers to "*move* such considerations *beyond* the well-worn debates that pit constructivism against realism, agency against structure, and idealism against materialism" and "*re*thin[k] fundamental concepts that support such binary thinking."[63] Barad's verbs here—move beyond, rethink—describe actions that replace by surpassing. Grosz also frames her project as a practice of moving beyond conventional modes of philosophical inquiry. Surpassing philosophy's conventional limits, her theoretical practice is, like existence itself, "a form of self-overcoming."[64] Putting it in less Nietzschean terms, Bennett argues that flexibility—both as the capacity to evolve beyond traditional configurations and the capacity to accommodate difference—distinguishes her vibrational ontologies from conventional modes of philosophical inquiry. For example, arguing that her project is grounded in a "performative contradiction" (120) in which humans "both are and are not" (114) extra-human nature, Bennett presents vibratory ontologies as flexible enough to accommodate the very thing philosophy excludes: the reality of both A and not-A. Grosz, Bennett, and Barad all choreograph their counter to philosophical representationalism as a replacement and surpassing. In this respect, they're representative of new materialism generally, which, as Steven Epstein describes, understands itself as operating "*in place of* a linguistic process of representing the world."[65] Key here is the "in place of": new materialism's founding gesture situates it as replacing and upgrading some older practice, a practice that is limited in specific ways: it's hierarchical, dualistic, and abstract. New materialism isn't just different from crusty old philosophy — it evolves beyond it, countering "old" philosophical representationalism's binaries and hierarchies with the performance of "newness."[66] Stepping past or beyond hidebound philosophical representationalism, the choreography of new materialism's founding gesture establishes new materialism as a member of Spence's first category: those who already have reformed and adapted to new ideas of mixing and diversity rather than hierarchy.

Although new materialism is supposedly better than representationalism because it prizes diversity over purity and includes what gets excluded by representationalist hierarchies — that is, because it replaces hierarchical discontinuities with resonant continuity — the vibratory materialisms I study in this chapter mark a break in this continuity that creates an exceptional class or population. Grosz and Bennett explicitly identify classes of unhealthy and dysgenic resonance. For example, Bennett emphasizes that her theory of matter departs from representationalism because it values hybridity over purity, but it then marks out certain classes of hybrids as pathological. Regarding the first part of that claim, she argues that her notion of vibrant materiality allows philosophers to "recas[t] the self in the light of its intrinsically polluted nature."[67] Unlike representationalist hierarchies, which use binary distinctions to maintain pure categories, "vital materiality better captures an 'alien' quality of our own flesh. . . . My flesh is populated and constituted by different swarms of foreigners."[68] Vibration counters old commitments to purity with new commitments to hybridity.[69] However, even this diversity is exclusive of genres associated with populations stereotypically incapable of adaptation to bourgeois ideals of respectability.[70] Distinguishing aesthetically pleasing from aesthetically displeasing wildness, Bennett makes a similar break in the continuity of vibrant matter: "The irresistible wildness of a lively woodchuck" is invigorating, she argues, yet "the repellent uncleanliness (in the sense of dirty, slimy, gooey) of its corpse" dampens vibrations with its viscosity.[71] Likewise, in her reading of Thoreau, she argues that we ought to privilege healthy mixes over pathological ones. According to Bennett, Thoreau "strives to confederate with a set of bodies . . . that render his own body finer, leaner, and more discerning — better able to sense the force of things."[72] Attunement to matter's vibratory patterns makes Thoreau more receptive to the things philosophy abstracts away. However, Thoreau associates himself only with the bodies that maximize his health by curing ailments caused by traditional philosophical practices. Patterns of behavior that don't exhibit this gesture of supersession (i.e., of overcoming representationalist skeptical melancholy) are dissonant with the frequencies at which matter vibrates and unworthy of admission into the confederation of vibratory matter. This is a politics of exception: it ties social inclusion to the performance of reform and flexibility, and it pathologizes supposedly static and unreformable phenomena.

Like Bennett, Grosz distinguishes between eugenic and dysgenic patterns of variability. This is most clearly evident in her comparison of music/resonance to Darwinian sexual selection: "Music," she argues, "belongs more to the order of sexual than natural selection."[73] According to Grosz, natural selection is truly random, like a "gamble" or an "accident."[74] Sexual selection, which Grosz defines as "the active but useless competition between males of the same species to attract the attention and discernment of females (or vice versa),"[75] shapes evolutionary accidents into rational and irrational patterns of variability. Rational patterns are consonant with other existing group norms and distributions (like binary gender and heterosexuality); irrational ones are dissonant with them. In Grosz's view, sexual selection is a process that amplifies patterns of chance and variability that are consonant with large-scale distributions of privilege and domination, life and death.[76] Likening music to sexual selection (as she does above), Grosz defines music as a kind of variability that is consonant with large-scale social structures; the rest, so to speak, is noise. If we apply this rubric to her own attempt to introduce a successful evolutionary variation within philosophy, then the "newness" of her new materialist practice must be consonant with existing norms and distributions of risk, vulnerability, success, and so on. In fact, the performance of newness is what makes new materialism consonant with those existing norms and distributions.

In the politics of exception, the demonstrated or potential capacity to reform oneself in accordance with newly dominant logics is what distinguishes those included in and protected by society and those it punishes and excludes as exception. Marking resonance, vibrance, and diffraction as *"new" vis-à-vis "old" Western (post)modernity*, new materialism both performs the behavior necessary for elite status in neoliberal institutions and defines any type of vibrancy or resonance that is not the result of overcoming past commitments to hierarchy, subject/object binaries, and other aspects of representationalism as exception.[77] Lacking demonstrable evidence of reform, adaptation, or overcoming, theories of vibratory resonance in intellectual traditions outside

103

new materialism qualify as an exceptional class, a class supposedly incapable of demonstrating the behaviors necessary for inclusion in the big diverse mix of voices.[78]

Most notably, new materialism marks as exception work in black studies and Africana philosophy that theorizes about and through various ideas of resonance and vibration, often in explicitly nonideal ways. Because these theoretical practices don't present themselves as having overcome Western post/modern visual representationalism, they don't exhibit the adaptive overcoming that the politics of exception demands of its constituents and are thus relegated to either Spence's second or third class. As Zakiyyah Iman Jackson explains, new materialism's "gestures toward the 'post' or the 'beyond' effectively ignore praxes of humanity and critiques produced by black people"[79] because those praxes and critiques don't situate themselves as superseding or overcoming traditional Euro-Western modernity. As a result, "potentially transformative expressions of humanity are . . . cast 'out of the world' and . . . rendered void or made to accord with Man's patterned logics by acts of presupposition."[80] Theory by black people is either normalized ("made to accord" with large-scale patterns of domination) and put in Spence's second class or rendered as exception ("cast out") and put in Spence's third class. Thus, Jackson concludes, this gesture of overcoming ironically reinstitutes the very thing it claims to supersede: stratifying theory into "new" and not-new, new materialist "appeals to move 'beyond' . . . may actually reintroduce the Eurocentric transcendentalism this movement purports to disrupt."[81] Instead of instituting that transcendentalism as a hierarchy, new materialism executes it as a politics of exception, a distinction between theories that have or can move beyond European post/modernity and those that purportedly can't or won't.

This choreography of supersession establishes or "justifies" (to use Kristie Dotson's term)[82] a project *as* philosophy. Theoretical practices that do not execute the gesture are unfit for inclusion within "philosophy" because they do not exhibit the behaviors that sync up with large-scale patterns of social privilege and domination. Both a turn away from representationalism and a turn *toward* acoustic resonance and the mathematical relationships it translates, the gesture is evidence not just of philosophy's capacity to reform but also of its ability to adopt and accord with dominant patterns of thought and distributions of value. There are lots of other ways it does this; I'll highlight some of the most significant.

As data-driven statistical normalization becomes an increasingly dominant mode and type of abstraction across corporate and government sectors, philosophy, with its old-fashioned theoretical and conceptual abstractions, is pressured to make itself over to keep up with the times and prove its continued relevance. For example, the rise of big data and advances in AI led magazines like *Wired* and *The New Scientist* to speculate about "the end of theory."[83] Faster, more comprehensive, and certainly more spectacular than mere human thought, algorithms threaten to make traditional modes of theoretical abstraction obsolete. What better way to prove philosophy's continued relevance than to make its methods of abstraction compatible with the statistical and probabilistic abstractions used across elite institutions? That's what new materialism does. Like the sonic episteme's other constituents, new materialism uses the concept of acoustic resonance to translate the kind of mathematical abstraction post-identity biopolitics uses — statistical normalization — into nonquantitative terms. For example, as Diana Leong argues, new materialism is fundamentally probabilistic. It "privileg[es] chance, contingency, and creativity in micro-level encounters" such that "matter and materiality are 'real' because they actively produce reality in unpredictable ways (Cheah, 2010)." Grosz's use of resonance to describe the emergence of signal from the chaotically noisy universe is an example of this. So is Barad's modeling of diffraction on the probabilistic math used in quantum physics. *New materialism uses the audiovisual litany to update the methods of humanistic inquiry so they work with qualitative versions of the quantitative abstractions used by probabilistic forecasts and normalized statistical distributions.* Their turn away from European modernity toward resonance is oriented not toward subaltern or subjugated knowledge practices but toward the newly hegemonic one. Bringing philosophy in accord with dominant practices of abstraction, new materialism leaves these other intellectual practices behind as unworthy of continued investment.

Similarly, new materialism's turn toward hard sciences like biology and physics has the effect of aligning philosophy with the most prestigious and well-funded fields in the twenty-first-century academy. Much like analytic philosophy in the twentieth century, which allied itself with the hard sciences *against* the rest of the humanities[84] just as these humanities fields began to incorporate feminist, queer, and critical race theory and scholars from those underrepresented groups, new materialism appears to be a turn toward hard science and all the prestige (which is not unrelated to its whiteness and cismaleness) that comes with it. As scholars like Leong and Jackson emphasize, this turn toward hard science for inspiration is a turn *away* from a long tradition of scholarship by black intellectuals that already addresses many of new materialism's main concerns. This commentary echoes Ahmed's critique of new materialism's founding gesture: it erases past feminist work. But as I have just shown, we can further refine Ahmed's point: the "newness" of new materialism is secured by creating "old" theory as exception, as what is static and incapable of reform. For example, as Leong argues, "the framing of the new materialisms as inherently more ethical generates, and is generated by, a disavowal or misreading of race as a stagnant analytical framework." By classifying theories that continue to pay attention to ongoing white supremacy as "stagnant" and "exhausted" (Leong) rather than "new" and adaptable, new materialisms use a single gesture to both abstract away from ongoing oppression and situate theories that treat vibration, diffraction, and resonance as descriptive models of an unjust society as insufficiently flexible and new—i.e., as exception.[85] Because "resonance" brings philosophy in accord with dominant epistemic and political models, intellectual practices that don't ground themselves in resonance or the math it translates appear dissonant and unworthy of further support and investment. Adopting acoustic resonance as its primary figure and method of theoretical abstraction, new materialism brings philosophy in accord with neoliberal biopolitics' epistemology, in terms of both how it thinks (the method of abstraction) and its distribution of what counts as scholarly knowledge. New materialism's gesture of supersession shows its ability to keep pace with—and garner prestige in—an academy that has itself embraced neoliberal market logics, data analytics, and the like, and to avoid the increasingly low status attributed to the humanities.

Because it is consonant with and effectively speaks the same language as neoliberal market logics and post-identity biopolitics, new materialism is easy to exploit for those purposes. For example, Bruce Braun argues that "modes of neoliberal governance" have "absorbed and deployed" new materialism's "notio[n] of non-deterministic nature."[86] Even though, as Braun repeatedly emphasizes, there is no *necessary* connection between neoliberalism and new materialism, "this redefinition is part of what others have argued is a shift toward a 'topological' approach to genealogy, one that identifies 'patterns of correlations' that lead to the formation of particular dispositions of unified heterogeneous elements (Collier, 2009)."[87] This shared focus on "patterns of correlations" is Braun's way of describing what I call their common method and type of abstraction: acoustic resonance as a nonquantitative version of probabilistic distributions. In effect, new materialism and neoliberal modes of governance speak different dialects of the same language of abstraction. As Braun argues, this is why it's easy for new materialist theory to be appropriated by and made to work for the interests of neoliberal modes of government. Braun identifies several co-presenting factors that led environmental philosophers to use the concept of ontological indeterminacy developed by new materialist theory as a tool for financializing our concept of nature and environmental policy (e.g., carbon emission exchanges). My argument is that various co-presenting factors exist in the academy, like, say, the neoliberalization of university administration (and thus also of the university's daily operations), the increasing pressures to secure external research funding and the disproportionate availability of funding for science-oriented scholarship,[88] the general prestige of science in the academy, calls from all around the academy (from data science to digital humanities) that "theory" is dead because we have statistics now,[89] or even calls from within the humanities that "critique" is obsolete (such as the "reparative reading" trend in literary studies).[90] These factors all contribute to a situation where it would be easy and rewarding to use new materialist theory in ways that both realize and naturalize the potential relationships with neoliberalism that their common language of abstraction makes possible.

We don't need to look beyond new materialist theory itself to find examples of this. As I have been arguing throughout this section, new materialism's founding gesture enacts a politics of exception. The politics of exception requires everyone to demonstrably adapt to neoliberal logics and ideals as proof that they're worthy of elite status. These logics use continuities to recreate the same basic relations of domination and subordination that classical liberalism creates with discontinuities. From this perspective, pointing out the existence of ongoing discontinuities such as race- and gender-based status differences demonstrates one's failure to adapt to neoliberal logics and ideals. In Grosz, Bennett, and Barad, new materialism's founding gesture presents resonant continuities as an adaptation beyond representationalist discontinuities and marks theories that continue to point to identity-based discontinuities as exception. Neoliberalism demands everything adapt to its logic of numerical continuity—even nonquantitative things like qualitative humanities scholarship. New materialist theory adopts acoustic resonance as its fundamental unit of reality and its model for philosophical practice in order to meet this demand. The ontological commitments it champions are appealing because neoliberalism makes them compulsory qualifications for elite status. This is yet another way Grosz, Bennett, and Barad use resonance to create qualitative versions of the same racialized status relations that neoliberalism and biopolitics create quantitatively.

As I discussed above, new materialism's capacity to translate the math behind neoliberal market logics and biopolitical normalization into nonquantitative terms makes it easily exploitable by and in service of those discourses. The next section argues that Grosz's, Bennett's, and Barad's use of resonance is especially susceptible to exploitation by neoliberal and biopolitical variations on white supremacist cisheteropatriarchal capitalism because they use an idealized model of acoustic resonance that, like neoliberal concepts of the market and biopolitical concepts of life, abstracts away from ongoing relations of domination and subordination.

4. New Materialism as Ideal Theory

Grosz, Bennett, and Barad use concepts of acoustic resonance that model how resonance works under perfect or ideal circumstances. In philosophers' terms, it is an idealized model of resonance. Charles Mills defines idealized models negatively against descriptive models. Whereas descriptive models capture "P's crucial aspects (its essential nature) and how it actually works,"[91] idealized models are "an exemplar, of what an ideal P should be like."[92] Idealized models figure how things *ought* to work in a *perfect* world. The problem is, of course, that the world isn't actually perfect, and its imperfections and their consequences are disproportionately distributed to oppressed groups. Beginning from *ought* rather than *is*, idealized models "abstract away from relations of structural domination, exploitation, coercion, and oppression."[93] Theories modeled on a perfect world cannot account for systemic domination, and when they are applied to our imperfect world(s), they make that domination worse. As idealized models, new materialist concepts of acoustic resonance do precisely this.

Grosz, Bennett, and Barad use idealized models of acoustic resonance grounded in how music, vibration, and diffraction ought to work in perfect conditions. For example, as scholars such as Stephen Zepke, Jussi Parikka, and Marie Thompson have shown, new materialist concepts of matter are based on other theorists' ideas of what art is in the abstract rather than on the description of art and media objects and practices. Zepke points out Grosz's "silence about 'actual art'" in favor of philosophers' theories of art.[94] Thompson argues new materialism's "turn away from lived differences, social mediation and historicism and toward . . . the pure productivity of matter mirror[s] the rhetorical and material formations of 'post–civil rights,' 'post-racist,' 'post-sexist,' 'post-class,' 'post-identity' capitalist society" by treating identity-based inequity as something that this very turn toward resonance and away from representationalism overcomes.[95] Parikka contrasts new materialism's habit of ignoring media objects and practices with a nonideal account of materiality grounded in the description of those phenomena. Unlike new materialism, which models how vibration works in perfect circumstances, this descriptively modeled materiality would foreground the imperfections ideal theory abstracts away, such as "de-powering . . . bad encounters that reduce the vitalities of material assemblages in such encounters."[96] As these criticisms show, new materialism is a type of ideal theory because it treats music, vibration, and diffraction as an idealized model of a perfectly functioning world.[97] Though diffraction and vibration often describe actual physical processes, when these physical processes conducted in relatively ideal *experimental* conditions are used as models for processes conducted in thoroughly nonideal *social* conditions, these concepts of acoustic resonance function as idealized models.

Even though Bennett and Barad do at times refer to particular cases (unlike Grosz, who only reads other philosophers' accounts of music and resonance), these cases are conceived solely from the perspective of the white Western philosophical canon. Modeling voice, vibration, and resonance only on white Western philosophical figurations of these concepts, new materialism adopts accounts of voice, resonance, and vibration grounded in the experiences and cultural practices of systematically advantaged groups, groups who, because of their advantages, "experience the least cognitive dissonance between ideal-as-idealized-model and ideal-as-descriptive-model."[98] These nominally descriptive models are still idealized ones because they fail to describe and account for systematic social disadvantage. John Gillespie Jr.'s reading of Bennett points out one way this happens. He argues Bennett's concept of voice is modeled on white Western notions of voice and vibration to the exclusion of theories of voice in black intellectual and aesthetic traditions. Bennett's project thus "cannot accept that Non-Human/Incommunicable standpoints might have a completely different system of being and knowing" and "does not engage with the possibility that the 'object/witness' may have an entirely different system of interest"[99] because they, as Diana Leong explains, already "have had to think within and through the categories of the non-human and the inhuman to pursue new ways of being in the world." In nonwhite intellectual traditions, sonic concepts and practices are shaped by experiences of racism and institutionalized white supremacy.[100] Grosz's, Bennett's, and Barad's new materialisms are ideal theory because they model resonance on the theories and practices of white people, whose experiences come closest to fitting neo/liberal ideals, such as the ideal of a universally inclusive social continuity "where all subjects have been granted equal access to western humanity."[101] As much as they claim to revolutionize philosophy, new materialisms continue to rely on idealized models that abstract systemic domination away.[102] In new materialism, "resonance" functions analogously to neoliberal models of the market and biopolitical concepts of life, which like idealized models put everyone on the same continuity and thus abstract away from the very social discontinuities they produce.

I have just shown several ways new materialism uses ideas of acoustic resonance to create qualitative versions of the same relations that neoliberalism and biopolitics produce quantitatively. But this doesn't mean all vibratory, resonant, and sonic ontologies are doomed to the same mistakes new materialism makes — there are better choices. The rest of this chapter builds on chapter 2's discussion of in-the-red sounds to consider some of the vibratory ontologies new materialism renders exception. Specifically, I focus on theoretical practices where resonance is a descriptive model of patterns of living that black women have developed within the registers of existence which white supremacist patriarchy perceptually codes out of its reality.

III. Vibratory Resonance in the Red

Christina Sharpe's concepts of wake and vibration and Ashon Crawley's concept of choreosonic vibration are abstractions of the same general shape or type as new materialist vibration/diffraction, but they are ideal-as-descriptive models that account for the structuring reality of white supremacy as experienced by black people. These phonographic concepts of vibratory resonance inhabit parts of the spectrum that capital-P Philosophy (the institution of academic philosophy) perceptually codes out of scholarly transmission.[103] They model methods of abstraction that compress lived experience according to a different "mathematical model of hearing," one that prioritizes the transmission of knowledges black women have developed to survive amid white supremacist patriarchy and that abolishes the logics of enclosure Philosophy uses to appropriate and extract surplus value from intellectual traditions outside the white Western canon. To explain how this works, I first unpack Crawley's concept of choreosonics and the aphilosophical kind of compression one must use to hear those phonographic resonances. Then I show how Sharpe's 2016 book *In the Wake* and Beyoncé's 2016 visual song "Hold Up" use literary and musical devices to translate that mathematical model of hearing into nonquantitative terms.

1. Choreosonics

In *Blackpentecostal Breath*, Ashon Crawley uses vibratory sound as a model for an "aphilosophical" theoretical practice. Metaphysically, Crawley's concept of vibration is generally the same as the other theories of vibration I've discussed in this chapter: a rhythmically patterned oscillatory movement. "Vibration," he argues, is "the displacement of air" (20) that falls into patterns figured either as "movement away from and to" (19) or as "pace, speed, [and] rhythm" (96). His primary model for this patterned displacement of air pressure is breath: "the always more than double gesture of inhalation and exhalation" (36) mirrors the repeated condensation and rarefaction of a vibrating waveform. Breath is an oscillating movement, such as the relationship between inhale and exhale or between call and response. This is a rhythmic relationship that parses a performance, text, or experience into irregularly sized sections and creates a phase space within which aleatory experiences can occur.[104]

Unlike new materialists, Crawley doesn't claim to offer a general or universal theory of vibration. Instead, he's using vibration as a descriptive model for a specific practice of abstraction used in Blackpentecostal aesthetics. Crawley takes the stylized form of preaching called "whooping" as an example of this kind of abstraction. Whooping adds extra syllables or other vocalizations to the ends of phrases, extending and embellishing them. For example, punctuating the end of some lines with "yeah … wooo" (1:42–1:44), "um" (1:14), "uh" (1:26), and the like, Rihanna's 2016 single "Love On the Brain" does something similar to whooping.[105] Though traditional philosophical and musicological abstractions would analyze vocal performances for their words or notes, whooping draws attention to what gets abstracted away in the study of words (philosophy) and notes (musicology/theory): "the intentioned apportioning of breathing" in vocalists' "varied breathing patterns" (Crawley, *Blackpentecostal Breath*, 42–43, 35). Paying attention to the patterns vocalists use to portion out their breaths, we can identify differences between whooping and the patterns of breathing common in white Protestant congregational singing, where it is common for congregations to pause every two or four bars and add a beat on which everyone takes a breath. Unlike this "catechismal" (170) breathing, which disciplines practitioners to a preordained script, whooping is a kind of "choreosonic" (147) abstraction that "br[eaks] — while giving — form" (170). Like "the cut" in hip-hop aesthetics, choreosonic vibration ruptures regular, disciplined form to create "otherwise form."[106] It is "a disruption of grammar" (163) that does not rationalize these disruptions into a higher-order distribution. For example, whooping adds to the length of a phrase, but not in any regularizable, predictable pattern. (In fact, whooping's unpredictable patterning echoes the technique Sharpe and McKittrick apply to the motives of "wake" and "she says she was born free" in their own writing. I discuss these later in the book.) Between inhale and exhale, call and response, whooping creates phase spaces within which random events can happen. As Crawley explains, "the pause or the break when one prays or preaches … creates a gap wherein the voices of congregants can 'fill' the otherwise than 'empty' silence" (43). Responding to the speaker's call, congregants create a vibratory phase within the speaker's larger-scale inhale-exhale pattern that is almost like a har-

111

monic or partial to the speaker's initial frequency, but of variable and indeterminate length. Whooping thus illustrates how choreosonic vibrations both parse the overall text into sections of indeterminate length and articulate a phase space that invites indeterminate events in response to its calls.

Choreosonic vibration is a practice of abstraction grounded in a descriptive model of black people's aesthetic practices. It is not an idealized model of sound in general. Nor does it translate the math behind neoliberal biopolitics into nonquantitative terms. Crawley emphasizes that choreosonic approaches to indeterminacy are "centrifugitive." This portmanteau combines "centrifuge" with a Motenian concept of fugitivity.[107] Unlike normalized statistical distributions, which compare the frequencies at which chance occurrences happen in order to find the most frequent frequencies, centrifugitive practice "is against the notion of centering"[108] — it doesn't take this meta-step of measuring the frequency of frequency patterns and privileging the most frequent one as a center around which all other rhythms are distributed. For these reasons, they are not a part of the sonic episteme — and, just to be clear, that's a good thing.

In their "refusal of being centered," centrifugitive practices like choreosonic rhythm "dispers[e] with the spatiotemporal geometric logics of western civil society" (*Blackpentecostal Breath*, 107). Normalization is one of these logics; enclosure is another. Enclosure refers to the practice of transforming the commons into private property, often through a Lockean mixing of one's labor with nature. Crawley's gesture toward enclosure and new materialism's gesture toward representationalism point to the same part of the Western philosophical canon. Much like Barad, Crawley characterizes "normative modes of . . . philosophical" practice as "reflection" (7). He also thinks that philosophical reflection is grounded in a logic of hierarchical exclusion and its attendant "desires for purity," and this leads practitioners to abstract away from material life (11). For example, he argues that "the representation of the object by the displacement of materiality before encounter is constitutive of philosophic thought" (118). Focusing attention on language, words, or "just the notes," philosophical abstractions practice a type of objectifying vision that leaves the conditions of textual or musical production — such as breath patterns — on the cutting-room floor.

Even though both Crawley and new materialist theorists think philosophy overlooks materiality, Crawley's claim is more narrow — philosophy perceptually codes choreosonic and centrifugitive materiality away into the red. First, Crawley argues that philosophy isn't the refusal of materiality but is itself "a movement of the mind" (112), "a material way to be, and thus to think about being, in the world" (111) defined by its negative orientation or "aversion" to choreosonic materiality (93). For example, Crawley discusses how Kant's philosophy is modeled on certain material practices, such as the clockwork regularity of his walks. However, Kant's characterizations of his routine omit the "the sounded movements . . . the moving sound" he made as he walked around and the ambient sound of the streets he moved through (113). Focused primarily on the regularity of his walking schedule, Kant's account of his material practice doesn't just omit but actively suppresses its choreosonic aspects—both the sounds his body makes as he walks (his breath, his footfalls, the swooshing of his clothes or jangling of accessories) and the "improvisational" (111) interactions one has with whomever or whatever one encounters along the way. This example illustrates how philosophy's material practices abstract away from choreosonic materiality.

Philosophy's material practices perceptually code choreosonic materiality into the red because this materiality, even if it were mixed with philosophical labor, couldn't be efficiently transformed into private property. As Crawley argues, "Philosophical thought is simply another enclosure of and on thought" (119) because it treats thinking as the labor of transforming common sense into an author's or the discipline's private property. Academic philosophy's "culture of justification"[109] is a clear example of philosophical enclosure that also connects enclosure to white supremacy and anti-blackness. The crux of this culture is the expectation that work not immediately legible as philosophy (e.g., as related to a canonical figure or topic) establish, to use Kristie Dotson's phrase, "how this paper is philosophy." In responding to the "how is this paper philosophy?" demand, scholars mix their labor with "uncultivated" material,[110] improving that material and transforming it into something that both the author and the field own.[111] This is a racializing (and cisheterogendering) practice in two ways: First, because Western philosophical canons are overwhelmingly defined by white (cis, hetero, able-bodied) male authors and their trademarked concepts (Hegelian dialectic, the Gettier problem, etc.), answering "how is this paper philosophy?" or "what does this have to do with Hegel?"[112] processes supposedly raw intellectual material into terms whiteness and white supremacist institutions can capitalize on. Second, just as white people experience the advantages white supremacy grants them as a private property interest, philosophy turns this private property interest into a theoretical practice.[113] Scholars inherit the discipline's capital—institutional recognition and prestige, tenure, etc.—by demonstrating their work's filiation with "Philosophy."

Traditional methods of philosophical abstraction don't abstract away

113

materiality in general. As Crawley shows, they target material racially coded as black (black people, choreosonic rhythm, centrifugitive performance) with respect to whiteness as a private property interest. New materialism's failure to engage black studies and work by black scholars is another instance of philosophical aversion. New materialist theories of resonant vibration may tune into aspects of materiality that representationalist methods abstract away from, but they likewise actively ignore centrifugitive and choreosonic materiality. In this way, new materialism's founding gesture isn't just a turn away from the established philosophical canon, but also an aversion to theories of sound that don't advance philosophy's project of enclosure. This is one significant reason why new materialist theory has, as Leong, Gillespie, Jackson, and others have shown, actively ignored research in black studies and by black scholars. New materialism's aversion to this work and to these scholars isn't just the result of institutional and/or authorial bias. Rather, the mechanics of the theory itself is designed to rehearse this aversion. Crawley's distinction between choreosonic vibration and resonance points us to the specific part of new materialist theory that's responsible for the active inattention to black thinkers and black thought. Though new materialism claims to recover materiality for philosophy, its turn toward material vibration is also a turn away from or aversion to choreosonic vibration and centrifugitive material, phenomena that can't be efficiently enclosed by and for philosophy.

Choreosonic methods of abstraction are "aphilosophical" because they tune into parts of the spectrum of existence that philosophy's methods of abstraction perceptually code out of scholarly attention. For example, though Crawley treats "philosophy and theology as abstractions *against* which Black-pentecostal aesthetics evade" (109), he repeatedly emphasizes that the practices of evasion he studies are "ongoing otherwise possibilities. I do not say new" (6) and that evasion, "rather than a turn to the new, is the production of otherwise . . . possibilities already enacted, already here" (34). Choreosonic and centrifugitive abstractions descriptively model practices with long histories. Their practitioners understand themselves not as replacing or progressing past white intellectual norms but as inhabiting parts of the spectrum those norms perceptually code out of scholarly conversation.

Crawley offers Harriet Jacobs's listening practices as an example of tuning into these "otherwise" bandwidths. Jacobs was a slave whose memoir detailed how she lived for seven years in her grandmother's attic/crawlspace. This space let her hide from her master and still be near to and keep abreast of family. Jacobs was totally hidden from view and could not see out of the attic; she could, however, hear what went on both in and outside her grandmother's house. Crawley describes this "forced looking away that heightened her awareness of sound in and around her" as a kind of "compression" (155). Removing what is conventionally treated as the dominant and most important sensory frequencies (sight), Jacobs's method of compression flips the script on perceptual coding, which compresses signal by removing redundant frequencies. Circumstances compel her (this is a "forced looking away") to tune in to those conventionally redundant or "discarded" (155) frequencies and modes of perception. This method of compression allows Jacobs to access "a different spatial and temporal measure than western thought allows" (155) — i.e., the "otherwise" of choreosonic and centrifugitive practice. Rather than seeking envoicement, which is ultimately a politics that seeks recognition by and from dominant institutions, Jacobs's style of compression evades dominant modes of perception, hiding out in the "B-sides of the record, the underside and the underground" (99). Neither Jacobs nor Crawley treat sound as something that replaces or progresses past sight; it is, rather, what racist, heterosexist circumstances make available as a space to escape surveillance. Instead of superseding the dominant status quo, compression treats that status quo as redundant signal, tuning it out in order to tune in to ongoing below-the-radar work.

Grounding his method in Jacobs's style of compression, Crawley brings into focus precisely the theories and practices that new materialism's founding gesture renders as exception: vibratory abstractions that people have practiced and continue to practice below Philosophy's radar and which do not aim to progress past or replace Philosophy's conventional methods of abstraction. Like new materialist concepts of resonance, choreosonics are vibratory abstractions that distill phenomena down to periodic, oscillatory relationships. However, because they are nonideal models grounded in oppressed people's epistemic and aesthetic traditions, they (a) more accurately diagnose the problem with the Western philosophical canon, (b) avoid doubling down on the political problems and inequities new materialist theories of vibratory resonance claim to solve, and (c) model intellectual practices that both affirm black epistemic traditions and contribute to relationships, structures, and institutions that are existing, ongoing alternatives to white supremacist cis-heteropatriarchy. If you want to work with vibratory abstractions, Crawley's method has many advantages over new materialism's.

2. Wake

Like Crawley's theory of choreosonic vibration, Christina Sharpe's concepts of wake and aspiration are nonideal vibratory abstractions that descriptively model both the ongoing effects of slavery and the aesthetic practices black people have developed in response to those effects. Attending to the choreo-sonics and the sonics of verbal texts, Sharpe demonstrates a method of abstraction that tunes in to the ontologies and patterns of existence that black people have developed in the frequencies white supremacy perceptually codes out of conventional archives.

Though she ascribes to "wake" a propositional content, Sharpe also uses choreosonics to define that term. Reiterating various definitions through the text, in italics, she creates a wake-like refrain throughout the book's structure — i.e., a choreosonic pattern that parses out the text's large-scale form in irregular sections.[114] (Katherine McKittrick uses a similar strategy in her "Mathematics of Black Life," which Sharpe cites in *In the Wake*[115] and which I discuss extensively in the next chapter.) To highlight this refrain, I'll list several variations of Sharpe's definition together and then discuss the content of individual sentences (all italics in the original):

— "*Wake*: the track left on the water's surface by a ship; the disturbance caused by a body swimming or moved, in water; it is the air currents behind a body in flight; a region of disturbed flow." (3)

— "*Wake*; the state of wakefulness, consciousness." (4)

— "So, the same set of questions and issues are presenting themselves to us across these historical periods. It [is] the same story that is telling itself, but throughout the different technologies and processes of that particular period (Saunders)." (5)

— "*Wake*: grief, celebration, memory, and those among the living who, through ritual, mourn their passing and celebrate their life in particular the watching of relatives and friends beside the body of the dead person from death to burial and the drinking, feasting, and other observances incidental to this." (11)

— "One aspect of Black being in the wake as consciousness . . . to be in the wake is to occupy and to be occupied by the continuous and changing present of slavery's as yet unresolved unfolding." (13–14)

— "Take up the wake as a way toward understanding how slavery's continued unfolding is constitutive of the contemporary conditions of spatial, legal, psychic, and material dimensions of Black non/being as well as Black aesthetic and other modes of deformation and interruption." (20)

— "The amount of time it takes for a substance to enter the ocean and then leave the ocean is called residence time. We, Black people, exist in the residence time of the wake, a time in which 'everything is now. It is all now.'"[116]

The refrain of wake-iterations gives Sharpe's text a periodicity, like the periodicity of a wave or a column of vibrating air. And within the fundamental — the period of the book from introduction to conclusion — there are subperiods — the recurrence of individual definitions of "wake" (wake as consciousness, as a ship's disturbance, as death rituals) acts almost like harmonics or overtones, subfrequencies within the fundamental frequency.

Like Crawley, Sharpe uses breathing patterns to illustrate the choreosonic character of the wake's vibratory patterns. As an empirical phenomenon, aspiration is the patterned flow of fluid (like water or air) in and out of lungs; our throats and vocal cords and sinuses and tongues and mouths sonify that flow. Transforming the empirical phenomenon into a metaphor, Sharpe thus emphasizes its "complementary sense" as both "the withdrawal of fluid from the body (and the taking in of foreign matter usually fluid) into the lungs with the respiratory current, and as audible breath that accompanies or comprises a speech sound" (109). Aspiration is both a patterned flow of intensity (sucking in or pushing out fluid) and the sonification of that pattern as it vibrates the bodies that contain aspirating lungs. Aspiratory sounds include things like the sound of someone inhaling right before they begin speaking or singing, the pauses in a singer or speaker's flow to grab a breath, and breath itself as a nonverbal vocalization, like rapper Nicki Minaj's extended inhales in "Anaconda," or the laugh in the chorus of Grandmaster Flash and the Furious Five's "The Message." Sharpe uses aspiration to theorize the same phenomenon Crawley calls choreosonic vibrations — the breathing patterns that accompany vocal utterance. Her definitions of wake create aspiratory patterns within her text. This structure or form is just as central to her definition as the attributes these sentences describe.

The content of her repeated definitions of "wake" echo new materialist concepts of resonance, vibration, and diffraction, but they are nonideal rather than idealized models. For example, the first of Sharpe's definitions listed above — wake as disturbances in water and/or air — closely tracks Barad's definition of diffraction; those patterns of disturbance *are* diffractions. However, Sharpe uses wake as a descriptive model of a nonideal social ontology. Specifically, wake models a society that continues to be "haunted" or "possessed"[117] by phenomena whose effects persist beyond the dismantling of their original

117

material-discursive arrangement. As the last few quotes on the above list show, the wake is a way of theorizing "slavery's continued unfolding." In direct contrast to new materialism's founding gesture, which carves out a "new" against the old, Sharpe's theory of the wake emphasizes the interweaving of past, present, and future. Citing Toni Morrison here, Sharpe's prose performs the temporal logic it describes: Sharpe takes Morrison's words and reiterates them in the now, illustrating the residence time of past patterns (here, of prose) with current . . . currents. Like a ship's trail in water or rituals surrounding the death of a person, Sharpe's concept of wake highlights the ongoing nature of supposedly past events.[118]

Sharpe notes that the practices that create such wake patterns — Middle Passage and its afterlives — are the foundations for contemporary capitalist technologies such as "the mathematics of insurance" (38). These practices also inform, or at least share common elements with, another capitalist technology that, though less violent and deadly than the slave trade, is nevertheless a white supremacist project: perceptual coding. For example, both perceptual coding and Middle Passage are "about shippability and containerization and what is in excess of those states" (30) — that is, about transmission, circulation, and their relationship to surplus value. And in both cases white Western norms (about speech and about personhood) ground logics of disposability that create an "excess" that doesn't need to be transmitted. Sharpe's analysis of slave ship records reveals that slave traders applied a kind of perceptual coding to the information they recorded about their enterprises. As Sharpe points out, slave ship ledgers counted individual slaves as "ditto" rather than by assigning them names. The word "ditto" codes out individual identity and personhood, reducing slaves to abstract quantities. "*The ditto ditto in the archives*"[119] creates rhythms and patterns that transmit what white supremacy thinks is most essential about black people and blackness: their status as fungible property. Sharpe argues that this "ditto ditto" reappears in the twenty-first century as "the rapid, deliberate, repetitive, and wide circulation on television and social media of Black social, material, and psychic death."[120] Whether ledgers from slave ships or Twitter hashtags, media in the wake of slavery circulate only flows of black nonpersonhood and code black people's personhood out of transmission.[121]

Like Crawley's choreosonic compression, Sharpe's method of wake analysis tracks these patterns of erasure and also points to the "dimensions of . . . non/being" (14) these patterns perceptually code out into the red and the strategies black people confined to these zones have used to "insist . . . being into the wake."[122] Sharpe identifies one such strategy, a literary device that appears in literary and theoretical archives. Like the practice of sounding that I discussed in the last chapter, this device effects a pivot in medium and sensory register from text to sound. Sharpe shows how M. NourbeSe Philip's poem "Zong! #15" uses homophones to make this pivot. As Philip writes, "where the *ratio of just / is* less than / is necessary / to murder / the subject in property / the save in underwriter / where etc tunes *justice / and the ratio* of murder / is / the usual in occurred."[123] Philip uses homophones "justice" and "just / is" to create a distribution or pattern of *sounds* that doesn't align with the poem's distribution or pattern of *words*. Because they are different words that sound the same, homophones create patterns in the text that don't exist in its verbal form or content — sounds will repeat where words and meaning do not. Taken together, these sounds form frequency patterns that are perceptually coded out of the poem's verbal form and content. As Sharpe puts it, this frequency is "beyond the logic of the ledger, beyond the mathematics of insurance."[124]

In this way, the poem expresses a fundamentally different mathematical relationship than the white supremacist biopolitical calculus that rationalizes slave ship ledgers and actuarial tables.[125] This math structures the repetition of names throughout the poem, which records captives thrown overboard as names — as people — rather than as abstract quantities.[126] As Sharpe explains, Philip structures the poem's form so that there are two long lines, one about midway through the text and one at its end, and under each of these lines she puts five "names for those Africans on board the *Zong* who had no makes that their captors were bound to recognize or record."[127] The frequency of black personhood in the poem "Zong #15" is thus significantly higher than the frequency of black personhood in the *Zong*'s ledgers. Philip's poem performs the same perceptual work Rihanna's "BBHMM" does: it both articulates and aesthetically represents frequency patterns that are coded out of white supremacy's modes of existence and which black people have used to build alternative ones.

Beyoncé's visual song "Hold Up" illustrates how the methods of abstraction Crawley and Sharpe work in practice.[128] Unlike the philosophical "Begriff" — the German word for concept, which is rooted in the word for grab or hold (*greifen*) — Beyoncé's "Hold Up" models intellectual filiation and inheritance (ways of holding on to and grasping ideas) that avoid the practices of enclosure found in both new and old philosophical abstraction. I also attempt to model an aspect of this practice in my own writing: by treating songwriting and vocal performance as theoretical practices — not as applications or examples of theories, but as doing the same ontological, metaphysical, epistemological, ethical, and aesthetic work that Sharpe and Crawley do in their theoretical writing—I avoid taking up songwriting and vocal performance as the unimproved "nature" that the philosopher labors over to transform into properly philosophical material, reinvesting and renewing philosophy.

3. "Hold Up" Instead of "Begriff"

A part of *Lemonade*, Beyoncé's 2016 visual album about marital infidelity, "Hold Up" is ostensibly about its narrator's anger at her husband's cheating. The choreosonic aspects of its songwriting and vocal performance tell a slightly different story. A complement to Beyoncé's 2008 "Single Ladies" video, which uses Afrofuturist imagery to critique the gendered, raced property relations behind traditional heterosexual marriage,[129] "Hold Up" articulates a centrifugitive method of abstraction that tunes into the choreosonic materiality that Philosophical logics of enclosure perceptually code out of transmission. In this way it models ways of holding on to and grasping ideas without transforming them into private property.

"Hold Up" gets its centrifugitive method from African American women's vocal performance traditions. Crawley identifies this method in Billie Holiday's and Nina Simone's work. According to Crawley, "Holiday and Simone breathed in such a way as to melodically break down the theological-philosophical conception of enclosure."[130] This technique is evident in each singer's approach to "Strange Fruit," a song about lynching first recorded by Holiday in 1939.

Crawley argues that the vocal performance choices each singer makes—the specific melodies they sing, each variations on the same text—create centrifugitive relationships rather than ones of categorical difference and enclosure. As Crawley explains, "utilizing the same song and sound" as Holiday, Simone "produces inflection, accent, and most importantly, critical distance from other performances."[131] A vocalist's inflection and accent create different diacritical patterns in the melody (i.e., patterns in pronunciation and accent), much like the way Philip's homophones articulated diacritical sonic patterns above and beyond the text's verbal patterns.[132] And while these different diacritical patterns can be used to make a private property claim when they are taken as markers of categorical difference (think of Vanilla Ice's 1990 MTV interview, where he argues that the riff in "Ice Ice Baby" "is not the same bass line" as in Queen and David Bowie's "Under Pressure" and thus not the basis of an intellectual property lawsuit),[133] they can also be taken as markers of the antiphonal oscillation that constitutes choreosonic vibration. Each singer's melodic and interpretive choices are to be heard as a departure from other versions that also recalls those versions—hence, antiphonal oscillation. This back-and-forth approach does not treat one version as the unimproved re-source that the current singer labors upon and makes her own. It thus enacts a mode of relation that "breaks down" practices of enclosure.

Creating antiphonal oscillations to black women's artworks, reimagining how black women might understand their inheritances of black women's creative traditions outside white supremacist patriarchal kinship, "Hold Up" adopts this approach to black women's expressive traditions. This approach is evident in its patterns of accent and breathing sounds; articulated amid visual and verbal text that's ostensibly about heterosexual marriage (which is a racialized, gendered private property relation), these patterns model ways to acknowledge those inheritances without transforming that work into private property.[134] Though birth and marriage are two key themes of "Hold Up," the video's choreosonic sounds obliquely pivot from these white supremacist heteropatriarchal private property relationships to antiphonal oscillations that open out centrifugitive ways of relating to other people and their ideas.

The first component of this antiphonal oscillation, the initial "call," is in the section of *Lemonade* titled "Denial," which serves as "Hold Up's" preface.[135] Here, the narrator plunges into water as the titles tell us she's in a state of denial. Her submersion visually represents her pre-woke consciousness still invested in fairly traditional ideas about femininity and marriage. For example, she swims around a submerged bedroom as she recites one of Warsan Shire's poems recounting traditional feminine disciplines like dieting, chastity, and, above all, silence. Right after the stanza about falling silent (about 0:50), the narrator breathes in and out: she blows bubbles of air out her nose, exhaling into the water, and then we see some reversed footage that makes her appear to inhale bubbles of air from the water. This breathing pattern accompanies but does not sync with the rhythm of the poetry the narrator recites. The narrator's breath thus creates an alternate rhythm than the one articulated by the poetic meter, one that is both in a different medium (visual rather than sonic) and dissonant with those other rhythms. This is the first hint that this song is working in registers of experience beyond the painful gendered logics the lyrics describe.

The video then cuts to one of these registers. We are now outside the submerged bedroom, facing double doors at the top of a stone staircase. As the narrator opens these doors, water rushes out, roaring and gushing down the stairs as she walks out the door. In this realm, we can hear the sounds previously muted by the water and the denial it represents. This sequence of scenes evokes birth: the bedroom is the womb, the doors are the birth canal, and the water is the broken water that comes at the start of labor.[136] The narrator has

121

been reborn: she has left the state of denial and entered one of awareness. The variable audibility of the choreosonic sounds (of breath, of water) aesthetically represents this pivot from sleep to wokefulness. In the state of denial, choreosonics are inaudible; in the state of wokeness, we can hear them, and we hear them repeatedly.

The repetitions of these choreosonics build up to the first response to that call. Beginning with the whoosh of water rushing out the doors, the choreosonic sounds continue throughout the song. They don't appear as the sounds of water or breath but as percussion ornaments that accompany the blows of the narrator's bat "Hot Sauce" as she hits cars, fire hydrants, and, at the song's two most key structural points, cameras.[137] The first of these licks happens when Beyoncé's narrator takes hold of the bat that's handed to her by another woman; the hand-off suggests that the narrator is drawing on and working with the help of other women's work. This cymbal roll next appears when she takes her first swing at a car window. The next several instances switch up the instruments, but in all cases there's a short roll up that lands on the accented downbeat as the bat hits on its target.

Each time the bat takes down a camera—a surveillance camera at the end of the song's bridge, and the camera-as-spectator-surrogate at the very end of the video—there's a more elaborate sonic buildup. First, at the end of the bridge when the narrator takes down the surveillance camera, the number of percussive events increasingly intensifies in order to build tension, which is then released on the downbeat of the next chorus. There are four measures of quarter-note snares, a dub siren on 1 and 3 of the penultimate measure of this four-bar phrase, and, in the last measure, a steel drum riff leading into the downbeat of the song's final refrain/chorus. During this last chorus, the bat hits and corresponding percussion licks are significantly more frequent than they were earlier in the song: at the beginning, there's a hit at the downbeat of every phrase, and the last phrase has multiple hits. This leads us into another quasi-soar in the song's outro.[138] Here the rhythmic intensification happens both in the vocals—the syllabic laughter[139] and the repetitions of "what's up"—and in the dub siren. These build up to a hit that cuts away the soundtrack—we hear the bat hitting the camera and clanking on the pavement as on-camera sound unrelated to the song—and cuts down the camera that frames the video. Like the meta-coda of "ʙʙʜᴍᴍ," these intensifying patterns push into the red and effect an oblique pivot in perceptual dimension, represented here by the breaking of the sonic fourth wall. The broken fourth wall represents a similar transition from disavowal to awareness of the video's conditions of production. "Hold Up" thus concludes with a return that also varies—an antiphonal oscillation.

These antiphonal oscillations in the song's form represent, in aesthetic terms, the method the artwork uses to grasp and pick up the artistic ideas that inform it. Traditionally, African American women's productive and reproductive capacities are treated as a commons that anyone else can enclose into private property. "Hold Up" picks up and works with black women's expressive traditions in a way that doesn't enclose them into private property. For example, the aesthetic choices on "Hold Up" are part of what Zandria Robinson describes as *Lemonade*'s

> writ[ing] black women back into national, regional and diasporic histories by making them the progenitors and rightful inheritors of the Southern gothic tradition. . . . *Lemonade* is a womanist sonic meditation that spans from the spiritual to the trap, with stops at country soul and rock & roll in between. . . . The film signifies on *Eve's Bayou* and Julie Dash's *Daughters of the Dust*, centers sacred Nigerian body art practices, draws on the words of Warsan Shire and grandmothers' reflections.[140]

123

According to Robinson, *Lemonade* draws on black women's creative traditions in a way that alters white supremacist patriarchal practices of inheritance and filiation, which give white men disproportional credit for things like the Southern gothic tradition and rock and roll and writes black women's contributions out of the archives. Tuning in to those written-out creative legacies, "Hold Up" writes such legacies in another register, a register perceptually coded out of those archives. Calling on and recalling Holiday's and Simone's centrifugitive use of accent to break logics of enclosure, "Hold Up" uses antiphonal oscillation—the calling out to, echoing, but varying in accent and inflection—rather than categorical distinction and enclosure.[141]

These patterns of antiphonal oscillation in "Hold Up" sketch out possible techniques for addressing ideas without transforming them into "Philosophical" private property.[142] For example, the relationships among the antiphonal patterns model diacritical rather than categorical difference. Within the large-scale antiphonal oscillation from beginning to end, the percussion riffs count out smaller oscillations as each riff both recalls and varies those that came before it. Both at the large and small scale, and in the interaction between the two, the antiphonal oscillations between call and response mark out a phase space that measures a cycle of departure *and return*. This choreography differs from both Philosophy's choreography of enclosure and new materialism's founding gesture. In the former case, it marks a difference of degree rather than a categorical difference in kind; moreover, the cycle of departure and return makes aversion (the turn to Philosophy as a turn away from blackness/what cannot be enclosed) impossible. In the latter case, it treats response as both departure and return, not as a counter-claim that departs and supersedes. New materialism's founding gesture articulates a categorical difference between itself and "old" ways of doing philosophy; antiphonal oscillations on "Hold Up" articulate diacritical differences between sourced and versioned material. The song's structural background and ornamental foreground articulate centrifugitive patterns, patterns of accent and inflection that mark diacritical rather than categorical difference, the kind of difference necessary to enclose something as one's private property.

So one way those of us whose intellectual practice takes the form of writing rather than music might adopt this model is to recognize, especially in our patterns of citation, the diacritical relationships our work has to scholarship outside our discipline, both within and beyond the academy. This is what new materialism's founding gesture precludes it from doing ("new" marks a categorical difference from the old) and why it doubles down on conventional philosophical enclosure. Greater awareness of research outside conventional disciplinary boundaries will also help us situate the works we address as contributions to ongoing conversations, not as "raw material" or unimproved nature that we, especially we philosophers, labor upon and enclose for Philosophy. We can also analyze texts (of whatever sort) for their internal patterns of diacritical difference and antiphonal oscillation, as, for example, I have done with Sharpe's definition of wake and with the choreosonic sounds in "Hold Up." This song's use of antiphonal oscillation to mark diacritical difference illustrates how we might draw on other texts as descriptive models for our theories of oscillation, vibration, and resonance without also appropriating those model texts as the private property of us as authors or of any specific academic discipline.

New materialist concepts of vibratory resonance use acoustic resonance to reinvigorate Philosophy so that it is more compatible with both the modes of abstraction performed by quantitative tools used across government and business and the structures of domination that those tools create. Beyoncé's "Hold Up," Crawley's choreosonics, and Sharpe's wake are all theories of vibratory resonance that offer concrete alternatives to new materialism's two main methodological problems: its ideal theory and the choreography of its founding gesture. Modeling its abstractions on black people's aesthetic practices, these phonographic theories of vibratory resonance develop lines of inquiry that have been perceptually coded out of Philosophy's canon because they do not advance the discipline's property interests/whiteness. Though it is definitely not "new," this "aphilosophical" practice is evidence that we can theorize with and through sound-based methods of abstraction without committing ourselves to new materialism's reinvestment in Philosophy and all the oppressive politics that come with it. As in the previous chapter, these phonographic approaches to sound attune us to gendered, racialized property relations and think outside traditional structures of property-in-person. Attention to sounds that are conventionally inaudible or disposable — choreosonic sounds, aspiratory patterns — reveals patterns of living that count on different models of relationality and value than the ones measured by neoliberal market logics and biopolitical statistics. In the next chapter, I focus on how these quantitative relations — both the normalized statistics of neoliberal biopolitics and the centrifugitive patterns in black aesthetics — translate into structures of subjectivity.

125

4

Neoliberal Sophrosyne

Acoustic Resonance as Subjectivity and Personhood

They expect the strictest of virtue ethics to arise spontaneously
from the immanent action of market forces.

— Melinda Cooper, *Family Values*

I. Chill Pop and Feminine Excess

In the early 2010s, neoliberalism's demand to intensify risk and maximize reward had pop culture riding a maximalist high.[1] People wore T-shirts and baseball hats emblazoned with neon YOLOs (You Only Live Once) and listened to
a seemingly endless number of tension/release-heavy pop songs about "molly"
(the postmillennial term for MDMA).[2] But by 2016, YOLO was out and chill
was in. For example, an August 2016 headline in *Dose* celebrates the fact that
"Chill Pop Is the New Music Trend That Isn't Going Anywhere."[3] The Chainsmokers, the most successful EDM artists on the pop charts in 2016, are commonly described as "chilled-out"[4] and "lukewarm."[5] As *Slate* music critic
Chris Molanphy explains, the fact that their megahit "Closer" turns its first
"drop—the thunderous climax of club-rattling electronic dance music"—into

a "downshift" instead signals a "comedown" from all that YOLO maximalism, "the end of an era."[6]

The pop charts' pendulum swing from early-decade maximalism to late-decade chill is symptomatic of the U.S. and U.K. electorate's broader dissatisfaction with seemingly ever-intensifying risk. For example, British social theorist Will Davies argues that "the entire practice of modelling the future in terms of 'risk' has lost credibility" because, as he puts it in his analysis of pro-Brexit and Trump voters, "people ... have utterly given up on the future."[7] According to Davies, these voters are groups of whites whose experiences have disconnected them from cost/benefit rationality. On the one hand, there are those for whom the ever-more-neoliberalizing economy isn't keeping its end of the deal and rewarding their risk with adequate returns. On the other hand, there are those so insulated by white privilege that, regardless of their dissatisfaction with the present, they cannot imagine any shock that would put *their* future at risk. Both cases share an underlying capitalist realism that cannot imagine the future as possibly presenting an alternative to the present. However, after Leave and Trump won, lots of people on both sides of the Atlantic felt the future would more than likely be a whole lot worse. In the United States, for example, PBS's *Newshour* reported about "post-election distress disorder,"[8] ProPublica and the Southern Poverty Law Center reported a significant uptick in hate crimes after the election,[9] and escalating tensions between the United States and North Korea have people fearing nuclear war for the first time since the Berlin Wall fell.[10] Popular attitudes about risk have changed. It's no longer a source of reward and pleasure but of anxiety. "You only live once" feels less like a rallying cry and more like a threat.

Washington Post pop music critic Chris Richards argues that in "today's freaked-out America," pop stars, like the rest of us, turn to drugs like Xanax "to numb the agony of existence."[11] According to Richards, pop audiences like to hear a similarly numbing effect in music: "Comfort zones are hard to find in Donald Trump's America. . . . We used to want to have our minds blown. Now, we'd prefer to have our minds massaged." He points to trends in songwriting and listening habits as evidence. First, songwriting now aims to "mitigate intensity" rather than build it, and stays well within "comfort zones . . . instead of forging new sounds or fresh styles."[12] As Steven Shaviro has argued, neoliberalism turns aesthetic transgression from a revolutionary strategy into a new norm and mode of surplus-value extraction; now that we're all expected to transgress, it isn't fun but a chore. This leads artists like Lana Del Rey, Kygo, and The Weeknd to write songs that emphasize "a smoothness, a softness, a

127

steadiness" that creates a "cushiony" and "soft" feel.[13] Second, Richards argues that the architecture of music streaming services creates a "fluid, frictionless listening" that "is designed to feel cool and undisruptive." Algorithms normalize the range of sonic and aesthetic variation listeners experience so that "even when you don't know exactly what's coming next," you know it won't deviate significantly from past song selections.[14] There's still an element of chance, but statistics have made chance something quantifiable and controllable. Moderation, specifically moderating risk, is the thread that runs through streaming's use of statistical normalization, pop's toned-down soars and drops, and the popularity of anti-anxiety medicine.

Those anti-anxiety medicines help people maintain a level of chill self-control in an otherwise outrageous environment. Outrage is for people with low social and cultural capital, like President Trump, leader of the so-called deplorables. As Elizabeth Keenan noted, "plenty of people were comparing Trump to a capricious, mean 13-year-old girl" because both are perceived to be irrationally outrageous.[15] Chill, however, is a desirable quality because it demonstrates reasonableness and self-control. For example, an Internet forum explaining English slang terms defines "chill" as the "ability to act in a rational manner"[16] such that one refrains from excess; examples of "no chill" excess include "reckless" behavior, being overly invested in a romantic partner ("When a girl bases her every choice on a single guy she likes"), typing in all caps, and overeating.[17] As Alana Massey argues, "Chill is a sinister refashioning of 'Calm down!' from an enraging and highly gendered command into an admirable attitude."[18] Chill is admirable because it signals masculinity, mastery, and self-mastery. "Being a chill woman is the opposite of being a hysterical one."[19] Chill is the ability to rein in feminine and feminized excess.

The (re)feminization of emotional, affective, and aesthetic excess is evident in both the songwriting choices in and critical reactions to former One Direction member Harry Styles's 2017 single "Sign of the Times."[20] This is the lead single off Styles's first solo album, which critics regard as a step toward a maturing style that appeals to both his original fan base (teen girls) and broader pop audiences.[21] In a profile for *Rolling Stone*, Cameron Crowe writes,

> Asked if he spends pressure-filled evenings worried about proving credibility to an older crowd, Styles grows animated. "Who's to say that young girls who like pop music — short for popular, right? — have worse musical taste than a 30-year-old hipster guy? . . . Teenage-girl fans — they don't lie. If they like you, they're there. They don't act 'too cool.' They like you, and they tell you. Which is *sick*."[22]

Styles counters (white, middle-aged, male) rock critics' assumption that what Crowe elsewhere describes as "the white noise of adulation" and "mania" of teen girl fandom is something to be outgrown and left behind in the pursuit of authentic art with the view that girls' unchill, unrestrained adulation is preferable to the affective restraint and emotional distance of "30-year-old hipster guy[s]."[23] Styles values fans' feminine and feminized excess. He also incorporated such excess in "Sign" itself.

A quiet-loud-quiet[24] rock ballad with lots of overt and unrestrained climaxes, the single stands out from the competition as distinctly unchill. From the Chainsmokers' "Closer" to Ed Sheeran's "Shape of You" (the track "Sign" displaced from a thirteen-week run at the top of the U.K. chart),[25] recent hits have featured severely toned-down soars. Soars usually combine rhythmic intensification (in percussion and sometimes in the repetition of phrases in the lyrics) and timbral intensification and a drop (a pause filled with a bass wobble, a vocal melisma, or some other vocal); the buildup and the pause make the return of the next downbeat hit harder. The main soar of "Closer" softens the rhythmic buildup by keeping the percussion at a steady tick (a bass drum hit on every eighth note) under increasingly frequent repetitions of a phrase in the lyrics. "Shape of You" eliminates rhythmic intensification altogether; it does not soar up to its drop.[26] "Sign," on the other hand, climaxes *hard* and it climaxes *a lot*. About a minute and eighteen seconds into the song and again just before the three-minute mark, the last two beats leading into the downbeat of the first chorus feature a loud percussion fill and an ascending guitar gliss that clears the way for that downbeat and makes it (and all its string backing and belted vocals) hit harder. Though the percussion doesn't intensify the way an EDM soar does, it serves the same purpose. The bridge is a series of climaxes spaced about fifteen seconds apart. First, at around three minutes fifty-five seconds, the song prepares for the bridge's first downbeat the same way it has prepped for the choruses. Then at around 4:15, there is a chorus of ascending "OH-oh-oh-oh-OH-oh-oh-oh"s over a rhythmically intensifying drum fill; this repeats again at around 4:30, but without the ascending vocals. Fifteen or so seconds later, there's an ascending whoosh up to another climax of repeated "we've got to get away!" that extend to the five-minute mark; here, just when the truncated repetitions of "we got to, we got to" might lead one to think the song is about to resolve, it goes on for another fifteen seconds before ramping down to its coda. With four climaxes in a row, "Sign" outdoes even the most crass, maximalist EDM soars (e.g., the one in Psy's "Gangnam Style"), which, for all their intensity, have only one huge climax.

The frequent and intense climaxes of "Sign" are, when compared to the

129

laid-back soars in "Closer" and "Shape of You," extremely unchill. And to the extent that "chill" is a gendered concept, an ideal of masculine self-control against feminine emotional and affective excess, this song's unchillness genders it feminine. So when rock critics object to its "wild melodramatic balladry"[27] and mock it as "a bombastic slice of bombastic piano pop that builds bombastically to a bombastic ending,"[28] they're objecting to its feminine and feminized excess. Even though "Sign" doubles down on the conventionally masculinized classic rock gestures and allusions, it uses them to depict an unchill excessiveness that, in a pop culture context that privileges chill as a sign of both masculine self-mastery and especially girls' and women's ability to lean in to relative patriarchal privilege, reads as undesirably feminine. As Massey argues, "chill" women don't act in stereotypically feminine ways, in particular, "demanding accountability" from heterosexual romantic partners (i.e., men). Chill women are the ideal postfeminist subject: independent, self-possessed, sexually adventurous, but unbothered by and not a bother about pesky things like sexism.

"Chill" is a twenty-first-century update on the ancient Greek concept of *sophrosyne*, which is commonly translated as moderation or self-mastery. As Anne Carson explains, sophrosyne was a gendered practice designed to keep men from embodying feminine irrationality and to prevent inherently and irreparably irrational women from sonic, political, and sexual insubordination.[29] As part of its redrawing lines of social inclusion/exclusion around (supposedly) individual performance rather than group-based social identity, neoliberalism and biopolitics use sophrosyne as a gendered racializing practice designed to keep feminine people from sonic, political, and sexual insubordination. However, unlike the ancient Greeks, who thought women exhibited sophrosyne when they were silent, neoliberalism and biopolitics think people on the femme spectrum exhibit sophrosyne when their voices are consonant with and amplify its ideal distribution of personhood and privilege.

Neoliberal sophrosyne is a constituent of the sonic episteme because it uses ideas of sonic harmony to translate normalized statistical distributions into structures of subjectivity and criteria for moral and political personhood.[30] As I've argued briefly in chapter 2 and will develop further in this chapter, Plato's concept of sophrosyne was grounded in the idea of musical harmony as hierarchically ordered geometric proportion, and neoliberal biopolitics updates this concept by switching the math used to calculate harmoniousness, replacing geometry with statistics. In both cases, a music-math analogy translates mathematical relationships into nonquantitative senses of selfhood and personhood. Because sophrosyne ultimately expresses a relation of subordination, neoliberalism's reworking of sophrosyne replaces one kind of subordination — a hierarchy — with another kind of subordination: the normal distribution. Chill and other variations on neoliberal sophrosyne translate normalized statistical distributions of risk and reward, cost and benefit, into nonquantitative terms we can understand in extra-cognitive ways, like through habits, routines, aesthetic preferences, and so on.

The first part of the chapter argues this in more detail. To begin, I establish the traditional relationship between sophrosyne and musical harmony in Plato and explain how he uses it to express a relation of subordination. Moving into the twenty-first century, I examine various academic and popular calls for "moderation" in professional ethics and neoliberal discourses of personal responsibility to demonstrate some of the ways sophrosyne is a part of the culture of neoliberalism. I then use the case of neoliberal popular feminism to develop the relationship between neoliberal sophrosyne and contemporary notions of musical harmony and explain what relationship of subordination it expresses. The second part of the chapter argues that Katherine McKittrick's concept of "demonic calculus" establishes modes of mathematical and political relation that are insubordinate to neoliberal sophrosyne. Using McKittrick's concept of demonic calculus as a rubric for reading some compositional strategies used in the songs on Beyoncé's 2016 album *Lemonade*, I clarify how the music part of demonic calculus's music-math analogy works, and how it's different from the music part of neoliberal sophrosyne's music-math analogy.

I. Sophrosyne
1. Plato's Sophrosyne

Sophrosyne was a common concept in ancient Greek thought, but I'm limiting my discussion to Plato for two reasons. First, as I mentioned in chapter 2, Rancière claims that neoliberal postdemocracy embodies Plato's concept of sophrosyne specifically. He does this because Plato treats moderation not as a mean between extremes but as a ratio and a proportion. Plato's articulation of the concept is thus most closely tied to ancient Greek theories of musical harmony as a series of hierarchically ordered geometric ratios. But before I get to the music theory, I will first explain what Plato means by sophrosyne.

a. Sophrosyne as a Practice of Personhood

According to twentieth-century American philologist Helen North, "the basic, etymological meaning of sophrosyne is 'soundness (or health) of mind' — or rather of the *phrenes*, an organ of uncertain location."[31] Practicing sophrosyne results in sound-mindedness. For Plato, sophrosyne is what makes citizens free from enslavement to the pleasures and thus fit to be politically free from enslavement to another human master.[32] Though the ancient Greeks didn't have our exact concept of "the subject," Plato did have a concept of personhood, and sophrosyne was central to it. Moderate sound-mindedness is the capacity one must demonstrate to be granted full membership in society, to be seen as a citizen and a free man.

For Plato, the free man is not liberated from mastery;[33] rather, he follows the best master of all, the truth.[34] Sophrosyne is the practice of subordinating yourself to the True. Because you can't actually *know* the True while you have a physical body,[35] the True isn't an authority that issues commands so much as a model one must approximate. Even though mortals can't know the True itself, we can see its form or logic everywhere in the physical world and strive to embody that form or logic. Sophrosyne is the True put in practice; this is why Foucault calls sophrosyne an "orthos logos," a practice of truth. In fact, *Republic* 3 suggests that imitation — the thing that Plato notoriously hates — isn't actually bad *if (and only if)* it's the imitation of *moderate* behavior.[36] As North explains, "the philosopher-statesman who gazes at the order and harmony of the eternal realities (the Forms) tries to imitate them and to liken himself to them as far as possible."[37] The point is to imitate the relationship the True has to the physical world by putting soul in command of body. One structures one's self or person by subordinating one's body to one's soul and one's soul, in turn, to the True. As Foucault explains, Plato "define[s] the *sophron* as the man in whom the different parts of the soul are *in agreement and harmony*, when *the part that commands and the part that obeys* are at one in their recognition that it is proper for reason to rule and that they should not contend for its authority."[38] This clarifies that Plato's sophrosyne is not a mean or an average but a relation of subordination of the less true to the more true.

More accurately, sophrosyne constitutes a specific type of subordination: "a hierarchy by which the rational part of the soul 'rules' the irrational"[39] or "a *symphonia* of the naturally inferior and the naturally superior [*Republic* 432a]."[40] But Plato also describes sophrosyne as another type of relationship. "Acquiring moderation," Plato writes, means bringing every aspect of your existence "in *proportion* as soul is more honorable than body" (*Republic* 591b; emphasis added). The soul or the intelligible isn't the main focus here — it's the proportional *relationship* between the soul and body. This is why Foucault describes sophrosyne as "the right sense of proportion."[41] Similarly, Plato's divided line expresses both a hierarchy of the intelligible over the visible and a ratio between them, namely, "the ratio of their comparative clearness and obscurity" (*Republic* 509d). Likewise, his myth of the metals — the idea that the just city is divided into three castes: gold, silver, and iron and brass (*Republic* 415a) — describes a relationship that is a ratio (the "gold" get the most responsibility) and a hierarchy at the same time (the gold are on the top). For Plato, sophrosyne is both a distribution of authority or status (a ranking) and a geometric or material distribution (a ratio). Practicing sophrosyne means instituting and maintaining those ranked ratios.

Plato constantly uses musical terms to describe the relationship sophrosyne maintains between the parts it governs. He likens "acquiring moderation" (σωφρονήσειν) to "concord" (συμφωνίας) and "harmony" (ἁρμοττόμενος), and he says that "moderation resembles a kind of harmony."[42] That kind of harmony is a consonant one, συμφωνίας of the greater and lesser, higher and lower. These are not metaphors but direct descriptions of the kind of geometric or material distribution sophrosyne creates. "Plato's later definition of sophrosyne," the one in the *Republic* and *Laws*, appears "in unmistakably Pythagorean terms as harmonic proportion (Rep. 431D)."[43] Plato used the geometric ratios Pythagoras discovered when fretting a string into different lengths as models for the ratios sophrosyne maintains among the parts it governs.[44] So digging deeper into Plato's theory of music will give us a more accurate sense of what he means by sophrosyne.[45]

b. Musical Harmony

As Plato says in *Republic* 430e, sophrosyne "bears more likeness to a kind of concord and harmony than the other virtues" because "moderation," like musical harmony, is all about maintaining proper proportions. There is no one theory of harmony in ancient Greek philosophy — it was actually a matter of much contention. Though it was mostly agreed that musical harmony was measured with ratios and proportions, there was disagreement about both what the proper proportions and ratios were and how to calculate them — some used arithmetic, others geometry.[46] Plato was team geometry.[47] In this view, ratios aren't calculated numerically (arithmetically) but derived from geometric relationships. For example, fretting a string in a 2:1 ratio (basically dividing it in two equal halves) produced the interval of an octave, and dividing a string into a two-thirds/one-third ratio produced the interval of a fifth. For Plato, *musical harmony doesn't measure sounds but mathematical relationships*. To treat harmony as a comparison of sounds is to put the part that should obey, physical senses, in charge of the part that ought to rule, ideas.[48] This is why Plato says "measuring audible consonances and sounds against one another . . . puts ears before understanding" (*Republic* 531a–b). Hierarchies must be respected even and especially in determining what ratios are harmonious and which aren't: the math commands and auditory perception obeys.

In this framework, dissonance is effectively insubordination, such as putting the body in charge of the soul or sounds in charge of math. This is evident in Plato's disdain for the aulos, which depends on the instrumentalist's body, not the geometric construction of the instrument, to produce properly tuned pitches.[49] A double-reeded instrument somewhat similar to the modern oboe, the aulos (αυλους) is Plato's favorite example of a geometrically disproportionate instrument. Playing either aulos or oboe, getting each note perfectly in tune often requires minute physical adjustments (of embouchure, of fingering, etc.) idiosyncratic to each pitch. This is what Plato is referring to when he says: "in the case of flute-playing, the harmonies are found not by measurement but by the hit and miss of training, and quite generally music tries to find the measure by observing vibrating strings. So there is a lot of imprecision mixed up in it and very little reliability" (*Philebus* 56a). Sounds made by auloi are the product or effect of *bodily* relationships ("the hit or miss of training," i.e., muscle memory), not mathematical ones. The actual body of the instrumentalist, rather than math, commands the sounds, and the hierarchical part of harmonious proportionality is out of whack. With the body in charge, the part that commands and the part that obeys aren't in their proper order; the body is behaving insubordinately.

As the example of the aulos demonstrates, Plato's sophrosyne is both a mathematical relationship and a power relationship: it measures both geometric proportion and hierarchical subordination. Just as music translates this hierarchical series of proportions into terms we can hear and feel, sophrosyne translates that same series of proportions into a nonquantitative philosophical concept. Practicing sophrosyne brings your patterns of behavior in accord with the patterns of subordination and dominance that structure society at large. Contemporary ideas of sophrosyne emphasize this aspect of the concept.

2. Neoliberal Sophrosyne

Like Plato's philosophy, neoliberalism treats sophrosyne as a practice of the self and uses it as a tool to distinguish those who are sound-minded and capable of ruling themselves and others from those who are economically irrational and in need of additional supervision. It also models sophrosyne on musical harmony, but its concept of harmony is acoustic rather than Pythagorean. Neoliberal sophrosyne switches out the old math (geometry) for newer math (statistics), and the old relations of subordination (slave-owning patriarchy) for newer relations of subordination (post-identity biopolitics, especially statistical normalization).[50]

a. Neoliberal Sophrosyne as Orthos Logos

As I discussed above, practicing sophrosyne organizes the self to mimic the True's logos. Neoliberal sophrosyne replaces Plato's concept of the True with one that combines modernity's epistemological notion of truth and Plato's structural and ontological model of truth. Plato thinks the True is the fundamental unit of reality: all true things embody its order or structure, making their structure isomorphic with that of the True. Thus, sophrosyne is the practice that will give your life the same *form* that the truth has. An epistemological concept of truth treats truth as a knowable *content*. For example, in the third essay of *On the Genealogy of Morals*, Nietzsche argues that both science (*Wissenschaft*) and religion are competing manifestations of the same underlying will-to-truth. They think truth can be known, if only you follow the right method. Either belief or empiricism/rationalism will reveal true epistemological content. In neoliberalism and biopolitics, the market and normalized statistical distributions function *both* structurally and epistemologically; however, they replace old structures and content with new ones.[51] First, they update truth's form or logos, replacing geometric proportions with cost/benefit calculus and normalized statistical distributions. They also update the ideas of what we know and how we know it: knowing is predicting, and probabilities are the content—the what—that is known.

135

For example, neoliberalism's enterprising *Homo economicus* uses cost/benefit analysis to structure his life, and that same cost/benefit calculus is the one reliably knowable thing about him. As Andrew Dilts emphasizes, original Chicago-school neoliberal economist Gary Becker was interested not in accurately representing an individual's past behavior but in successfully predicting future behavior.[52] As long as the predictions worked, it didn't matter whether the data behind the predictions was correct. So the point isn't to have an account that correctly corresponds to someone's actual actions, but to have a metric that successfully forecasts future behavior. Similarly, philosopher Gordon Hull argues that data scientists approach big data analytics "not as knowledge generating in any traditional sense, but as action guiding. . . . In other words, the question is not whether we 'know' that people who like Hello Kitty tend to be low on emotional stability. . . . It's that we want to know if the correlation is robust enough to justify some sort of action."[53] The point here isn't to have accurate knowledge of subjects' emotional state but to predict who needs mental health services. In both cases, knowledge isn't justified true belief but the ability to make successful predictions. And those predictions are made using a specific kind of math: the market logics and statistical normalization that define neoliberalism and biopolitics. Something is "true" if it successfully controls for chance occurrences. Thus, in updating the idea of truth one practices, neoliberal sophrosyne also updates the kind of mathematical relation behind the concept.

Just as Plato's sophrosyne translated the math behind his idea of musical harmony into nonquantitative terms, neoliberal sophrosyne translates the math behind neoliberal market logics and biopolitical governmentality into nonquantitative terms that we understand and implement at the level of social norms rather than statistical norms. As habit, affect, ethics, aesthetic preference, etiquette, and so on, these social norms govern our relation to ourselves and to others.

I consider several such practices below: moderation as an ethical ideal, neoliberal discourses of personal responsibility, and the difference between "moderate" and "loud" feminist voices. Whereas the rest of the constituents of the sonic episteme appeal explicitly to acoustic resonance, these discourses of moderation, responsibility, and feminist respectability indirectly appeal to acoustic resonance via the idea of sophrosyne. Because it historically carries connotations of musical harmony and consonance, sophrosyne is the middle term that connects these various concepts of responsibility and moderation to acoustic resonance. This will be especially clear in the latter case, where consonance and overcompression both produce and naturalize biopolitical relations of domination and subordination.

b. Moderation as an Ethical Ideal in the Twenty-First Century

The traditional social contract is an exchange of freedom for security. Neoliberalism reframes this as an entrepreneurial investment: I exercise my freedom in choosing among various options and their attendant costs and benefits. An entrepreneurial society reduces all relationships and values to risk and reward: the riskier the investment, the greater the reward. However, every venture has a point of diminishing returns where the cost just isn't worth the benefit.

Because cost/benefit calculus requires balancing maximal reward with acceptable risk, some management and public administration scholars have argued that sophrosyne is a useful practice for managing markets and market-based decision making. For example, in his article "Agonistic Moderation: Administrating with the Wisdom of Sophrosyne," Dragan Stanisevski does the exact thing I'm claiming that neoliberalism in general does: he reworks the ancient Greek concept of sophrosyne and argues that this nü-sophrosyne is the best way to ensure that competition and competitive markets don't encourage the kind of excessive risk-taking that enabled "the blind excesses on Wall Street that led to the housing bubble and the subsequent financial crisis" and "the scandalous excesses that led to and ensued during the Iraq War."[54] A similar appeal to sophrosyne appears in an anonymously authored post on the Experian (one of the three major U.S. credit bureaus) corporate blog about the 2008 financial crisis. Like Stanisevski, the author uses a concept of sophrosyne to describe how investors ought to act:

> In the past several years, we have experienced excesses in commercial real estate, residential development and subprime mortgages. It is now these excesses that are creating the problems that we are dealing with today. Bringing back these limitations — in other words, reestablishing the discipline in our portfolio risk management — will go a long way in avoiding these same problems in the future. As I learned early in my banking career: "... soundness, profitability and growth ... in that order."[55]

This idea of sound-mindedness or sound behavior recalls one of the earliest and most literal meanings of sophrosyne as related to *phrenes* or a mode of *phronesis*. According to this post, sound-minded, disciplined, responsible risk management is what pre-2008 banking lacked and what led it to unsustainable excesses. Self-disciplined "soundness" is, as the last sentence indicates, the primary attribute of successful investing because it lets bankers distinguish between acceptable and excessive risk.[56] In a financialized market where risk is the source of surplus value, eliminating risk isn't an option. Thus, it's up to market actors to manage that risk responsibly. Sophrosyne is one way people frame this idea of responsible risk management.

Whereas Plato ties sophrosyne to a transcendental limit (the True), neoliberals reframe it as a limit internal to the market. This reframing parallels Foucault's description of the difference between classical and neoliberalism as "a shift from exchange to competition in the principle of the market."[57] For example, Stanisevski defines "moderation" as "an agonistic struggle in which the individual striving for greatness is matched by the countervailing ambition of an opposing rival in a contesting community."[58] Agonistic moderation uses competition itself as the limiting factor: the point is to keep one's own success *proportionate* enough to the success of one's competitors so that nobody scores a definitive, final win and competition can continue. Similarly, in a 2013 editorial, the editors of the "Ethics Forum" section of the journal *Pain Medicine* use

137

the idea of sophrosyne to define an editorial vision that refrains from imposing external limits but instead uses agonistic competition to separate out the
signal from the noise in ethical debates. This "Platonic/Socratic approach . . .
will be one of 'point-counterpoint,' with scientifically based opinions offered
by thought leaders whose views on the pressing ethical issues in pain medicine are not necessarily consistent with each other's."[59] The agonistic competition among viewpoints or voices is the practice that produces consonant
signal from noisy dissonance. Thus, this approach is "Platonic/Socratic" not
so much because it is dialogic but because it frames truth as a "*consonance . . .
among groups of supply-side stakeholders and between supply- and demand-
side stakeholders*"[60]—i.e., as sophrosyne.

Neoliberal sophrosyne builds relations of subordination into generic
competition by making a distinction between natural inferiority and superiority, thus limiting who is even capable of success in the first place. Stanisevski's
definition of sophrosyne as "agonistic contest that conjoins rivaling *geniuses*
in striving for greatness"[61] assumes a pre-given and self-evident distinction
between geniuses and the rest of us poor slobs. Similarly, the Ethics Forum
editors limit competition to "thought-leaders." The role of sophrosyne in
maintaining class-based status hierarchies is also evident in Elizabeth Currid-
Halkett's theory of the twenty-first-century "aspirational class." Reviewing
Currid-Halkett's book, J. C. Pan argues that early twenty-first-century elites
eschew conspicuous consumption (which is generally associated with black
people and the middle class) in favor of "inconspicuous consumption. Their
understated expenditures signal that they are knowledgeable and moral."[62]
Inconspicuous consumption demonstrates consumers' ability to make value
judgments that balance risk and reward. For example, buying ethically sourced
coffee or local, organic, heirloom produce demonstrates the ability to balance
your pleasure and enjoyment with the consequences your consumption patterns have on the environment, laborers, and so on. Inconspicuous consumption is effectively respectability politics applied to consumer behavior: racialized class distinctions are cut along lines of chastity and modesty. Understood
as a feature of neoliberal markets and market logics, sophrosyne retains its
ancient role in establishing relations of subordination but establishes them
with new techniques. Agonistic competition is one of those techniques; "responsibility" is another.

c. From Rights to Responsibility

As both political scientist Lester Spence and surveillance scholar Simone
Browne emphasize, neoliberal biopolitics grants political membership and

full personhood only to individuals who can demonstrate "responsible" behavior. Classical domination contracts used gender and race as markers of preordained (ir)rationality and regulated political membership and personhood on these bases.[63] Neoliberal biopolitics deregulates those things, letting "the market" decide who is rational and responsible enough to deserve society's protections and privileges. As Spence puts it, "the neoliberal turn swaps out 'rights' for 'privileges'—people don't have an inherent 'right' to the city unless they perform the way the city and city elites need them to perform."[64] In this framework, political membership and the protections that come with it (i.e., rights) aren't something individuals choose to opt into (as in the classical social contract) but something granted to those who have demonstrated a history of rational, "responsible" choices. For example, Browne argues that state ID documents like permanent resident cards "are about border control and self-control, where the successful card applicant is realized as responsible, strategizing, rational choicemaking, and self-controlled."[65] Possession of a card is proof that one's past patterns of behavior—"employment, residences, detailed comings and goings"[66] and relationships with citizens of that state—either follow the rules or successfully manage the risks that come with breaking those rules.[67] These neoliberal concepts of "responsibility" are a kind of sophrosyne: self-control or self-mastery understood as cost/benefit rationality, human capital development, and risk management.

Neoliberal discourses of responsibility emphasize another aspect of sophrosyne: doing what is proper to one's place or position and obeying the large-scale distribution of roles and status. Analyzing a case where a U.S. customs agent thought a Canadian woman's permanent resident card was fake because it attributed a Hispanic-sounding surname to an Indian national, Browne highlights the fact that "rationality" is a judgment of both the choice itself (did it successfully balance risk and reward?) and the raced, gendered social status of the person making that choice. As Browne recounts, "even when she produced other symbols of . . . the 'stable self' (her driver's license and health card) she was still subjected to the discretionary power of the border guard,"[68] who perceived a dissonance between the race implied by her name and the race implied by her visible race. So even though this woman exhibited the self-control necessary to obtain a card, the customs agent thought the card was fake because the information on it wasn't consonant with the patterns of racial markers that the agent used to judge the woman. Responsible people exhibit several aspects of sophrosyne: self-control and submission to large-scale distributions of status and relations of subordination.

As these cases show, neoliberal approaches to management, banking,

139

democratic deliberation, and political membership/personhood both explicitly and implicitly appeal to an idea of sophrosyne. Like its predecessor, neoliberal sophrosyne frames sound-mindedness as respect for institutionalized relations of subordination. This is especially easy to demonstrate in the case of gender because we can build on Anne Carson's account of the relationship between gender, sound, and sophrosyne in ancient Greek literature.

3. Sophrosyne and Women
a. Old-School Sophrosyne

Anne Carson's "The Gender of Sound" studies the women of classical Greece. They are presented as "a species given to disorderly and uncontrolled outflow of sound."[69] Unless carefully managed by husbands and the law, women's loose lips (in both senses of the term) will upset the overall "harmonious" order of the city.[70] Emphasizing the relationship the Greeks drew between sonic harmony and social harmony, Carson's analysis of gendered sounds hinges on the concept of sophrosyne. According to Carson, the ancient Greeks thought women's voices were immoderate and lacked sophrosyne because they exhibited excessive frequency: they could either talk at too high a pitch or just talk too much. Such excess "characterize[s] a person who is . . . deficient in the masculine ideal of self-control,"[71] of which "verbal continence is an essential feature."[72] This ideal of self-control is sophrosyne.

(Certain kinds of) men were thought to be capable of embodying (masculine) sophrosyne, of comporting their bodies in accord with the order of the city, the cosmos,[73] and, as I discussed earlier, the True itself, so that when they did speak, their speech contributed to social harmony and orderliness. Women (and slaves, and some other kinds of men) were thought to be incapable of embodying this logos and transforming their bodies into microcosms of the ideal mathematical order. Women couldn't bring their bodies in accord with the logos because, like the aulos, they had "the wrong kind of flesh and the wrong alignment of pores for the production of low vocal pitches."[74] Focusing on the "alignment of pores," Carson's description of what the ancient Greeks thought was problematic about women's bodies echoes what Plato thought was problematic about the aulos: "the rough relationships between trumpemata [finger holes] and mouthpiece" and their "correspond[ence] to the possible ratios between the pitches produced by those trumpemata."[75] Plato thought this was a problem because it meant playing the instrument in tune was more a matter of players' muscle memory and less one of strictly mathematical relationships: it put the part that should obey — the body — in charge. Just as aulos playing was a form of insubordination, women's speech was likewise a form of insubordination: in both cases, the body was in charge, not the logos. Women's voices are immoderate because they upset the proper proportion between what should rule and what should be ruled. This is why "female *sophrosyne* is coextensive with female obedience to male direction and rarely means more than chastity. When it does mean more, the allusion is often to sound. A husband exhorting his wife or concubine to *sophrosyne* is likely to mean 'Be quiet!'"[76] By remaining silent, women would remain subordinate to the part that should rule: men, the logos, etc.

Carson shows that ancient Greek sophrosyne was a patriarchal technology used to police and maintain women's subordination. That patriarchal social order used ideas of geometric proportion to distinguish those who should rule from those who should be ruled. In the twenty-first century, the patriarchal social order cuts this line differently. It's not a hierarchy that requires women's silence; rather, it's a normalized distribution that requires some women to make a certain amount of noise. From the perspective of neoliberal biopolitics, that noise serves as evidence that the old mechanisms of silencing marginal groups are out of commission. Women practice sophrosyne when their behavior is consonant with overall distributions of social subordination.

b. Neoliberal Sophrosyne

X-Ray Spex's 1977 feminist punk classic "O Bondage, Up Yours!" opens by citing the old adage "little girls should be seen and not heard." Following that statement with a scream so forceful it cracks her voice, lead singer Poly Styrene uses loud sound to push back against the adage's sexist stereotype and against women's bondage generally.[77] Nearly forty years later, social norms seem to be reversing themselves: the mainstream media explicitly praises women for their loudness, especially when that loudness is the sound of feminists busting out of the misogynist chains that once held them back. Rebecca Solnit, author of the "Men Explain Things to Me" essay that gave rise to the term "mansplaining,"[78] wrote that 2014 was, for feminists, "a year of mounting refusal to be silent. . . . It has not been a harmonious time, but harmony is often purchased by suppressing those with something to say. It was loud, discordant, and maybe transformative, because important things were said—not necessarily new, but said more emphatically, by more of us, and heard as never before. . . . Women have voices now."[79]

Solnit thinks "women's voices have achieved a power" strong enough to disrupt the previously harmonious functioning of rape culture. Lindy West titled her 2016 memoir, *Shrill: Notes From a Loud Woman.* One reviewer's description of the book as "a primer on the development of her fat-accepting, feminist consciousness"[80] hints at how the title uses a revaluation of a traditionally sexist term for women's excessively loud and high-pitched voice — "shrill"—to represent West's defiance of sexist norms that traditionally devalue women with excessively large bodies. Similarly, the title of Anne Helen Peterson's book, *Too Fat Too Slutty Too Loud: The Rise and Reign of the Unruly Woman*, frames women's insubordination to patriarchy as a matter of sonic excess.[81] Writing in 2013, Amanda Hess argues that the growing influence of women's metaphorical voices in politics and business leads their literal voices — their speech patterns and vocal aesthetics — to be louder and more influential: "As women gain status and power in the professional world, young women may not be forced to carefully modify totally benign aspects of their behavior"—such as vocal fry and uptalk—"in order to be heard. Our speech may not yet be considered professional, but it's on its way there."[82] The idea that women and girls shouldn't be afraid to be loud because old-fashioned sexist attitudes won't hold them back anymore is mainstream enough that advertisers feel safe using it to brand women's products, like soap (Dove's "Speak Beautiful" campaign) or maxi pads (Always's #LikeAGirl videos).[83] Neoliberalism and biopolitics domesticate literal feminist noise: because we've traditionally equated women's silence with their oppression, "loudness" has become a metaphor for and measure of their progress. Women should speak up and be heard.[84]

At the same time that the media celebrated women's feminist envoicement, there was evidence that such envoicement was not uniformly well-received. In 2014 *Harvard Business Review* published a study that found "male managers we interviewed were well aware that women often have a hard time making their otherwise strong voices heard in meetings, either because they're not speaking loudly enough or because they can't find a way to break into the conversation at all," and when they did, "'they pipe up at the wrong moment, and it sounds more like noise to some of us.'"[85] These businessmen thought their women colleagues used their voices inappropriately—they spoke, but it was noise, not signal. This accusation doesn't come only from men. The same year as this *hbr* article, Michelle Goldberg published a now infamous article titled "Feminism's Toxic Twitter Wars." Here, she argues that "feminists" who "are calling one another out about ideological offenses" create a hostile climate that silences women: "'Everyone is so scared to speak now,'" one of her sources says.[86] From Goldberg's perspective, feminists are too loud because the rate at and tone in which they call out women's feminist deficits is dissonant with the proper feminist distribution of women's voices — its frequency pattern masks the feminist message of envoicement, producing a frightened silence just as noise-canceling headphones mask disruptive ambient sound.[87]

In a 2017 interview, musician Solange Knowles explains how black women in particular are commonly felt to be disproportionately loud: "I still often feel that when black women try to have these conversations [about, as she says earlier in the interview, 'all of these ugly things that are staring us in the face,' like ongoing racism and sexism], we are not portrayed as in control, emotionally intact women, capable of having the hard conversations without losing that control."[88]

In other words, black women are perceived as lacking the moderation or self-mastery—the sophrosyne—necessary to ensure that what comes out of your mouth is consonant and syncs up with the rhythms of white supremacist patriarchy. For Solange, performances of vocal control can counteract the tendency to perceive black women's discussions of ongoing oppression as excessively loud and in the red. "It was very intentional that I sang as a woman who was very in control, a woman who could have this conversation without yelling and screaming," she explains. Her voice's sonic moderation, which she describes as a "happy medium," affects the perceived rationality of the content of the words she sings. Sonic moderation means singing so that one's voice is "direct and clear," as Solange describes it, or, in the words of her interviewer Beyoncé Knowles, as "the sweetness and the honesty and purity in your voice." Clearness, purity, fidelity, or honesty are metaphors for expertly rationalized signal, signal without any irrational dissonance or noise. But even though Solange and Beyoncé present such clarity as something the singer creates through practices of self-control and moderation, recording and engineering also play a significant role. For a recorded voice to sound clear and pure, the ambient noise must be minimized or eliminated (e.g., with acoustic foam in the studio or with behind-the-glass processes like equalization or noise removal). Ignoring the role ambient noise plays in a recorded voice's clarity is the equivalent to abstracting away the background conditions within which *Homo economicus* makes bets and takes entrepreneurial risks. Even though her lyrics talk about ongoing structural oppression, her voice *sounds* moderate and controlled because it aesthetically represents the ideal neoliberal subject, the black woman whose success is seen purely as a matter of individual responsibility and not as a matter of institutionalized relations of subordination. Solange's sonic sophrosyne softens the impact of the lyrics' verbal content and discourages the stereotypical interpretation of her as a loud, immoderate, irrational black woman. Society both values and devalues loud women and feminized loudness: women can be loud when their voices rationally sync

143

up with the rhythms of white supremacist patriarchy and amplify its signal, but this loudness is dangerous when their voices don't rationally sync up with those rhythms and introduce dissonance and noise.

Neoliberalism and biopolitics use the concept of sophrosyne to distinguish between consonant feminist subjects and dissonant ones. It conceives their dissonance in the same terms that neoliberalism uses to define exceptional populations: invariance and inflexibility, the failure to exhibit a normalized distribution. Dissonant feminist voices exhibit an abnormal distribution of volume. This is the same deficiency that audio engineers attribute to loud sound. Over the last decade, as the "loudness wars" have evolved, the aesthetic value of audio loudness has changed significantly, shifting from *maximalism* to *variability*.[89] Maximal audio loudness was fashionable in the late 1990s and the first decade of the twenty-first century. Due to advances in recording and transmission technology and an increasingly competitive audio landscape, "loud" mixes with frequencies of uniformly maximized amplitudes were thought to be more commercially appealing and effective than dynamically variable ones where not all amplitudes are maxed out. Compression is the technique audio engineers use to louden a mix; the highest-amplitude frequencies are brought down a bit so that the lowest-amplitude frequencies can be amplified without distortion and the amplitudes of all the frequencies can be maxed out to a uniform level.[90] This consistent and uniform maximization of all frequencies lets a loudened song cut through an otherwise noisy environment, like a crowd's din or competition on the radio dial; in turn, the record industry thought that loudness correlated to sales and popularity. But many now consider loudness to be passé and even regressive. Framed as a matter of "tearing down the wall of noise" or ending "a sonic arms race" that "makes no sense in the 21st century,"[91] anti-loudness activism aims to preserve the health both of listeners' hearing (not their ears, but their discernment) and the music (making it more robust and expressive). As one anti-loudness advocate puts it, "when the dynamic range of a song is heavily reduced for the sake of achieving loudness, the sound becomes analogous to someone constantly shouting everything he or she says. Not only is all impact lost, but the constant level of the sound is fatiguing to the ear."[92] Loud music feels like someone "shouting" at you in all caps; this both diminishes the effectiveness of the speech, and, above all, is unhealthy and "fatiguing" for those subjected to it. Dynamic range advocates fault overcompressed music for exhibiting an invariable, nonnormalized distribution of amplitudes.

"Dissonant" feminists are charged with the same flaws attributed to overcompressed music. Women, especially women of color who express feminist

and antiracist views on social media, are commonly represented as lacking actual dynamic range, as having voices that are always too loud.[93] As Goldie Taylor writes, unlike a white woman pictured shouting in a cop's face as an act of protest, "even if I were inclined, I couldn't shout at a police officer—not in his face, not from across the street," because, as a black woman, her shouting would not be read as legitimate protest but as excessively violent and criminal behavior. White supremacy grants white people the ability to be understood as expressing a dynamic range; whites can legitimately shout because we hear them/ourselves as mainly normalized. At the same time, white supremacy paints black people as always-already too loud. Taylor continues, "merely mention the word privilege, specifically white privilege, anywhere in the public square—including on social media—and one is likely to be mocked." These voices feel too loud because they are both *supposedly*, from the perspective of their critics, (a) lacking in range—they stay fixated on one supposedly overblown issue (social justice)—and (b) overrepresented among the overall mix of voices. Just as overcompressed music is thought to "sacrifice . . . the natural ebb and flow of music,"[94] loud feminist activists are thought to be insubordinate to the "natural" distribution of women's voices on social media and in society generally.

That distribution includes some feminist voices; the point isn't to silence and exclude those voices but to maintain the right level or proportion of them in the overall mix. When prestigious institutions and roles—roles that are not already devalued via feminization, like nursing or teaching or other pink-collar jobs—are seen as sufficiently inclusive of women, that's proof that society has fixed its sexism problem. As political theorist Christina Beltran puts it, "for many citizens, descriptive representation has a kind of beauty that feels and looks like a form of justice."[95] Descriptive representation is the idea that elite institutions should reflect the diversity present in the general population— they should be microcosmic representations of the social macrocosm. Another term for descriptive representation is "proportionalism"[96]—if you've read this far in the book you can probably guess why this is significant. When the proportion of women in elite roles aligns with *what you feel* is the correct or proper proportion of women in society at large, then women must not face any undue impediments. The catch is that this felt sense of proper proportion isn't necessarily connected to empirical reality. For example, in 2016 the producers of the *Stuff You Missed in History Class* podcast revealed that they are often and commonly accused of overrepresenting women in their episodes; for example, a listener complained that their "podcasts had become mostly about women."[97] The producers crunched some numbers and discovered that between March 2013 and June 2016, 45 percent of episodes had been about men or masculine things, 34 percent of things had been about ungendered things (like natural disasters), and 21 percent of episodes had been about women or feminine things. Even though women are just over half the population, one in five (20ish percent) sounded disproportionately feminine to many in the podcast's audience. Women ought to be included at levels that don't *feel* disproportionate, actual statistics be damned. Sophrosyne's traditional denotations as both a ratio and a hierarchical ordering highlights how relations of subordination rationalize our sense of proper proportion, so that 20 percent women feels disproportionate. White supremacist patriarchy normalizes our perception by distinguishing between acceptable levels of noisiness and in-the-red sounds that would distort social harmony. Thus, women's voices and even feminist noise are acceptable, as long as they are subordinate to that norm.

As in ancient Greece, twenty-first-century Western women are expected to practice sophrosyne. Those who do are granted some degree of personhood; those who don't, aren't. Just as white noise is an architectural feature used to mask office sounds that decrease productivity,[98] some kinds of feminist noise contribute to the productivity of white supremacist patriarchal society. Healthy feminist voices are moderate—they contribute to the "natural ebb and flow" of white supremacist patriarchy—but unhealthy ones are immoderate because they upset that flow, either arguing for or effecting the redistribution of that norm. That's what listeners accused *Stuff You Missed in History Class* of doing: redistributing the acceptable proportion of women in the mix of voices and topics they heard. Even though neoliberalism and biopolitics expect women to make some feminist noise, they must do so in ways that are consonant with large-scale relations of domination and subordination. Exhibiting the proper distribution of signal and noise, such feminine-presenting phenomena can "lean in" to patriarchal privilege and avoid the negative effects of structural feminization. Conversely, femininities that feel immoderately noisy or loud because they distort rather than amplify patriarchy are structurally feminized and perceptually coded into the red. Thus, sophrosyne helps patriarchy misrepresent women's ongoing subordination as their liberation.

The next section considers how black women have responded and developed alternatives to neoliberal sophrosyne. First, I argue that Katherine McKittrick's concept of "demonic calculus" describes practices that are superficially similar to sophrosyne—patterned rates and ratios—but are neither grounded in nor reproduce the relations of subordination that rationalize neoliberal sophrosyne. Whereas neoliberals update the math behind the ancient Greek concept of sophrosyne to accord with contemporary structures of domination, McKittrick replaces both of them with an insubordinate numeracy. The final section of the chapter identifies various ways Beyoncé's 2016 visual album *Lemonade* applies demonic calculus to music composition and songwriting. *Lemonade*'s demonic calculus counts out distributions of artistic credit, aesthetic value, and pleasure in ways that don't obey the relations of subordination that calibrate neoliberal practices of sophrosyne. In so doing, it rationalizes black women's experiences and ways of knowing (i.e., the things neoliberal sophrosyne normalizes out as irrational).

II. Demonic Calculus

In both its classical and contemporary forms, sophrosyne is a proportional distribution and a relation of subordination. That relation of subordination makes otherwise irrational distributions of chance, accident, risk, and precarity seem rational. The rationality beneath surface-level chance, this relation of subordination guarantees that the house always wins and even highly deregulated systems predictably (re)produce outcomes that bolster existing distributions of resources, health, personhood, and property. Neoliberal biopolitics transforms all relations into mathematical norms and probabilities, and the disproportionate distribution of life and death underwrites the success of these forecasts. For example, as Katherine McKittrick argues, "the premature death of black people . . . is entrenched in algorithmic equations" as the key to their predictive success.[99] The reliable certainty of the connection between blackness and (physical, social, civil) death is what makes it possible to predict the futures of (white) life. White supremacy is one of the intersecting relations of subordination that ground the mathematical truths that neoliberal sophrosyne puts in practice. Patterns that are consonant with that distribution of life and death will be accepted as true, whereas dissonant patterns will be treated as abnormalities in need of reform.

Studying black women's writing about epistemology, McKittrick identifies and riffs on a poetic technique that counts out an *orthos logos* whose quantization is dissonant with and insubordinate to neoliberal sophrosyne's logos. Building on Sylvia Wynter's concept of demonic grounds, which names black women's space-making practices, McKittrick calls this insubordinate numeracy "demonic."[100] If, as an orthos logos, sophrosyne is a practice of ordering oneself so that one may speak true things (that is, so that one can exhibit *parrhesia*),[101] then demonic calculus is a practice of ordering oneself so that one may make what would sound, to ears quantized by sophrosyne, like a counterfactual claim. "Noticing and reworking and mistrusting numerical data," demonic calculus is a kind of sounding: it feigns complicity with and obliquely pivots from the metrics that disproportionately distribute the social, civil, and physical death of black people to a "mathematics of black life" (McKittrick, "Mathematics Black Life," 18). McKittrick calls such pivots "truthful lies that can push us toward demonic grounds" (24). These claims sound like lies because their fidelity to black feminist epistemologies makes them insubordinate to the relations of domination that neoliberal sophrosyne codes into statistics, algorithms, forecasts, and markets. McKittrick argues that if we "trust the lies" instead of practicing sophrosyne's so-called truth, we can "begin to count it out differently" (23) and work from an insubordinate numeracy that pivots us to a register in which so-called lies sound like truths.

Demonic calculus is a poetic technique, so rather than explaining it, McKittrick models this counting differently in her writing: the structure of her prose is an instance of demonic calculus. Within the standard organization of a particular practice of truth—the academic article—McKittrick's develops a new pattern of prosody, a pattern that breaks with norms of both verbal repetition and analytical emphasis in academic prose. Between pages 20 and 25, McKittrick repeats "she says she was born free" or some variation in seven different places, for a total of twelve repetitions. Such repetition is generally frowned upon by academic editors and audiences. Nevertheless, McKittrick uses it to create a rhythm to her prose. The repetition of this phrase creates two kinds of choreosonic patterns—i.e., patterns in the poetic apportioning of her words and phrases—which is a literary register common scholarly methods abstract away in their focus on propositional content (for more on choreosonics, see chapter 3). First, there is a large-scale intra-repetition pattern that parses and "counts out" the article's overall form into shorter and longer sections. Second, because the phrase is varied and sometimes repeated directly in sequence, its repetitions also exhibit inter-repetition patterns and rhythms. These internal rhythms are easiest to analyze when you list each repetition together, in sequence:

— "She says she was born free. Says she was born free. She is not free. She says she was born free" (20)

— "The unfree nonperson says she was born free. She says she was born free. She says she was born free at Newtown, Long Island: she is not free. She says she is free" (20)

— "She says" (21)

— "She says she was born free. The archives are full of truthful lies" (21)

— "What if we trust the lies — she says she was born free — and begin to count it all out differently?" (22)

— "But again: What if we trust the lies — she says she was born free — and begin to count it all out differently?" (23)

— "She says she was born free" (25) [This is the last sentence in the article.]

Isolated from its appearance in the article and taken as a whole, the repetition and variation of this phrase reveals a rhythmic pattern — a pattern that doesn't rationalize or normalize itself into a regular distribution where readers can predict what variation will come next. There are only a few predictable things about this pattern: (1) the phrase starts with the subject: "she" or "the unfree nonperson"; (2) the main verb is in the present tense — she says — and the object of that verb is in the past imperfect: was born. This variation creates a rhythm among the iterations of the phrase. The phrase's intra-repetition pattern counts out a rhythm beyond or beneath the lines of the full prose article — a demonic calculus. McKittrick uses these repetitions to demonstrate "counting it out differently."

This recounting and repatterning isn't just about form: it affects the article's content, that is, McKittrick's argument. "She says she was born free" is the "true lie" McKittrick refers to: nominally it's a lie — this "she" was born a slave, a legal nonperson — but it's also empirically true; she found ways of counting her social death out differently and practiced a kind of freedom that wasn't grounded in or limited to self-ownership of one's property-in-person. McKittrick's demonic rhythms return our attention to this true lie, make it *proportionally the most frequently cited thing in the text.* This frequency redistributes what McKittrick identifies as the conventional rhythm of citation in black studies, which emphasizes black death and violent dispossession, such as the picture of a man's whipped back. In other words, whereas the archives McKittrick studies perceptually code black life out into the red, demonic calculus tunes in to those very coded-out frequencies. Shifting frequencies, McKittrick retunes the theoretical apparatus of black studies so that it can register more spectra of black existence than just social death and violence.

In addition to modeling demonic calculus in her writing, McKittrick explains how it "re-think[s] the mathematics"[102] behind biopolitical distributions and neoliberal market forecasts in order to tune in to frequencies

149

they perceptually code into the red. Neoliberal sophrosyne translates probabilities into nonquantitative terms; these probabilities work because normalized black subordination makes racially disproportionate distributions of risk and reward easy to foresee (for example, in credit scores or disease morbidity rates). Forecasting metrics like credit scores find patterns in past behavior and use those patterns to predict future performance. Because the past and present are organized by ongoing relations of subordination, these forecasting metrics project that subordination into the future.[103] Demonic calculus abandons the relations of subordination that make such probabilities and statistical forecasts rational in the first place. As McKittrick explains, "the demonic—in physics and mathematics—is a nondeterministic schema; it is a process that is hinged on uncertainty and nonlinearity because the organizing principle cannot foresee the future."[104] Demonic calculus can't foresee the future because it doesn't take past performance, practices, or patterns of behavior as models for future performance, practice, and behavior. Trusting the "lies" means understanding that black people's past strategies of survival "are not blueprints for emancipation, or maps to our future," but are practices that "uncomfortably enumerat[e] the unanticipated contours of black life."[105] This "uncomfortable enumeration" is a kind of dissonance, a frequency or rhythmic pattern whose contours don't mesh neatly with past and present distributions of life and success. Refusing to subordinate itself to the distributions of life and personhood that define neoliberal biopolitics, demonic calculus is a practice of truth that identifies and articulates the frequencies those distributions perceptually code into the red.[106] Demonic calculus counts out these dissonant frequencies as truths consonant with black women's practices of truth—the speaker of that above-cited "true lie" is a she, remember.

As many scholars and critics have noted, Beyoncé's 2016 visual album *Lemonade* "plac[es] the black woman at the center of the puzzle"[107] and "restor[es] black women to their human form."[108] Though most people focus on the visual centering of black women, this centering happens through the album's sound just as much as through its visuals. The album uses a sonic demonic calculus to articulate a concept of personhood that centers black women and their knowledges. The album's politics are complicated, and I am not making any general assessment of the album as a whole; I am making a claim only about the parts of the songwriting and composition in "6 Inch" and "Formation" that adopt the very same poetic techniques that McKittrick uses in her literary modeling of demonic calculus. Both of these songs use repeated repetitions of black women's vocal phrases to count out differently structures that assume black women's subordination, centering both black women's epistemology and their personhood.[109]

Emily Lordi's analysis highlights how the track "6 Inch" takes a sample from the women backup singers on Isaac Hayes's "Walk On" and uses it to count out the gendered relationship between featured and backup singers differently than it appears in the original. Like Nicki Minaj's "Anaconda," which repurposes the bass riff from Sir Mix-a-Lot's "Baby Got Back" to sonify femme sexual pleasure, "6 Inch" takes a famous sample — the "fierce network of ascending strings" in "Hayes's grand orchestral treatment" — and "harnesses" it "to a woman's story."[110] But it's another sample from that Hayes track that does the re/counting: "less dramatically but constantly, the track samples Hayes's three female backup singers singing 'walk on.'"[111] Proportionally, the women backup singers play a bigger role and appear more frequently in "6 Inch" than Hayes or the song's hook does. Like McKittrick's article on demonic calculus, "6 Inch" recounts the gendered frequency of citation to favor what "she says." Counting out the gendered rhythms of Hayes's original song differently, "6 Inch" opens new geography, one that black women don't have to flee to survive. As Lordi notes, "At the end of that song, Beyoncé echoes the backup singers' lyric 'walk on' but changes the words to 'come back.' Repeating the call like an incantation, she might be heard as not only addressing an absent lover but also hailing women themselves: those voices in the background of soul, and the backrooms of slave plantations."[112]

151

Transforming "walk on" into "come back," "6 Inch" finds the true lie hidden by practices of truth that relegate black women and their work to the background and compel them to walk away from a deck that's stacked against them. It does this by restacking or recounting that deck. The *come back*s increase in rhythmic intensity from once every other measure to once every measure; this echoes both the structure of the "walk on" samples and, more overtly, the soar at the beginning of the song. That soar represents the economic risk that requires black women like "6 Inch's" protagonist to constantly hustle, working both weekdays and weekends, and Hayes's backup singers to "walk on."[113] Revoicing this structure as a series of *come back*s, the song regraphs the sonic space of EDM and trap into what Zandria Robinson calls "a risk-free . . . space that sonically and visually highlights what we miss when we dismiss and neglect black women."[114] One of the things we miss is black women's aesthetic and kinesthetic knowledges, such as the knowledge and practice it takes to work and werk in six-inch heels as one strips in a club to soul, R&B, or trap.[115] Counting out song structures and gendered genre conventions differently,

"6 Inch" articulates an orthos logos that centers black women's voices and epistemologies and allows us to hear the true lies masked by white supremacist patriarchal distributions of personhood, which are rationalized by black women's multiple subordination.

"6 Inch" is one example of *Lemonade*'s sonic demonic calculus. "Formation" is another; its use of verbal repetition and repetition as a large-scale formal device also echoes McKittrick's use of "she says she was born free."[116] Both the song's background formal structure and its foreground lyrical rhythms articulate patterns of living and practices of truth Southern black women use to make what nominally sounds like a lie an empirical reality. "I slay" is Beyoncé's postmillennial update on her foremother's assertion that she was born free.

First, let's look at the large-scale form, the "background" or backbone of the song's overall structure. Joan Morgan argues that the album's "genius lies partially in form," and as the culmination of or coda to *Lemonade*, "Formation" proves Morgan correct.[117] In contrast to the conventional verse-chorus-verse-chorus-bridge-chorus-chorus form, "Formation" redistributes the typical balance among these parts. Here is a diagram of the song's form, where "x" stands for one 4/4 measure, assuming quarter note = 120ish:

———

INTRO: xxxx/xxxx

PRE-CHORUS: xxxx/xxxx   (same as the intro but with vocals)

                 xx/xx

                 xxxx/xxxx   (downbeat of first measure hits on "BAMA")

                 [unmetered vocals]

INTRO: xxxx/xxxx

PRE-CHORUS: xxxx/xxxx

                 xx/xx

                 xxxx/xxxx

CHORUS: xxxx/xxxx   (with marching percussion)

                 xx/xx

	xxxx/xxxx	("I slay" densely repeated every measure)
	xxxx/xxxx	
VERSE 1:	xxxx/xxxx	("I slay" at the end of every second and fourth measure in each phrase)
	xxxx/xxxx	
CHORUS:	xxxx/xxxx	
	xx/xx	
	xxxx/xxxx	("I slay")
	xxxx/xxxx	
VERSE 2:	xxxx/xxxx	(Percussion drops out; main backing is the synth from chorus.) [Note that there are eight bars missing in the second verse.]

[unmetered vocals]

_____

"Formation" quite literally counts out pop song structure differently: instead of interweaving verses and choruses, it batches them into proportionally uneven sections, with the "I slay"–filled choruses getting most of the space. This recounting of pop song form contributes to what Britt Julious calls its "off-kilter, even downright weird" take on trap.[118] That off-kilter, conventionally disproportionate form is one way "Formation" *musically* represents "the celebration of the margins — black bodies in motion, women's voices centered, black queer voices centered"[119] — that the video and lyrics express. "Formation" distributes a lot of sonic space to those usually counted out of the equation as exception, so the rationality of its background form will appear off-kilter, even downright weird, to ears tempered by a calculus whose rationality depends on and assumes the subordination of the voices "Formation" centers.

The musical foreground of "Formation" is similarly calibrated. Lyrical repetition is common in pop music, but, as I argued in chapter 2, excessive serial repetition of a lyric is one way Southern hip-hop aesthetics find alternative, more pleasurable and survivable patterns of living within the neoliberal imperative to hustle. An amalgam of early twenty-first-century Southern hip-hop (including cowriter Swae Lee's ATL-via-Tupelo sound, producer Mike Will's ATL trap, and Beyoncé's own Houston influences), "Formation" adopts this strategy in the second half of its choruses. "I slay" is repeated many times, in different variations: I slay, they slay—and both Beyoncé and the background vocalists respond with "all day" and "okay," whose two-syllable rhyme with the stress on the second rhyming syllable makes them sound like just another variation on "I/they/we slay." The overall effect here echoes the effect of McKittrick's collected repetitions of "she says she was born free." The choruses collect all the slays and put them in series, a nod to the lean aesthetics that share Beyoncé's Houston roots. The verses spread the slays out, dropping them at the end of every second and fourth measure. Spreading the "I/they/we slays" out to parse formal sections in the larger work, the verses of "Formation" echo the exact same strategy McKittrick uses in her prose.

Both in its foreground and in its structural background, the musical composition of "Formation" exhibits the exact type of demonic calculus McKittrick describes in her article. Beyoncé and McKittrick use similar rhythms to count out the distribution of citations so that what she says—be it "I was born free" or "I slay"—predominates. These phrases aren't just set similarly; their content resonates. Invoking "complete domination . . . even in the face of the very real forms of violence and oppression that [black women] face,"[120] "I slay" is a plausible variation on "I was born free," one rendered in twenty-first-century queer femme AAVE.[121] As McKittrick explained, "she says she was born free" is a "true lie," that is, a statement whose rationality depends upon being insubordinate to white supremacist patriarchal distributions of epistemic credence and calibrating practices of truth to align with the priorities of people who negotiate white supremacist cisheteropatriarchy with and through black women's bodies. For example, as Erica Thurman argues, Lemonade's "repetition of shared experiences reinforces [to black American women] that we are not crazy, that we have not imagined the slights"[122]—it reflects back to them as truth what otherwise gets discounted as a lie ("You're making things up/you're being too sensitive," etc.). "Formation," like Lemonade in general, uses demonic calculus to count out an orthos logos that allows black women to trust the "lies" she says: I slay, I was born free. These are both forceful assertions of agency and self-determination—i.e., of personhood. Demonic calculus is a tool black women have used to conceptualize and experience a kind of personhood that doesn't subordinate them to white supremacist patriarchal logics.

Lemonade is not just an example of demonic calculus; it also hints at its relationship to sophrosyne. Bringing Carson's essay into the mix makes that relationship more explicit. As Carson explains, women's immoderate, "disorderly[,] and uncontrolled outflow of sound" was often represented as "a loud roaring noise as of wind or rushing water . . . 'she who pours forth.'"[123] As I discussed in the previous chapter, *Lemonade*'s opening movements rely on a similar equation of immoderate femininity and gushing water. First, the litany of personal austerity in the "Denial" section is easily interpreted as a kind of feminine sophrosyne in the most classical sense: Beyoncé's narrator ticks off some forms of extreme self-mastery she practiced, like keeping her mouth closed, not eating or speaking, and not having sex. All her lips are tightly closed. This scene takes place in her bedroom, which is also underwater. This scene equates contained bodies of water with women's contained bodily flows. However, at the beginning of "Hold Up," which is the song where Beyoncé's character bashes representatives of all the men that have kept her down with a baseball bat named Hot Sauce, she opens double doors and lets out a gush of water as she leaves home and heads out for her cathartic promenade. In the meantime, she busts open a fire hydrant with Hot Sauce, letting loose another gush of water. The video represents the movement from lemons to lemonade — the pivot between registers — as the unleashing of previously contained flows of water. Robinson argues that these "baptismal waters" both impart and represent "a theretofore unrealized freedom to be emotionally human."[124] Learning to count it out differently means smashing the tools that people use to restrict and subordinate water's flow, be they fire hydrants or concepts and practices of feminine sophrosyne. Let loose, water/demonic calculus can even sink the white cisheteropatriarchal state. That's what Robinson sees at the end of "Formation," where Beyoncé's character "vanquishes the state, represented by a NOPD car,"[125] by using her body to sink it in floodwater. If we follow the flow of water — lemonade is a liquid after all — *Lemonade* is a story of turning sophrosyne into demonic calculus. This is why it's possible for Ashley Ray-Harris to interpret *Lemonade* as embodying all the flaws critics attribute to "loud" feminists. She writes, "In Lemonade, Beyoncé boldly reclaims her right to express her black self outwardly. . . . The black woman who demands accountability is referred to as upset, aggressive, or angry. The black woman who expresses joy is too loud or inappropriate."[126] Voices that count out demonic calculus are immoderately loud because they don't subordinate themselves to neoliberal sophrosyne.

As both McKittrick and Beyoncé practice it, demonic calculus is a practice of rhythmic patterning that: (1) weights the ratio of citation to black women, and (2) rejects the relations of subordination that make white supremacist patriarchal distributions of chance, risk, and precarity seem rational,

155

natural, and fair. Demonic calculus is a technology black women use instead and in place of statistical normalization and sophrosyne. If neoliberalism upgrades ancient Greek sophrosyne by replacing old math with new math, McKittrick and Beyoncé replace that new math with their own math, their own style of counting and their own orthos logos. As a practice of truth, demonic calculus makes black women's personhood perceptible in what otherwise sound like lies, falsehoods, and impossibilities. Similarly, whereas the sonic episteme uses sound to translate the math behind neoliberal biopolitics into nonquantitative terms, *Lemonade* uses sound and music to translate the math behind demonic calculus into nonquantitative terms. Demonic calculus is not a zero-sum game. It does not replace or supersede dominant practices of truth; rather, it tunes in to the frequencies those practices perceptually code into the red, such as the "come back" coded out of "walk on." As a version of "sounding," it feigns complicity with white supremacist patriarchal practices of truth while at the same time going around, above, and below them to craft transmission networks for insubordinately tempered ears. For this reason, *Lemonade* can be both a commodity and capital-building enterprise for Beyoncé while also working with and against capitalism's racialized, gendered distributions of personhood-as-property.

156

Like the ancient Greeks, contemporary Western culture uses the idea of sophrosyne to enforce women's subordination and police their voices. The shape of that subordination is different: instead of a hierarchy that excludes women, neoliberal biopolitics uses a Gaussian curve or normalized distribution to manage the (conditional and instrumental) inclusion of women's/feminist voices that amplify overall patterns of domination and subordination. It grants personhood only to these consonant voices. Updating the music-math analogy in Plato's original concept, the concept of sophrosyne captures how this normalization translates from metaphysics of numbers (as Mader describes) to a metaphysics of personhood. Neoliberal sophrosyne is the sonic episteme's theory of personhood: it models personhood on acoustically resonant sound. Demonic calculus, on the other hand, models personhood on frequencies this concept of sophrosyne perceptually codes out of circulation. I'm no mathematician, but by analyzing the sonics and choreosonics of McKittrick's and Beyoncé's works, I've shown what the music part of demonic calculus's music-math analogy looks like. It is a non-zero-sum accounting that counts out proportions, ratios, and frequencies that center black women and that do not subordinate themselves to white supremacist patriarchal distributions of personhood.

This chapter explained how the sonic episteme updates Plato's music-math analogy and uses that analogy to translate from neoliberal biopolitics' metaphysics of numbers to a metaphysics of personhood. Plato applied this analogy at both the micro, individual level and the macro, cosmic level. The next chapter addresses the sonic episteme's use of this analogy at the macro level. Twenty-first-century popular science writing, especially accounts of big-data–style "social physics" and the physics of string theory, uses acoustic resonance to translate the math behind that physics into layperson terms; however, this risks naturalizing the math behind neoliberal biopolitics as an objective feature of the universe. Following McKittrick's ongoing work on "demonic calculus" or "wicked mathematics,"[127] I show how she counts out some of the fundamental ideas in big data–style social physics differently.

157

5

Social Physics and Quantum Physics

Acoustic Resonance as the Model for a "Harmonious" World

So far in this book I've shown how various constituents of the sonic episteme use acoustic resonance as the foundation for theories of the market, political ontology, materialist ontology, and subjectivity or personhood. This last chapter focuses on constituents of the sonic episteme that appear in pop science accounts of social and cosmological physics. They appeal to concepts of musical harmony to translate the math behind the physics into layperson's terms. In both big data–style social physics and string theory, these appeals to acoustic resonance naturalize the very same mathematical relations neoliberal biopolitics uses behind an apparently apolitical concept of "harmony."

The connection between these two disciplines isn't just in the name "physics" or in their shared ontology. They are genealogically related: social physics comes from astrophysics. Adolphe Quetelet adapted astronomers' method of estimating the location of a planet in space into a tool for thinking probabilistically about populations. Originally, astronomers used Gaussian averages as a way to address irremediably imprecise measurements of things in outer space. Because it was impossible to get a single accurate measurement of, say, a planet's distance from Earth, they would gather a number of measurements and used the Gaussian distribution to establish a range of normal measurements for that distance. As Mary Beth Mader explains, "Quetelet is credited with first applying the Gaussian error curve, or 'bell curve,' to social objects in his 1835 book, *Sur l'homme et le développement de ses facultés, ou Essai de physique sociale*. . . . This extension of the mathematical law of error to social objects ushers in the nineteenth-century era of 'social arithmetics,' 'social mathematics,' and 'social physics.'"[1]

Quetelet's *physique sociale* "gave us the mean and the bell-shaped curve as fundamental indices of the human condition."[2] Though many advances have been made since the nineteenth century, both social physics and astrophysics are rooted in this basic math. Pop science accounts of both types of physics commonly appeal to ideas of harmony and resonance to translate that math—the normalized statistical distribution—into nonquantitative terms. This makes them constituents of the sonic episteme.

To show how they do this, I trace how MIT data scientist Alex Pentland and astrophysicists Brian Greene and Stephon Alexander appeal to "harmony" in their popular science writing. Though nobody explicitly appeals to acoustic resonance in my sense of the term, I will show that they use harmony as a metaphor to describe things that fit under that rubric. As constituents of the sonic episteme, these pop science narratives use "harmony" to hide the relations of inequity created by neoliberal biopolitics behind a supposedly apolitical idea of sound. Pop science accounts of string theory are particularly troubling on this count because they pass off the mathematical relationships neoliberal biopolitics uses to structure society as facts about the fundamental structure of the universe.

As in the previous chapters, I conclude this one by discussing phonographic approaches to the phenomenon that is the chapter's focus—here, that's the math behind big data–style social physics and string theory. Building on earlier discussions of McKittrick and Weheliye, I show how their coauthored analysis of the TR-808 uses the choreosonic dimensions of twentieth- and twenty-first-century hip-hop and R&B as models for a different kind of math. This math counts out the quantitative relationships in Pentlandian idea flow (and neoliberal biopolitics more generally) differently. This work is evidence that the problem with the sonic episteme isn't that it uses sound to translate math into qualitative terms, but rather with the specific kind of mathematical relationships acoustic resonance translates.

159

I. Big Data–Style Social Physics

The concluding chapter of Alex Pentland's book *Social Physics* is titled "Design for Harmony: How Social Physics Can Help Us Design a Human-Centric Society."[3] "Harmony" is Pentland's metaphor for the kind of world that results when we apply "a mathematical, predictive science of society" (191) to study and influence people's behavior.[4] He never explicitly defines what he means by "harmony." However, because he uses "harmony" to describe the outcome or telos of his style of social physics, we can infer this from his explanation of how that social physics works. I begin this section by doing just that. After establishing what Pentland means by "harmony," I will argue that Pentland's account of social physics uses "harmony" as a conceptual *jacquemart*: it hides ugly mechanics behind an aesthetically pleasing concept of harmony or resonance.

1. Sound as a Metaphor for Statistics

Pentland is not the only person to use sonic metaphors for big data. Scholars in sociology have proposed "symphonic social science" as a method of combining traditional sociological research methods with those of big data. For example, Susan Halford and Mike Savage use "resonance" as a model for the kind of argument such social scientists make: "a cascading and elaborating argument which comes to have resonance through repeat motifs spliced with telling (partial) counterfactuals."[5] Unlike claims for correlation or causation, symphonic arguments compound evidence much in the same way interest compounds in an investment. An intensifying cascade that builds up to an interruption, the structure of symphonic arguments strongly resembles the soar-drop structure commonly used in postmillennial EDM-influenced pop music.[6] Halford and Savage use resonance to describe soars, not acoustics or acoustic resonance. This is because sound isn't translating the mathematical operations they use to analyze data but is the way that data is used to make arguments in scholarly research. More commonly, when resonance is used as a metaphor for big data, it refers to the math part of data science. For example, there is a startup named Resonance that "appl[ies] the latest Cognitive Computing and Big Data techniques to the problem of finding, quantifying and analysing key reputational data."[7] The company name uses resonance to represent the number crunching and human capital forecasting service the startup provides. Pentland does the same thing but in a much more detailed way. "Harmony" is his metaphor for the statistics social physicists use to study and shape people's behavior.

According to Pentland, "social physics is based on statistical regularities that span the population" (*Social Physics* 189). In his version of social physics, scientists use big data to redescribe relations among people as a specific kind of relation among numbers: a normalized statistical distribution of frequencies across a population. "Social phenomena," he explains "are really made up of millions of small transactions between individuals. There are patterns in those individual transactions that are not just averages . . . [but] micro-patterns" (10–11). These micro-patterns are rates or frequency ratios, such as the rate at which an employee talks with their coworkers. Though these individual micro-patterns may appear irregular or aleatory, when "analyzed . . . across many people" they "explain many things—crashes, revolutions, bubbles— that previously appeared to be random 'acts of God'" (9). After identifying individual micro-patterns, social physicists then collect them and identify the "social norm" they express or ought to express (21). Norms are different than averages: they aren't just the mean or median of a range of values but the range of individual patterns or frequencies that amplify specific macro-patterns, like distributions of wealth, personhood, and so on. Pentland's idea of the "healthy wisdom of the crowd region" is an example of such a norm: this region maps out the range of rates of idea flow that optimize productivity and profit (38). Pentlandian social physics has a fundamentally mathematical understanding of the social; it takes frequencies as the fundamental unit of society and imagines that society as a normalized distribution of those frequencies.

Pentland uses sonic metaphors to translate that math into "a human-scale" phenomenon that nonexperts have an "intuitive understanding of" (189). Echoing Du Bois's descriptions of statistics as measurements of the rate and rhythm of chance events, Pentland explains that social physics observes the "rhythm[s] of [people's] daily habits" (142), "the rhythms of a city" (144), or other "activities [that] have rhythms that are predictable across days and weeks" (141). Rhythm is a metaphor for the micro-patterns social physicists identify in individual behavior. Though he does not name them directly, Pentland also appeals to several aspects of acoustics to explain what these "micro-patterns" are and how they work. For example, "idea flow" is both a flow that "oscillate[s] between exploration and engagement" (100) and an abstraction that describes "the *proportion* of users who are likely to adopt a new idea introduced into the network" (83; emphasis added). Just as acousticians measure oscillating waves and express that oscillation as a frequency, social physics measures oscillating flows and expresses that flow as a proportion comparing individual rates across a group. Moreover, because twenty-first-century physicists use acoustics to study the flow of energy (electrical, kinetic, etc.) through

161

fluids, Pentland's claim that "just as the goal of traditional physics is to understand how the flow of energy translates into changes in motion, social physics seeks to understand how the flow of ideas and information translates into changes in behavior" (5) states that social physics applies the laws of acoustic resonance to society. So even though this comparison doesn't directly name sound or acoustics, it nevertheless uses the fundamental concepts in acoustics to explain the role of rate and frequency in social physics.

Pentland points to various concepts of harmony to explain how these rhythms or frequencies relate. Rhythmic patterns of individual behavior or idea flow "mesh together like pieces in a puzzle" (62), smaller micro-patterns nesting together in "synchrony" (111) with one another and with larger-scale social patterns.[8] Similarly, Pentland's appeal to Zipf's law (162) to explain the relationship among the subpatterns and overall patterns sounds a lot like contemporary understandings of how overtones relate to primary tones. Zipf's law holds that the frequency of phenomena within a bounded set, like "the distributions of the sizes of cities, earthquakes, solar flares, moon craters, wars and people's personal fortunes all appear to follow power laws."[9] Power laws describe exponentially proportional relationships.[10] The relations among overtones are exponentially proportional. In fact, mathematicians identify Zipf distributions as a type of harmonic series.[11] So, if Pentlandian social physics thinks the relationships among individual patterns follow Zipf's law, then it treats those relationships as a type of harmonic series. Even though the word "harmony" only appears in the title of the book's last chapter, the concept of harmony as consonance or rationally related phase patterns runs throughout *Social Physics*, translating the quantitative relationships Pentland and his team use to measure and manage social phenomena into lay terms.

Pentland doesn't use the language of acoustics, but his theory of social physics is grounded in the key components of acoustic resonance as I define it in this book: frequency ratios, oscillatory motion, proportional flows, and Gaussian distributions.[12] Like the other constituents of the sonic episteme, Pentland's appeal to harmony and resonance is a conceptual jacquemart (a clock equipped with mechanical bell-ringing puppets that are supposed to disguise a sound made by an ugly machine as one made by aesthetically pleasing one) that hides ugly mathematical and managerial mechanics behind a metaphor for sonic and musical pleasure. In the next section, I'll explain why those mechanics are ugly.

2. Pentland's Revamped Social Contract and Post-Identity Biopolitics

All constituents of the sonic episteme oppose themselves to some aspect of Western modernity or postmodernity and claim to fix the problems that follow from that canon's mechanics while actually reinstituting new forms of those problems. Pentland's book is full of phrases that indicate a departure from "the old vocabulary" (8), "the traditional language" (x), "the standard . . . approaches" (5), or "old-fashioned . . . thinking" (24). Philosophical representationalism and its emphasis on propositional content is one example of such old-fashioned thinking.[13] But Pentland's main target is the classical social contract. First, social physics changes the type of agreement that grounds social cooperation from a contract to a norm. This entails a further revision in the scope of what the agreement covers, extending the range of the legitimate exercise of government (and corporate) authority over individuals from the rule of law to social normalization.

a. From Contract to Norm

Pentland explicitly offers social physics as a replacement for classical liberalism and social contract theory. According to Pentland, "our culture and the habits of our society are *social contracts*" (61; emphasis added). However, this contract isn't constituted through reasoned individual consent but through "the attitudes, actions, and outcomes of peers, rather than by logic or argument. Learning and reinforcing this social contract is what enables a group of people to coordinate their actions effectively" (61). For Pentland, social cooperation takes the form of synchronously coordinated micro-patterns that mesh into rational macro-patterns. The kind of agreement that grounds this form of cooperation is "*a bargain* between individuals to adopt behaviors that are *synchronized* and compatible" (62; emphasis added). Even though he refers to this bargain as a contract, he uses that term to describe norms. Like contracts, norms are economic metaphors; they're just metaphors for a different kind of economic interaction. Pentland understands norms as a type of population-wide cost/benefit calculus, a "consensus" that "account[s] for the cost-benefit trade-offs of everyone in the group" (63). Just as Rancièrian postdemocracy takes the phusis of enterprising man as community nomos, Pentlandian social physics takes that same logic of entrepreneurial investment as the basic element of society. From contract to norm and exchange to investment, Pentlandian social physics updates the kind of agreement that grounds social cooperation to fit with biopolitical and neoliberal frameworks.

This shift from contract to norm leads Pentland to rework other aspects of the classical social contract. The most important of these are the related concepts of property-in-person and consent. According to political theorist Carole Pateman, property-in-person is a "fiction"[14] invented by John Locke, who argues that "every Man has a Property in his own Person."[15] As Pateman explains, "the individual owns his body and his capacities as pieces of property, just as he owns material property."[16] So, for Locke and other classical contract theorists, personhood was a commodity that could be exchanged. Paralleling neoliberal economists' shift from the concept of labor power to human capital, Pentland reframes property-in-person by updating the *kind* of property individuals are understood to own. Human capital is just that—capital, an asset.[17] Arguing that "we need to recognize personal data as a valuable *asset* of the individual that is given to companies and government in return for services,"[18] Pentland redefines the kind of ownership one exercises over oneself. Ownership is an "investment in social ties" for the purpose of "building social capital."[19] I make different kinds of decisions about investments than I do about exchanges: my interest is less in fairness (e.g., a fair wage in return for my labor power) and more in risk management. As Pentland explains, "personal data . . . [is] under the control of the individual, as he is the one who can best judge the *balance* between the associated risks and rewards."[20] This shift in ownership entails a shift in our understanding of what it means to consent to a contract. I'm not exchanging freedom for security but placing a bet and making an investment. In this framework, consent isn't rational free will but cost/benefit calculus.[21] To consent is effectively to make a bet.

Even though he revises the kind of property one owns in one's person and how exactly one owns it, Pentland uses the same—if slightly displaced—sleight that Pateman identifies in classical uses of property-in-person. According to Pateman, the classical contract understands property-in-person as labor power, which is a commodity alienable from the body that performs such that "the individual can contract out any of his pieces of property, including those from which he is constituted, without detriment to his self."[22] However, as anyone who has had a job knows, you can't just send tiny packets of yourself off to work while you stay home and watch game shows in your pajamas: "Labour power, capacities or services, cannot be separated from the person of the worker like pieces of property."[23] This fake separability of property from person allows for the fiction that employees subordinate only parts of themselves to bosses, not their entire person. Pentland also uses a false separation between part and whole to pass off subordination as individual liberty. He argues that the best way to protect individual privacy is to allow individuals to maintain full ownership over the detailed, concrete content of their data and let others see only *abstractions* of those concrete details: "The code is shared not the [raw] data."[24] This distinction between raw and cooked data is the same whole/part distinction classical contract theorists draw between person and labor power: the distinction between raw data and code creates the illusion that "pieces of property in the person"—in this case, data as an asset— "can (be said to) be freely contracted out without detriment to the person who owns them."[25] But there are clear detriments. Primary among them is the fact that other people are extracting surplus value from my assets and not adequately compensating me—I might get something like increased convenience in return for sharing my data, but even though that company is making money from my assets, I'm not getting paid for the work I did to cultivate those assets.

Because Pentland updates the kind of agreement that grounds social cooperation from contract to norm, he must also update some of the contract's key components, like property-in-person and consent. In spite of these updates, they all still achieve the same purpose they were originally designed for: to make relations of subordination appear to be freely chosen, and thus legitimate and just. The changes he makes to this agreement's scope have the same result.

b. From Law to Opinion

Taking what the classical social contract explicitly excludes from the sphere of government and making it government's fundamental medium, Pentland's social physics upends the scope of the classical social contract. Separating "law" from "opinion" and limiting government to the former, classical liberalism can have its cake—full political emancipation and formal equality before the law—and eat it too. In this framework, ongoing private-sphere oppression is still acceptable because it doesn't fall under the scope of the law's power over individuals.[26] J. S. Mill's in *On Liberty* makes this exact argument. Though Mill thinks that the law's reach should be limited (the law can only prevent me from doing things that infringe on others' rights), he also argues that opinion can and should be applied without limitation to any kind of harm or slight. For example, he says that "the inconveniences which are strictly inseparable from the unfavourable judgment of others, are the only ones to which a person should ever be subjected for that portion of his conduct and character which concerns his own good, but which does not affect the interest of others in their relations with him."[27] Though the law may only interfere with actions which negatively affect the interests of others, opinion has free rein over any aspect of my life. Mill thinks it's totally legitimate to use opinion to govern where the law cannot reach, that is, where somebody's actions harm only one-self. As Marx argues in *On the Jewish Question*, this trick lets formal equality before the law pass as full emancipation while legitimating systemic inequities in the private sphere. For example, laws in the United States and France mandate secularism, but this doesn't eliminate private-sphere religious bias.

Whereas classical liberalism relies on the extra-institutional status of "opinion," Pentlandian social physics formalizes and institutionalizes it, making it the explicit medium of the social contract. "Alter[ing] idea flow by creating social pressure, increasing the amount of interaction around specific, targeted ideas," social physicists distribute the flow around a specific idea to make it more normal (*Social Physics* 66). "Social pressure" is Pentland's term for opinion; his use of "pressure" frames governmental power as flows of pressure waves through the social fluid, just as acoustic resonance is flows of pressure waves in air or water. "A function of the cost of any mismatch between the behavior of the individuals, the value of the relationship, and the amount of interaction" (69–70), social pressure exists when individual flows are not consonant with the population's normal patterns of behavior. Individuals whose patterns of behavior are irrationally and abnormally related to larger-scale social patterns feel the dissonance that generates as social pressure, pressure to become normal. "Us[ing] the tools of social network incentives in order to establish new norms of behavior, rather than relying on regulatory penalties and market competition" (191–92), social physics incentivizes people to adopt behaviors rather than punishing them for transgressions. Thus, normalization appears to be a kinder, gentler form of governance: social pressure goads individuals into *choosing* new behaviors. But this language of choice hides coercion and domination. First, the fewer advantages one has, the more significant the drawbacks are for not choosing to follow social pressure—if circumstances even allow you to do that in the first place. And second, the fewer advantages one has, the more dissonant they will be with the norm they are pressured to follow. So, even though they have fewer resources to draw on, oppressed people face stronger pressure to follow the norm and higher consequences for refusing. In Pentland's system, social pressure accomplishes what formal equality of the law does in classically liberal systems: it hides institutional domination behind the idea of individual choice or liberty.

Despite his repeated and explicit claims to replace the traditional mechanics of social cooperation with more accurate and inclusive ones, Pentland's so-called improvements are really just upgrades that makes these mechanics more compatible with neoliberal biopolitics. This compatibility is most evident in his argument for the superiority of idea flow over stereotypes.

Studying "idea flows rather than static divisions in society" (157) such as traditional identity categories and the "stereotypes" (185) grounded in them, social physics "*leap[s] beyond* demographics to directly measure human behavior" (141; emphasis added).[28] Replacing identity-based demographic abstractions with "idea flow," Pentland claims that social physics overcomes the social problems endemic to identity politics, problems like stereotyping, hierarchical inequality, and the division of labor (an odd claim, given that he doubles down on the idea of private property).[29] But as I have just shown, Pentland's social contract remakes those same relations in new forms. Like Cavarero, he explicitly marks nonhuman voices, or rather, rates of idea flow in nonhuman populations, as exception. According to Pentland, idea flow is a feature of all primate social groups: human and nonhuman, we all learn and adopt new ideas. However, in the case of nonhuman primates, "even though such idea flows bring innovation into their repertoires of habits, these primate cultures remain simple and static" (45). Pentland concludes that this stasis is due to the nonhuman primates' disproportionate and immoderate idea flow—the exploration-engagement ratio leans too far to engagement and not enough to exploration. The frequency of their idea flow isn't efficiently normalizable into the "healthy"—i.e., human—range,[30] so they appear as the exception incapable of reform. Though idea flow is supposedly a more inclusive metric than demographic or identity group, Pentland marks a break in this continuity that polices the same boundary conventionally policed by those old-fashioned categories (i.e., the boundary of humanity and personhood).

Pentland uses acoustic resonance to translate into nonquantitative terms the math that big data–style social physics uses to measure and normalize populations. Like the other constituents of the sonic episteme, he then leverages the supposed difference between resonance and traditional philosophical abstractions to hide ongoing domination—especially the politics of exception he articulates—behind claims of reform. Though Pentland uses sonic metaphors to obscure ugly mechanics behind concepts that connote aesthetic pleasure, they can also reveal what's so ugly about these mechanics. All you need is a technical understanding of resonance and harmony. Though harmony is aesthetically pleasurable, it is only possible because cultural practices subordinate some frequencies (dissonant ones) to others (consonant ones). A harmonious society is one structured by a relation of subordination. The mathematical tools that big data–style social physics uses to study and shape society create a specific kind of subordination: a politics of exception. Because these same tools are used in everything from machine learning to finance to policing, Pentland's metaphor reveals an important fact about an increasingly ubiquitous technology: even though they work very differently than the classical social contract, these tools nevertheless mold society into the same general relations of domination and subordination.

Pop science accounts of string theory use harmony and resonance to translate math that's quite similar to Pentland's into layperson's terms. This is even more dangerous than Pentland's project, because it risks legitimating the idea that "resonant" abstractions and methods of abstraction model objective, natural, unbiased relations, the kinds of relations that structure the universe itself.

II. Theoretical Physics

In the Western tradition, people have used musical metaphors to translate the math behind physics into layperson's terms since the ancient Greeks started using math to model physical reality. As Peter Pesic and Axel Volmar put it, "for the public understanding of science, musical metaphors seemed to offer opportunities to provide the imagination of the lay public with *affective* experiences of abstract mathematical theories."[31] First, because harmonic metaphors refer to sensory phenomena available to both hearing people (as sound) and nonhearing people (as physical vibration), they transform the ontology of numbers to the ontology of "normal" human perception. Second, because music relies on nonpropositional, affective abstractions, musical metaphors can translate mathematical abstractions into commonsense ideas people learn through exposure to music. Pop science accounts of the twentieth- and twenty-first-century genre of theoretical physics known as string theory are solidly within this tradition. Related to the physics Karen Barad uses to ground new materialist philosophy, string theory is a subdiscipline within physics that blends general relativity (which focuses on macrocosmic space-time) with quantum mechanics (which focuses on the workings of subatomic particles). It holds that the fundamental unit of existence is a one-dimensional vibrating string. Popular science writers commonly use acoustic resonance to translate the probabilistic equations physicists use to model string behavior into layperson's terms.

In this section I look at two representatives of this trend: the most well-known and foundational one, by Brian Greene, and a recent one by Stephon Alexander. Both accounts use acoustically resonant harmony as a metaphor for the probabilistic relationships string theorists derive from their mathematical analysis. This makes them constituents of the sonic episteme: they're using acoustically resonant harmony and probabilistic statistics as interchangeable abstractions or methods of abstraction. Though both authors are

168

explicit about their metaphorical and analogical methods, the thing that does most of the conceptual work is not a metaphor or an analogy but a *slippage* between two kinds of mathematical abstraction. Even though "the unheard cosmic music is not conceptualized in terms of ratios between celestial objects . . . but as the result of the various vibrational modes (or resonant patterns) of the tiny but highly energetic strings,"[32] Greene and Alexander insist on appealing to Pythagorean concepts of harmony to describe acoustically resonant vibrational patterns. This slippage between Pythagorean harmony and acoustic resonance hides the fact that string theory models the universe with the same mathematical tools neoliberal biopolitics uses to model society. So, after I first discuss the details of Greene's and Alexander's appeals to harmony and establish that they understand "harmony" in terms that situate them within the sonic episteme, I will argue that this slippage between Pythagorean and acoustic resonance encourages the idea that the *statistical* mathematical relationships for which acoustic resonance is a metaphor are benign natural relationships so fundamentally embedded in the nature of things that they are knowable even with the primitive science of the ancient Greeks.

1. The Music-Math Analogy

String theory is a branch of theoretical physics: its theorems are proven not through experimental observation but through mathematical calculations. Both Alexander and Greene explicitly state that they're using music to translate mathematical abstractions into terms a lay audience, especially those with "no training in mathematics or physics,"[33] can understand. Arguing that "it is hard to embrace quantum mechanics viscerally"[34] and that "sound" is a "*tangible* manifestation"[35] of the behavior of quantum strings, Greene and Alexander think music can bring mathematical abstractions down to earth and present them in noncognitive terms that don't require specialized knowledge to interpret. Alexander uses a fairly conventional audiovisual litany to frame the relationship between music and math: "putting into words subjects like general relativity and quantum mechanics" is less precise a translation of the math than analogies to music because words mediate and distance us from the "naturalness" of the mathematical relations among elementary particles and forces.[36] Words create representations of the mathematical patterns strings make, but music copies those exact patterns; music and math are literally analogues because they embody the same logos. The analogy between math and music thus requires one fewer layer of abstraction than it would take to put these mathematical relationships into words. Treating music as the best way to translate mathematical relationships into nonquantitative terms, Greene's and Alexander's accounts of string theory fit one criterion for inclusion in the sonic episteme.

More fundamentally, their versions of string theory are constituents of the sonic episteme because the "music" in their music-math analogy is a type of acoustic resonance. String theory argues that the elementary unit of existence is a one-dimensional looped string. Greene and Alexander compare the behavior of these strings to sound waves. According to Alexander, "sound is a vibration that pushes a medium, such as air or something solid, to create traveling waves of pressure," which can also be understood as "a series of compressions and rarefactions that propagate the wave through the medium."[37] Both Greene and Alexander frame the behavior of quantum strings in identical terms. Quantum strings are "resonant vibrational patterns" with "evenly spaced peaks and troughs."[38] A string can vibrate at a number of different frequencies, and the frequency determines the physical properties of the string (which particle or force it is). As Greene explains, "what appear to be different elementary particles are actually different 'notes' on a fundamental string."[39] Just as the frequency of a vibrating piano string determines its pitch, the frequency of a vibrating quantum string determines its material state. These frequencies interact via phase relationships. "The universe — being composed of an enormous number of these vibrating strings — is akin to a cosmic symphony"[40] because quantum strings, like consonant sound waves, have "synchroniz[ed] . . . phases."[41] Like all constituents of the sonic episteme, Greene's and Alexander's accounts of string theory understand "music" as rhythmically patterned intensities that interact in phase relationships and thus model sound on acoustic resonance.

2. The Analogy as Sleight

Comparing the behavior of quantum strings to the behavior of sound waves, Greene and Alexander use this analogy to translate the math scientists use to describe those strings into sensory terms laypeople are familiar with. They also compare quantum strings to three-dimensional strings, like "the strings on a violin or on a piano."[42] In this version of the musical string–quantum string analogy, science writers commonly conflate two different explanations of how strings produce musical sounds: the one contemporary music theorists and scientists use and the Pythagorean one. For example, Alexander claims that "in quantum mechanics, the *Pythagorean* theory of the harmony of the spheres was finally realized but on a microscopic, not macroscopic, level."[43] Though it is often associated with the relationships among celestial bodies, Pythagoras derived his theory of harmony by observing the behavior of a vibrating string as it was fretted in different proportions. For example, when you pluck one string, and then another string either half or twice as long, the strings will sound pitches that are an octave apart. He discovered a series of integer ratios that produced consonant harmonies: 2:1 (octave), 3:2 (fifth), 4:3 (fourth), 9:8 (whole tone). "These intervals are defined by the lengths of the *strings* being in a certain ratio"[44] — not by the relationship among the frequencies the strings emit. Pythagorean ratios compare geometric measurements of strings' lengths. String theory, on the other hand, measures the probability that a string vibrates at a given frequency. For example, Greene ultimately describes strings as "probability waves."[45] Similarly, Alexander uses the idea of jazz improvisation to represent the probabilistic character of string theory. "Improvisation," he argues, "provid[es] us with a tool for understanding" the "inherent uncertainties" of quantum matter.[46] String theorists do use ratios, but those ratios express probabilities and frequencies, not geometric measurements. Though they are rooted in the origins of string theory itself, string theorists' analogies to Pythagorean strings are actually disanalogies between two different types of measurements.[47]

This disanalogy is a sleight in Mary Beth Mader's sense — i.e., it uses misattribution to hide ugly power relationships behind pleasant appearances. As she explains, "sleights" are "conceptual collaborations that function as switches or ruses important to the continuing centrality and pertinence of the social category of" a political system like "sex."[48] Sleights, in other words, are slippages in the use of a term that render underlying hegemonic structures like cisheteropatriarchy coherent; they're logical errors that buttress the credibility of unjust social practices. To flesh out the mechanics of a sleight, Mader turns to a concrete example: sleights are, she argues, "conceptual jacquemarts."[49] Jacquemarts are effectively the Milli Vanilli of clocks: sounds appear to come from one overtly visible, aesthetically appealing source action (figures ringing a bell) but they actually come from a hidden, less aesthetically appealing source action (hammers hitting gongs).[50] The clock is constructed in a way to "misdirect or misindicate"[51] both who is making the sound and how they are making it. A sound exists, but its source is misattributed. This is *exactly* what happens in Greene's and Alexander's use of Pythagorean concepts of musical harmony to explain what is actually acoustic resonance: their outward accounting of sound misindicates its precise internal mechanism (i.e., the kind of math used). For example, when Alexander claims his analogy to Pythagoras works because in both approaches "the harmony of the cosmos was, simply, a manifestation of the relationships between numbers,"[52] his appeal to harmony, a term that connotes aesthetic pleasure, hides a slippage between two

171

different relationships between numbers. Presenting these Gaussian relationships as Pythagorean ones, string theory's sleight disguises the exact mathematical relationship that's at stake in this cosmology.

Though string theorists understand themselves as providing objective, factual accounts of pre-political reality, this sleight functions to obscure the fact that string theory reconceives the fundamental nature of reality in the same terms that neoliberalism and biopolitics use to conceive and control more obviously social phenomena like markets, subjectivity, and identity politics. I *do not* think pop science writers like Greene and Alexander are *trying* to pull a fast one on us, but I am concerned about the possibilities this slippage opens up — that is, I'm concerned with the kinds of social functionality this argumentative dysfunction makes possible. For example, neoliberalism reframes classical liberalism's "binary system of offense against the law" with a "gradational social space,"[53] and string theory is a gradational theory of actual, cosmic space. Relying on the same basic ontological framework as neoliberalism, string theory does for cosmology what social physics does for social science: it reconceives the universe and the relationships between its elementary particles in the same terms neoliberalism and biopolitics use to analyze and manage society, such as the bell curve.[54] The Pythagorean analogies hide the fact that string theory uses the same math that, when applied to people and social relations, creates relations of domination and subordination.[55]

Though theoretical physicists may not think of themselves or their theories as having any politics, this ontological framework is socially functional for a very specific kind of society: one whose social ontology, ethics, and aesthetics are modeled and managed as matters of statistical normalization. In a social and political context where normalized statistical distributions maintain white supremacist cisheteropatriarchal relations of domination and subordination, it's dangerous to take that same mathematical relationship as the fundamental structure of the universe — it risks naturalizing a contingent and unjust political relationship as *the* nature of existence itself. Again, I'm not arguing that individual string theorists are intentionally trying to justify white supremacist cisheteropatriarchal domination; rather, I'm saying that their understanding of the objective nature of reality is identical to the mathematical relationship neoliberalism and biopolitics use to structure and perpetuate white supremacist cisheteropatriarchy, and this similarity could be used to justify those unjust social structures as natural and objective. I'm not accusing string theorists of exploiting that correspondence, but I am arguing that they make it easy to do so. Who can object to statistical normalization as a political tool when it's just the way the physics of the universe works?[56]

Pop science writers use music to explain the math behind probabilistic statistics because the kind of abstraction that Western music requires listeners to make is the same kind of abstraction performed by these probabilistic statistics: the identification of relative frequency. Don't get me wrong: it's a *good* metaphor. But the act of comparison itself has dangerous consequences. As many music and sound scholars have shown, all sorts of embodied knowledges — metaphysics, ontologies, ethics, and politics, to say nothing of aesthetics — are coded into our practices of musical listening.[57] People's ability to hear and understand sounds and music is always oriented by a "listening ear." From a philosophical perspective, a listening ear is an epistemology of ignorance applied to aural perception and interpretation; from a sound studies perspective, it is a method of perceptually coding human hearing to facilitate the efficient reproduction of social inequity. Pop science appeals to music, listening, and hearing encourage the lay public to interpret the science through their listening ears; to do this, they assimilate scientific "facts" to the assumptions coded into those ears. Like the other constituents of the sonic episteme, these pop science accounts of social and theoretical physics reinforce the relations of domination and subordination that allow for the most efficient reproduction of a society ordered by neoliberalism and biopolitics.

173

Whereas Alexander, Greene, and Pentland use the figure of acoustically resonant sound to translate the probabilistic math social physicists and theoretical physicists use to model the world into terms laypeople can understand, phonographic approaches to math abstract mathematical relationships from vernacular applications of music technology and pop music aesthetics. So whereas pop science writers go from math to music, these phonographic theorists go from music to math. Likewise, whereas the expert/layperson distinction is key to the former approach, the latter approach treats pop music as inherently theoretical. The next and final section studies one example of this phonographic approach to math and sound.

III. Wicked Mathematics

Building on my analyses of phonographic alternatives to the sonic episteme's various constituents, this section considers McKittrick and Weheliye's use of choreosonic sounds to theorize what they call "wicked mathematics" and argues that it is a phonographic alternative to the math behind Pentlandian social physics and string theory. These wicked mathematics are oblique pivots from the exact kinds of mathematical relationships Alexander, Greene, and Pentland use sound to explain.

In their 2017 article "808s and Heartbreak," McKittrick and Weheliye study the choreosonic dimensions of twentieth- and twenty-first-century African American and Afro-Caribbean popular musics as examples of wicked mathematics; the choreosonics aren't metaphors for a supposedly more abstract and nonsensory math, they *are* the math. These mathematics model the relationship McKittrick and Weheliye call "Heart/////Break."[58] Building on their earlier work, much of which I have discussed in previous chapters, heart/////break refers to a pivot from the logics of neoliberalism and biopolitics to rationalities those logics perceptually code into the red. The "break" in heart/////break is a pivot from the math the sonic episteme translates to modes of calculation that black people have used to engineer alternative epistemologies and ontologies. These alternatives "emulate" hegemonic math in "inaccurate repetition[s]"[59] that unlock possibilities those conventions compress out of circulation.[60] Their work on heart/////break counts out the math behind big data–style social physics and string theory differently.

They do this in three main ways, which I will discuss in sequence. First, like *In the Wake* and "Mathematics Black Life," "808s and Heartbreak" is written so that the choreosonics of its prose create rhythmic patterns both among the article's subdivisions and in the repetitions of words and phrases. These patterns emulate Pentland's logics of "idea flow," counting the flow's distribution out differently so that readers/listeners can tune in to frequencies conventionally compressed out of that flow because they impede the efficiency of surplus-value extraction and enclosure. Second, their analysis of Rihanna's performances heart/////break on "We Found Love" and "Diamonds" shows that she emulates the logics of resilience in a way that sabotages their ability to generate profit from and enclose upon both black women's trauma and their care work; heart/////break is thus quite similar to what I identify, in these same works, as melancholy. Finally, their interpretation of the role of gambling in black culture shows that gamblers emulate probabilistic speculation in a way that alters the affective charge of black sociality from pure risk to (complicated, heartbreaking) pleasure.

McKittrick and Weheliye write choreosonics patterns into their prose and use these patterns to pivot to perceptual registers that academic prose otherwise codes out of circulation. They do this in two ways. First, they directly quote song lyrics in order to evoke (some) readers' memories of the sonic and choreosonic dimensions of those songs' recordings. For example, their argument that "heartbreak, then, is already part of the 808s Black circuitry, boomingly amplifying joy and pain, sunshine and rain,"[61] incorporates the lyrics of the hook to Maze's 1980 song "Joy and Pain," which has been sampled (or better, emulated) on Rob Base and DJ E-Z Rock's 1987 song of the same title, and was again reworked on Apexape featuring Josh Barry's 2016 dance hit "Joy and Pain." Reading along, I heard these songs in my head, pivoting back and forth from text to sonic memory. Similarly, they cite passages from Blaque and Brandy that "emulat[e] the sensation of the TR-808,"[62] such as Brandy's punchy, staccato delivery of "eight-oh-eight" as her vocals mimic the drum machine's famously dry beats.[63] Because this sensation is choreosonic—both aural and physiological/affective—it is "is difficult to cordon off into words on the page."[64] Just as Brandy's vocals emulate the sound of the 808, McKittrick and Weheliye's text emulates the sound of her voice, which is what does most of the work conveying "the fleshy neural feelings set off by the boom of the 808."[65] They transcribe this performance as "eeightt-ohh-eeightt/eeightt-eeightt,"[66] but readers have to pivot from the text to either a recording of those songs or their own memory of those recordings. For readers familiar with the songs they reference, this writing strategy expands the scope of the authors' analysis and argument to including the nonpropositional, kin/aesthetic, affective knowledges coded into these musical performances and recordings. In the songs McKittrick and Weheliye sample in their article, these knowledges tend to be ones common in Afrodiasporic communities but underrepresented in scholarly writing. Emulating hip-hop and R&B songs in their scholarly prose, the authors obliquely pivot to dimensions that conventional methods of philosophical abstraction code out into the red.

175

McKittrick and Weheliye use this technique to pivot to a specific type of knowledge, which they call wicked mathematics. Because these maths model frequencies that are compressed out of dominant circuits of communication, they can register "like a sssshhh—eviscerated, ear-piercing silence" (19), such as the literal silence of academic prose. However, as this quote demonstrates with its onomatopoeias, when we pivot from the text's words to its choreosonics, we can tune in to some of those in-the-red frequencies—this is the third way they incorporate choreosonics into their argument. For example, McKittrick and Weheliye use onomatopoetic emulations of the 808's sounds to count out patterns in the text's choreosonics. Similar to McKittrick's use of "she says she was born free" in an earlier article, these patterns both divide the prose into sections of uneven and irregular length and create patterns of repeated and varied words throughout the text. In the former case, they use words like "boom" (14) and "shhhh" (18) as section headings. In the latter case, you can see these patterns when I compress the text and remove everything but those onomatopoeias:

— "the boom-bap-blonk-clap of 808s" (13)

— "the thump of the 808-machine" (14)

— "the boom of racial-sexual violence. Heartbreak, then, is always already part of the 808s Black circuitry, boomingly amplifying joy and pain, sunshine and rain. The thump, the boom, create shivering circuits of pleasure laced with damage, loss, sorrow" (15)

— "the 808s and the mechanics of the deep boom" (16)

— "the deep boom, clap, blip" (20)

— "Blap. Squonk." (31)

— "This returns me to the 808s or the LinnDrum machines or eeightt-ohh-eeightt/eeightt-eeightt: here are mathematics—measured and unmeasured bam, drop, eeightt—that reveal a new or different register of black life (I hope!): That, perhaps, is wicked mathematics." (33)

McKittrick and Weheliye emulate the sound of the 808 in their text, and that emulation pivots the register of argumentation from prose and propositions to the sensory, aesthetic, and affective knowledges carried in the sonics and choreosonics of twentieth- and twenty-first-century hip-hop and R&B. Examples of such knowledges include the "meta/physical reverberations" (14) of familiar sounds or song hooks, or the "intonation" (30) of a behavior—how it "sounds" in Havis's sense.[67] Such knowledges are cumulative and experiential, a kind of sensory-muscle memory like the kinds DJs or drummers gain through practice—"something you do and can never possess" (16). McKittrick and Weheliye describe this knowledge as "not a noun" but "an aesthetic-physiological practice" that can be accessed only when we "exceed and unsettle the accumulative logic of cis-heteropatriarchal racial capitalism" (22) Like the care work that is disproportionately relegated to black women because it doesn't transform anything into private property,[68] wicked mathematics don't produce the kind of abstractions that can be disconnected from the experiential knowledges developed by subaltern and minority communities and transformed into private property by white cisheteropatriarchal institutions. They are what get left behind after propositional and formalist abstractions love-and-theft away whatever they can glean from hip-hop and R&B. Iggy Azalea may appropriate black women's vocal intonation, but she cannot use them to convey the knowledges they were designed to communicate. Incorporating the sounds of the 808 and recordings that use those sounds into their article,

McKittrick and Weheliye tap in to the flow of knowledges that traditional (white) scholarly methods perceptually code out of circulation yet which are central to the epistemologies elaborated in hip-hop and R&B.

Thus, the patterns in the article's choreosonics create a centrifugitive idea flow, a flow that can't be enclosed. As the last bulleted quote above argues, these flows, their rhythms, frequencies, and other patterns, exhibit the kinds of wicked mathematics that count out white supremacist cisheteropatriarchal distributions of success and failure, life and death differently. These idea flows model black people's strategies for "us[ing] sonics, or flows, to delineate this enunciation of life within the context of racial violence and modernity"[69]— i.e., for surviving and experiencing emotions, affects, and sensations that feel good (love, pleasure of all sorts) while they are nevertheless amid and subject to hurtful, painful oppressions. In this way, wicked mathematics emulate Pentlandian social physics, using its technology—idea flow—for unintended purposes to engineer physio-aesthetic practices in the frequencies those technologies otherwise compress out into the red.

They identify another example of wicked mathematics in the sonics on Rihanna's "We Found Love" and "Diamonds," which emulate logics of neoliberal creative destruction. Situating both songs in the context of Rihanna's response to media coverage of her highly publicized 2009 domestic assault, they interpret these songs as refusals of the overcoming narratives the media and the public expected from her. As I argued in *Resilience and Melancholy*— through an analysis of both of these songs—these "Look, I Overcame!" narratives subject the gendered damage women experience from patriarchy to enclosure. It is a gendered version of neoliberalism's "creative destruction, which uses crisis—such as a financial crisis or a natural disaster—as a mechanism for accumulation by dispossession."[70] Overcoming their damage, women transform trauma into profit and human capital. Neoliberalism turns redemption into a form of self-possession. In contrast, McKittrick and Weheliye argue that Rihanna's performances of heart///// break articulate something that "cannot be possessed [because it] does not follow the laws of redemption" (16). Much in the same way that "BBHMM" emulates pornotroping to rework its racialized, gendered property relations, Rihanna's vocal performances on "We Found Love" and "Diamonds" emulate resilience to rework its logics of enclosure.

In *Resilience and Melancholy*, I argued that the EDM-pop trope called the soar expresses resilience. Soars are compositional devices used to build and release tension. They intensify the number of rhythmic events (such as drum hits or hand claps, or the repetitions of a vocal phrase) in a Zeno's-paradox-

177

like rush to and sometimes past the implied limit of our ability to hear distinct events. This is followed either by silence or by some filler sound, like a siren or a scream, and then the gesture lands on the downbeat of the next section. Whereas blues-based harmonic conventions build and release tension by introducing dissonance and resolving it through assimilation, soars create and release tension by intensifying and overcoming damage. Soars are neoliberal "creative destruction" applied to music aesthetics.[71]

McKittrick and Weheliye identify such creative destruction in the soars of "We Found Love." They describe the soars as a "crescendo of cascading keyboards as well as a drum roll" that "generate[s] intense sonic tension so that the arrival of the bass drum registers as both like relief and like punishment."[72] Even though the song soars, the authors observe that Rihanna's vocals do not: "Fenty's voice . . . remains almost impassive, displaying a 'cool affect' that sounds like it is resisting the booming rush of the song structure/instrumentation."[73] I call this cool affect melancholy—it emulates resilience but feels like a failure rather than an overcoming because it doesn't turn damage into private property. It may mimic resilience, but its outcome is different: it is a "bad investment"[74] in oneself that creates a "continual, compounded draining of neoliberalism's batteries."[75] Just as McKittrick and Weheliye's "booms" emulate the 808 and pivot the text from Philosophical methods of abstraction and their logics of enclosure to the centrifugitive methods of abstraction found in the choreosonics of hip-hop and R&B performance, Rihanna's melancholy vocals emulate the soar's resilience. She is "not overcoming but surviving, living with, breathing in, subsisting through. Boom. Like an 808" (25). As I argued in *Resilience and Melancholy*, Rihanna's melancholic performance bends the circuits of neoliberal biopolitics; thus bent, these circuits tune into ways of living they conventionally code out of perception—the ways of surviving, living with, breathing in, and subsisting through that McKittrick and Weheliye point out. Emulating resilience, these ways of living are organized by a cost/benefit calculus that drains hegemonic institutions but benefits Rihanna. That cost/benefit calculus is another instance of wicked mathematics.

Though many of McKittrick and Weheliye's examples of wicked mathematics come from hip-hop and R&B, it's not exclusive to music and can be found across black popular cultures. Gambling is one of these cultures. It emulates neoliberalism's cost/benefit speculation but cooks the books so that black people's disproportionate exposure to risk feels, in this limited context, like something besides oppression. As I have argued earlier in this book, the mathematical tools neoliberal biopolitics uses to govern society distribute risk

178

and reward along conventional racist, cisheterosexist, capitalist lines; black people are exposed to more and greater risk and its negative effects, while white people and institutions reap the rewards of that risk. Ruth Wilson Gilmore's well-known definition of racism as the "production and exploitation of group-differentiated vulnerability to premature death"[76] captures the way white supremacy functions as a disproportionate distribution of risk: it makes it hard for black people to succeed and then bets on their failure. McKittrick and Weheliye argue that gambling, when practiced as a leisure activity in black communities, emulates that cost/benefit calculation in a way that brings them pleasure instead of just pain. Recognizing that gambling is a traditional and popular leisure activity in black communities, they ask if, in addition to the actual mathematical probabilities in the games, players are figuring a different set of numbers: "Is the playing the bug in the system, the conjuring of other a-systems?"[77] White supremacy has ensured their house will always win; however, when gambling becomes a site of sociality, it reaps rewards beyond the merely financial—the emotional, aesthetic, and social pleasures of being in communion with other people. McKittrick and Weheliye's gamblers may be losing money and/or social capital, but they're gaining something else—the sociality that white supremacy is designed to foreclose for them.[78] From this perspective, gambling emulates the math behind neoliberalism and biopolitics, pivoting from white supremacist distributions of life and social death to the very thing those distributions perceptually code out: black people's sociality and the pleasures that its participants experience.

179

As McKittrick and Weheliye make clear, the problem isn't math or numbers or quantification in itself. Numbers and relations among numbers are abstractions, and like all other abstractions they bring some things to the foreground and abstract other things away. The problem with the sonic episteme and its constituents, such as the social physics and theoretical physics I discussed earlier in this chapter, is the specific kind of quantitative abstractions they use, which foreground the kinds of relationships that facilitate the efficient reproduction of a society organized by the neoliberal and biopolitical versions of white supremacist cisheteropatriarchy and perceptually code other relationships out of circulation and renders them exception. In contrast, McKittrick and Weheliye present us with quantitative abstractions that tune in to the stuff that the sonic episteme codes out. The abstractions they study don't appear, at least at first, in numbers and equations. Rather, they appear as aesthetic phenomena—as the rhythm of choreosonic sound, as melancholy, as the pleasure of gambling and play. Just as acoustic resonance translates the math behind neoliberal biopolitics into nonquantitative terms, these aesthetic phenomena are nonquantitative expressions of mathematical relationships. The logics, aesthetic forms, subjectivities, social relationships, and cost/benefit speculations that express these mathematical relationships impede the efficient circulation and accumulation of all the advantages white supremacist cisheteropatriarchal capitalism gives its beneficiaries.

CONCLUSION

There are better and worse ways of theorizing with sound. The difference between the better and worse ways begins with what you think sound is and where you look for it. The better ways attend to sounds and sonic practices that Philosophy perceptually codes out of scholarly circulation because they do not contribute to the efficient reproduction of a discipline and a society structured by ongoing relations of domination and subordination. The worse ways treat existing Philosophical theories of sound as a supposedly radical alternative to the Philosophical status quo because this makes the reproduction of such a society more efficient and advantageous for those at the top. Taken as models for politics, ontology, subjectivity, or whatever it is you're theorizing, these different definitions of sound produce very different outcomes. The latter, Philosophical models misrepresent intensified relations of domination and subordination as the surpassing and repair of identity-based oppression. The former, phonographic models represent ideas and practices oppressed people use to create less oppressive realities in what Philosophy disregards as untheoretical. If you are interested in maintaining Philosophy's traditional boundaries and implication in systematic domination, then the latter approach to sound best fits your aims. But those are not my aims; that's why I think the former approach is better. I'm interested in methods of theorizing that both (1) go beyond philosophers' idealized concepts of sound and engage the kinds of nonpropositional, a-Philosophical abstractions pop songs use to communicate, and (b) contribute to an intellectual practice which feigns complicity with the disciplines, academy, and society that demand our subordination to white supremacist cisheteropatriarchal capitalism while building insubordinate ways of thinking and living under these institutions' radar. I have tried to do both of those things in this book.

The sonic episteme, however, does neither of those things. The sonic episteme rarely if ever goes beyond idealized accounts of sound. Misrepresenting acoustic resonance as sound itself (rather than a particular theory grounded in other values and assumptions) makes these methods of theorizing appear objective and neutral when really they aren't. They aren't objective and neutral because they produce theories that both naturalize the relations of domination and subordination that neoliberalism and biopolitics produce and create those very same relations within theory/scholarship. In this way, the sonic episteme is just a new version of European modernity's favorite trick, which misrepresents relations of subordination as freedom and equality.[1]

I'm skeptical that sound or sounds can be a model for revolutionary ontologies and epistemologies that completely eradicate ongoing relations of domination. First, these relations are systemic, and completely revolutionizing those relations means revolutionizing the systems that rest on them—and this involves more than just changing the object or mode of our theorizing. This is hard because many of us (myself included) are theorizing in institutions deeply structured by those systems. Second, there is no singular definition or understanding of "sound." Concepts of sound always exist in broader epistemic frameworks, the same frameworks that ground concepts of vision, text, and other media and sensory modalities. When theorists appeal to sound and its differences from vision or text or whatever, more often than not they're just appealing to a different component of the same epistemic framework that grounds the concept of vision or text they're working with. The sonic episteme does something slightly different: it overtly contrasts a contemporary definition of sound with old, representationalist definitions of sight and text, thus obscuring its reliance on now-hegemonic epistemic and ontological frameworks. More specifically, it presents a concept of sound grounded in nineteenth- to twentieth-century science as an alternative to a philosophical framework developed in the seventeenth and eighteenth centuries—a framework with its own, different concepts of resonance.[2] So even though acoustic resonance does exhibit different epistemological and ontological commitments than the ones behind classical liberalism and representationalism, it holds the same commitments as neoliberalism and biopolitics. It may be an alternative to past frameworks, but it fits right in with contemporary ones.

We can find other frameworks by tuning in to the sonic episteme's in-the-red frequencies and understanding how communities subject to these relations of domination survive and thrive under the radar. This means looking and listening and reading and talking and hearing outside capital-P Philosophy. Crawley, Havis, McKittrick, Sharpe, and Weheliye, along with the musicians and audiences they study, are already doing this. And we can follow their lead by asking questions such as: What frequencies, what patterns of behavior and rhythms of living, does the sonic episteme perceptually code out of circulation? How do these patterns and rhythms ground epistemologies, ontologies, and aesthetics that validate the communities that practice them and provide those communities with some of the resources neoliberalism and biopolitics deny them? There are as many ways to work in the red and under the radar as there are frequencies and overtones outside the sonic episteme's spectrum. This book addresses a portion of that in-the-red spectrum that registers in contemporary work in black studies and African American philosophy. There are plenty of others.

If my analysis of the sonic episteme has any lesson for how to theorize with and through sound, it's that sound never overcomes, fixes, avoids, or preempts power relations. Any project that offers sound as either ontologically prior to or surpassing politics reinvests and renaturalizes those power relations. If you want to excuse philosophy from addressing its participation in systemic injustices, then that's a great way to do it. But as I've shown, that's not the only way to do it. Hopefully we can turn more of our attention to these other ways. Doing so will require us to think and work in ways that eschew disciplinary prestige and legibility, in part because they will require attention to actual, concrete sounds, attention that isn't reducible to technoscientific or music-theoretical approaches to spectrograms or "just the notes." This will require inventive approaches to describing, explaining, documenting, and discussing those sounds. I have pointed to and attempted to practice such approaches in this book, and I look forward to future inventions of this type.

183

NOTES

Introduction

Epigraph: Pesic, *Music and the Making of Modern Science*, 284.

1   David Castro-Gavino, "Creating a Symphony from the Noise of Customer Data," *dunnhumby* (blog), April 27, 2018, https://www.dunnhumby.com /resources/blog/creating-symphony-from-customer-data-noise.

2   To clarify: by "musical understanding of sound" I mean an understanding of sounds shaped by sociohistorically local conventions. For example, as I discuss in chapters 2 and 4, ancient Greek concepts of musical harmony are completely different than the more familiar ones grounded in seventeenth- to nineteenth-century European music theory. Different cultures have different sets of musical conventions that shape how listeners parse signal from noise, consonance from dissonance.

3   Mader, *Sleights of Reason*, 56.

4   Supplementary Table: Trends in Suicide Rates among Persons ≥ 10 Years of Age, by State and Sex, National Vital Statistics System, 1999–2016, in "Vital Signs: Trends in Suicide Rates and Circumstances Contributing to Suicide — United States, 1999–2016 and 27 States, 2015," *mmwr: Morbidity and Mortality Weekly Report* 67, no. 22 (2018): 617–24, https://stacks.cdc.gov/view/cdc /53785.

5   As Dale Chapman emphasizes in his book on jazz metaphors in neoliberalism, economists such as Frank Knight realized as early as 1921 that probabilistic quantification often relies on qualitative judgments by mathematicians. As Chapman explains, distinguishing "risk," a situation where all the variables are known and defined, from "uncertainty," a situation where one can't appeal to clearly defined variables, economists identified a role for qualitative judgments in mathematical calculation: "situations of 'uncertainty' require the analyst to engage in a qualitative and intuitive judgment about the range of possible outcomes, before any probability can be calculated for each one." Chapman, *Jazz Bubble*, 37.

6   See for example Vinodh Venkatesh, "Malaysia 'Boleh'? Carles Casajuana and the Demythification of Neoliberal Space," *Romance Notes* 54, no. 1 (2014): 67–73; Luca Mavelli, "Widening Participation, the Instrumentalization of Knowledge and the Reproduction of Inequality," *Teaching in Higher Education* 19, no. 8 (2014): 860–69; Kate Hughes, "Transition Pedagogies and the Neo-

liberal Episteme: What Do Academics Think?," *Student Success* 8, no. 2 (July 2017): 21–30.

7   Winnubst, *Way Too Cool*, 32.

8   Winnubst, *Way Too Cool*, 34. Classical liberalism's commitments to white supremacy, patriarchy, and the like are juridical because they hinge on the idea of formal equality before the law, or what Marx calls mere political emancipation in *On the Jewish Question*. Treating materially unequal people as political equals naturalizes that inequality rather than fixing it.

9   Winnubst, *Way Too Cool*, 34.

10 Foucault, *Order of Things*, ix.

11 Sterne, *Audible Past*, 15.

12 According to Sterne, the audiovisual litany is traditionally part of the "metaphysics of presence" that we get from Plato and Christianity (*Audible Past*, 16): sound and speech offer the fullness and immediacy that vision and words deny. However, contemporary versions of the litany appeal to a different metaphysics. As Marie Thompson explains, "Against the 'staleness' of social theory, discourses of signification and representation, textual analysis and cultural critique, the ontological turn, in its abolition of the Kantian shadow over philosophy, promises a vibrant new line of flight" ("Whiteness and the Ontological Turn," 267). Flipping the conventional script, these versions of the litany associate sight and vision with the metaphysics of presence and its essentialisms and associate sound with dynamic, generative, relational processes that refuse essentialism. For example, Cavarero argues that privileging vision over sound is the foundation of the metaphysics of presence (*For More Than One Voice*, 57). For more on the sonic episteme and the audiovisual litany, see chapter 3.

13 For example, they argue that "the properly musical content is plied by becomings-woman" (Deleuze and Guattari, *Thousand Plateaus*, 248) and that "musical expression is inseparable from a becoming-woman" (299). "Woman" is their quintessential example of a minoritarian status: "It is perhaps the special situation of women in relation to the man-standard that accounts for the fact that becomings, being minoritarian, always pass through a becoming-woman" (291). To say that music is a becoming-woman thus means that music occupies the same status with respect to traditional European philosophy that women occupy in patriarchy.

14 See Sterne, *Audible Past*, 16–18. Thompson addresses this in a work in progress that she tweets about here: https://twitter.com/DrMarieThompson/status/1001400206506774528.

15 The desire to appear other than modernity (which is visual, linguistic, representational, etc.), to both revolutionize it and recuperate its minoritarian discourses, is why theorists don't offer revised version of the visual or language but instead pick sound (or, often, affect). As Deleuze and Guattari suggest in *A Thousand Plateaus*, music's otherness to modernity is isomorphic with femininity's otherness to modernist patriarchy. (I develop this point in chapter 3.) So the turn to sound is motivated primarily by sound's minoritarian status in

modernity; any number of senses, including vision, could be understood to work as neoliberalism understands sound to work.

16   Foucault, *Order of Things*, xii.

17   Attali, *Noise*, 113.

18   Friedman and Friedman, *Capitalism and Freedom*, 15.

19   Rancière, *Disagreement*, 106.

20   Barad, *Meeting the Universe Halfway*, 195.

21   Grosz, *Chaos, Territory, Art*, 33.

22   Foucault, *Order of Things*, ix.

23   This meme juxtaposes a picture of Foucault, captioned "I'm not saying every-thing is bad, I'm saying everything is dangerous," with a picture of Adorno, cap-tioned "I AM saying everything is bad." An example can be found here: https://imgur.com/gallery/ouZXy, accessed February 8, 2019.

24   Rose, *Black Noise*, 74.

25   Rose, *Black Noise*, 75.

26   Weheliye, *Phonographies*, 200.

27   Sharpe, *In the Wake*, 13.

28   This is what distinguishes it from ancient Greek theories of cosmic harmony, which use a different concept of sound. I explain the differences in more detail in chapters 2 and 4.

29   Helmholtz, *Sensation of Tone*, 3.

30   Olson, *Music, Physics, and Engineering*, 4.

187

31   As the website *Physics Classroom* explains, "The representation of sound by a sine wave is merely an attempt to illustrate the sinusoidal nature of the pressure-time fluctuations. Do not conclude that sound is a transverse wave that has crests and troughs. Sound waves traveling through air are indeed longi-tudinal waves with compressions and rarefactions. As sound passes through air (or any fluid medium), the particles of air do not vibrate in a transverse man-ner. Do not be misled—sound waves traveling through air are longitudinal waves." *Physics Classroom*, "Sound Is a Pressure Wave," http://www.physicsclass room.com/class/sound/Lesson-1/Sound-is-a-Pressure-Wave, accessed Febru-ary 8, 2019.

32   Audiopedia, "What Is Acoustic Resonance," *YouTube*, December 21, 2016, https://www.youtube.com/watch?v=5nhZf13Wq_w.

33   *The South Bank Show*, season 30, episode 12, "Steve Reich," directed by Matthew Tucker, Sky Arts, aired December 10, 2016.

34   Dissonance or out-of-tune-ness is how we humans perceive out-of-phase sound waves, and consonance is how we perceive sound waves that are in phase. This out-of-phaseness is sometimes described as "roughness" or "beating"; these metaphors imply that dissonance is the perception of clashing, incongruent phase patterns.

35   Spence, *Knocking the Hustle*, 3.

36   For example, Foucault distinguishes among German ordoliberalism, French neoliberalism, and American neoliberalism in *Birth of Biopolitics*. Simi-

larly, scholars such as Craig Willse and Melinda Cooper distinguish between welfare-state biopolitics and neoliberal biopolitics.

37   This neoliberalism-biopolitics conjunction is different from the neoliberal biopolitics that Melinda Cooper studies in *Life as Surplus*, in part because those neoliberalisms and biopolitics use slightly different though still overlapping math (e.g., tranching instead of Gaussian distributions of risk). Cooper distinguishes between a "state biopolitics [which] speaks the language of Gaussian curves and normalizable risk" and neoliberalism-biopolitics, which is "more likely to be interested in the non-normalizable accident and the fractal curve" (*Family Values*, 10). Cooper and I examine different varieties of neoliberalism and biopolitics: Cooper studies neoliberalisms that begin after those Foucault studies in *Birth of Biopolitics*, whereas I am primarily focused on the Chicago-school-influenced neoliberalism he addresses toward the end of the book and the French neoliberalisms that Attali was referring to in his work from the late 1970s and early 1980s. It is also a different biopolitics than the one Naomi Waltham-Smith discusses in her forthcoming book *The Sound of Biopolitics*. She relies primarily on Giorgio Agamben and the relationship between his account of biopolitics and Derridean deconstruction, whereas I rely primarily on Foucault and the relationship between his account of biopolitics and the neoliberalisms that appeal to the same probabilistic methods of quantification. Similarly, Huw Hallam's work on sound, music, and biopolitics foregrounds the Agambean notion of bare life, whereas I foreground the Foucauldian idea of normalization. See Huw Hallam, "The Production of Listening: On Biopolitical Sound and the Commonplaces of Aurality," *Journal of Sonic Studies* 2, no. 1 (May 2012), https://www.researchcatalogue.net/view/227912/227913.

38   Attali, "Interview with Jacques Attali," 11.

39   Foucault, *Society Must Be Defended*, 246.

40   Winnubst, *Way Too Cool*, 102, 101.

41   Mader, *Sleights of Reason*, 56.

42   Mader, *Sleights of Reason*, 65.

43   Mader, *Sleights of Reason*, 45.

44   Plato, *Republic* 509d.

45   Mader, *Sleights of Reason*, 45.

46   Mader, *Sleights of Reason*, 44.

47   Mader, *Sleights of Reason*, 52.

48   Because audio normalization means something else than what Foucault means by normalization, whenever I say normalization here I mean it in Foucault's sense, not in the sense commonly used in audio engineering.

49   Hicks, "Audio Compression Basics."

50   White, "Advanced Compression Techniques."

51   Kerr, "Compression and Oppression."

52   Sterne, *mp3*, loc. 775 of 8252.

53   Sterne, *mp3*, loc. 558 of 8252.

54   See Winnubst, *Way Too Cool*; Rancière, *Disagreement*.

55   McRobbie, "Post-Feminism and Popular Culture," 256.

56 See Mills and Pateman, *Contract and Domination*.

57 Mader, *Sleights of Reason*, 58.

58 Mader, *Sleights of Reason*, 46.

59 According to Mader, "Foucault contrasts two forms of social control in the West, one that works by exclusion and another that works by inclusion" (*Sleights of Reason*, 46).

60 Sterne, *mp3*, loc. 575 out of 8252.

61 Spence, *Stare in the Darkness*, 15.

62 James, *Resilience and Melancholy*.

63 See Darling-Hammond, "Race, Inequality and Educational Accountability."

64 Chow, "Video Calls Out Catcallers."

65 Sexton, *Amalgamation Schemes*, 6.

66 I discuss this song more extensively in James, "Listening to Sounds."

67 Spence, *Stare in the Darkness*, 15.

68 Sterne, *mp3*, loc. 165 of 8252. MP3s, the object of Sterne's study, are also frequency ratios. "MP3s are measured in terms of the bandwidth they require when played back, which is kilobits per second (kbps)" (Sterne, *mp3*). To clarify: I'm not, as Sterne cautions against, "replac[ing] a grand narrative of ever-increasing fidelity with a grand narrative of ever-increasing compression" (*mp3*). My claim here is that the same technique manifests in one sphere as signal compression and in another sphere as biopolitical normalization. The idea of the sonic episteme lets us talk about how this technique manifests as a logic that structures heterogeneous practices, ideas, and values. An episteme isn't a grand narrative—it's a specific bundle of techniques with common conceptual roots.

189

69 Mills, "Ideal Theory as Ideology."

70 Weheliye, *Phonographies*, 8.

71 I refer to pop musicians by the name under which they release music. As scholars such as Steven Shaviro have argued, the pop star persona—"Rihanna" or "Madonna" or "Grace Jones"—is the effect of a collective creative project: it involves producers, songwriters, graphic designers, stylists, video directors, dancers, studio musicians, PR and marketing professionals, and lots of other collaborators. The pop star persona is basically a corporate person. Robyn Fenty certainly contributes the majority of work that goes into creating Rihanna, but Fenty is not identical to Rihanna. Fenty is like the CEO of the corporate person that is Rihanna, and I'm talking about that corporation, not its CEO. Thus, when artists release music under just a single name, I will refer to that artist by that stage name to clarify the distinction between persona as corporation and artist as CEO. This is not designed to devalue black women artists by referring to them by first name but everyone else by last name; rather, it is to be precise about exactly to whom I am referring.

72 Sharpe, *In the Wake*, 13.

73 This chapter significantly reworks and expands my *Culture, Theory and Critique* article in which I reread Jacques Attali's 1977 book *Noise: The Political Economy of Music* through Michel Foucault's lectures on neoliberalism and biopolitics.

74 For example, I argue that Attali claims that "a more properly statistical vision of

reality, a macrostatistical and global, aleatory view, in terms of probabilities and statistical groups," that we see in "the kind of theorizing one finds in macro-economics" is "organically related to that whole dimension of non-harmonic music . . . which involves the introduction of new rules and in particular those of chance" ("Interview with Jacques Attali," 11).

75 Winnubst, "Queer Thing," 96.

76 Sterne, *mp3*, loc. 562 of 8252.

77 Stoever, *Sonic Color Line*, 7.

78 Code-switching is the practice of strategically shifting cultural communica-tion styles, often between a hegemonic style (such as standard white American English) and a subaltern style, such as African American Vernacular English (AAVE). For example, President Obama addressed white audiences differently than he did predominantly African American audiences: he used a different tone of voice, pattern of diction, vocabulary, and body language. For more on the history of African American women and code-switching, see Lorna Williamson Nelson, "Code-Switching in the Oral Life Narratives of African American Women," *Journal of Education* 172, no. 3 (1990): 142–55.

79 Feminist new materialism is a reaction to the perceived overemphasis on lan-guage and linguistic analysis in feminist theory in the late twentieth century; it argues that feminists ought to focus less on words and more on concrete, often biological and physiological matter, and that all matter is fundamentally equal or "univocal." Rosi Braidotti defines new materialism thusly: "Thus "neo-materialism" emerges as a method, a conceptual frame and a political stand, which refuses the linguistic paradigm, stressing instead the concrete yet com-plex materiality of bodies immersed in social relations of power." "Interview with Rosi Braidotti," in Rick Dolphijn and Iris Van Der Tuin, *New Material-ism: Interviews and Cartographies* (Ann Arbor, MI: Open Humanities, 2012), 21.

80 Ahmed, "Some Preliminary Remarks," 23.

81 By "personhood" I mean full civil and political status. Persons are granted the full protection of the laws and institutions that govern them, whereas sub- and nonpersons are seen as unworthy or undeserving of such protections. For ex-ample, so-called terrorists are often represented as undeserving of basic rights to due process.

82 The theory of the divided line in the *Republic* expresses this structure. Though the True itself isn't knowable or perceptible to living humans, we can know and perceive articulations of its structure: Forms, thoughts, physical things, and images (these are the four categories of things on the line in descending order from most to least real). The line is first divided to reflect the reality of ideas as compared to material things, and then each section is again divided by the same ratio, such that intelligible : visible :: forms : thoughts or things : images.

83 Pentland, *Social Physics*, 193.

84 Pentland, *Social Physics*, 142, 144.

1. Neoliberal *Noise* and the Biopolitics of (Un)Cool

Portions of this chapter are revised and updated versions of my articles "Neoliberal Noise" in *Culture, Theory, and Critique*, and "Is the Post- in Post-Identity the Post- in Post-Genre?" in *Popular Music* (special issue *The Critical Imperative*).

1   Nyman's piece is built on harmonies (called the "ground bass") from English baroque composer Henry Purcell's opera *King Arthur*.

2   Pet Shop Boys, "Love Is a Bourgeois Construct," on *Electric*, x2 Recordings, September 1, 2013. Arpeggios are figures that play all the notes of a chord in ascending or descending sequence rather than simultaneously; church bells are a commonly heard arpeggio.

3   James, *Resilience and Melancholy*.

4   Harvey, "Neoliberalism as Creative Destruction." My claim that soars are analogous to neoliberal markets is further supported by N. Adriana Knouf's description of noise artist collective RYBN's sonification of a crashing stock market. The collective took data describing market behavior during a famous crash (called the "Flash Crash" of 2010) and sonified it (i.e., they assigned a sound to each data point and then played these sounds in chronological sequence). Knouf describes the lead-up to the crash in terms that are basically analogous to my description of the soar: "Four minutes from the end, the high-frequency pulses become louder and more rhythmic, sounding as if the spaces between them were slowly decreasing. A few seconds before the sonification ends, the pulses rapidly start to smear together until they merge into a continuous sound, thereby ending the piece" (*How Noise Matters*, 46). RYBN's sonification shows that markets in the throes of creative destruction behave exactly like soars do.

5   See Shaviro, "Accelerationist Aesthetics."

6   Attali's position on noise is in line with then current trends in economics. As Knouf explains, "It was not until the late 1970s and early 1980s that most financial economists began to realize that noise was an additional factor that needed to be accounted for. Noise upset their understanding of the market as entirely signal. . . . Yet like good capitalists, financial economists and traders alike learned how to profit from this noise, a profiteering that continues today via high frequency trading (HFT) algorithms" (*How Noise Matters*, xi–xii).

7   Attali, "Interview with Jacques Attali," 11.

8   Stahl, "Evolution of the Normal Distribution," 104.

9   Stahl, "Evolution of the Normal Distribution," 99.

10 Stahl, "Evolution of the Normal Distribution," 108; Mader, *Sleights of Reason*, 53. Quetelet's book is titled *Sur l'homme et le développement de ses facultés, ou Essai de physique sociale*; "physique sociale" translates to "social physics."

11 "A word must be said about the origin of the term normal. Its aptness is attested by the fact that three scientists independently initiated its use to describe the error curve. These were the American C. S. Peirce in 1873, the Englishman Sir Francis Galton in 1879, and the German Wilhelm Lexis, also in 1879" (Stahl, "Evolution of the Normal Distribution," 111–12).

12 Attali, *Noise*, 115.

13 Attali, *Noise*, 113. I argue later in this chapter that what Attali calls repetition is more commonly known as neoliberalism.

14 Knouf, *How Noise Matters*, 50.

15 Knouf, *How Noise Matters*, 44.

16 Keohane, "Neoliberal Institutionalism."

17 Attali and Knouf are not isolated examples of the sonic episteme's application to political economy. Writing in 2010, Steve Kennedy argues that sound and sonics are a better model for late capitalist society than the "representationalist" (or what Rancière calls "metapolitical") models conventionally used in the discipline of "political economy." He understands himself as building on Attali's attempt "to engage political economy sonically." Kennedy argues that, unlike Attali, his concept of sonic economy "appl[ies] sonic thinking to the statistics as well as to festivals" ("Sonic Economy"). Kennedy is misreading Attali slightly: the *Noise* author clearly articulated continuities between acoustics and statistics, as I have cited in this chapter.

18 Attali, *Noise*, 32.

19 Winnubst, "Queer Thing"; Winnubst, *Way Too Cool*.

20 Winnubst, *Way Too Cool*, 111.

21 Spandau Ballet, "True," on *True*, Chrysalis Records, April 14, 1983; Taylor Swift, "Shake It Off," on *1989*, Big Machine Records, 2014.

22 Attali, *Noise*, 129.

23 For example, he argues that repetition includes the period in the early twentieth century when "mass production began to demand a radical recasting of the industrial apparatus" (*Noise*, 85). It's possible to read the slippage in Attali's use of the term "repetition" as unintentionally marking the shift from standardized mass production to statistical forecasting and financialization that intensified as late-1970s deindustrialization really kicked in.

24 Foucault, *History of Sexuality*, vol. 1, 148.

25 Winnubst has a similar breakdown of the key elements of Foucault's theory of neoliberalism: "The central categorical and epistemological transformations that, Foucault argues, occur in the shifts from classical to neoliberalism: the sites and mechanisms of truth (from the contract to the market . . .); dominant social values (from utility to human capital); concepts of freedom (from Rights of Man to subjects of interests); concepts of subjectivity (from 'citizen' to 'entrepreneur'); and modes of rationality (from juridical to calculative)" (*Way Too Cool*, 21).

26 Foucault, *Birth of Biopolitics*, 118.

27 Marx, *Capital*, vol. 1.

28 Foucault, *Birth of Biopolitics*, 118–19.

29 See Nealon, "Empire of the Intensities."

30 Foucault, *Society Must Be Defended*, 246.

31 Attali, "Interview with Jacques Attali," 11.

32 Foucault, *Society Must Be Defended*, 244, 246.

33 Attali, *Noise*, 115.

34 Foucault, *Society Must Be Defended*, 246.

35 Attali, *Noise*, 107.

36 Harvey, "Station to Station."

37 James, "Cloudy Logic."

38 Foucault, *Birth of Biopolitics*, 323.

39 On mass biopolitics, see Mario Tronti, "Towards a Critique of Political Democracy," *Cosmos and History: The Journal of Natural and Social Philosophy* 5, no. 1 (2009), http://www.cosmosandhistory.org/index.php/journal/article/view /127/236.

40 Foucault, *Society Must Be Defended*, 249.

41 Attali, *Noise*, 89; emphasis added.

42 Attali, *Noise*, 126.

43 Foucault, *Society Must Be Defended*, 216.

44 Attali, *Noise*, 122; emphasis added.

45 Attali, *Noise*, 136; emphasis added. In this way, *Noise*'s approach to musical noise is consistent with the approach to deviation, randomness, and irregularity that Attali adopts in the rest of his work on economics. As Eric Drott explains, "the image of transfigurative disruption — or rather, its idealization of the principle of order from noise — stands at the center of Attali's economic thought . . . a disjunction, a break, was in fact regeneration" (Drott, "Rereading Jacques Attali's Bruits," 741).

46 Attali, *Noise*, 114.

47 Foucault, *Birth of Biopolitics*, 140.

48 The section at the end of the chapter on repetition — "The Political Economy of Repetition" — reads, nowadays, as a rather standard description of branding. For example, Attali argues that mass production means that "considerable labor must then be expended to give [a commodity] a meaning, to produce a demand" (*Noise*, 128).

49 Nealon, "Empire of the Intensities," 79.

50 Attali, *Noise*, 107; emphasis added.

51 "Repetition . . . totally obstructs communication by way of object-related differences" (Attali, *Noise*, 121).

52 Horning, "Primitive Accumulation."

53 Horning, "Primitive Accumulation."

54 Winnubst, *Way Too Cool*, 102, 101.

55 Drott, "Rereading Jacques Attali's Bruits," 725.

56 Attali is not the only person to claim that sound and statistics are isomorphic. As Nick Seaver explains, "for [Gabriel] Tarde, not only are the senses statistical, but statistics is sensory." Nick Seaver, "Every Sensation Is Only a Number," paper presented at the American Anthropological Association meeting, San Francisco, CA, November 2012, http://nickseaver.net/papers/seaverAAA2012 .pdf.

57 Attali, "Music as a Predictive Science" (n.d.).

58 This is consistent with Drott's reading of *Noise*, where "music take[s] over the role previously assigned to the information/energy pair" ("Rereading Jacques

Attali's Bruits," 733) in Attali's previous book, *La Parole et l'outil*. In that book, Attali uses a "probabilistic" (730) theory of information to argue that information is the signal that emerges from all the noisy entropy of energy consumption (731).

59 James, "Cloudy Logic."

60 Attali, *Noise*, 142.

61 Foucault, *Birth of Biopolitics*, 223.

62 Attali, *Noise*, 142.

63 Attali, *Noise*, 144; emphasis added.

64 Foucault, *Birth of Biopolitics*, 226.

65 Attali, *Noise*, 143; emphasis added.

66 Attali, *Noise*, 142.

67 Attali, *Noise*, 6.

68 Shaviro, *Post-Cinematic Affect*, 48.

69 Reich, "Gradual Process."

70 Reich, "Gradual Process."

71 Reich, "Gradual Process."

72 Winnubst, "Queer Thing," 95.

73 "'Surplus value' is another way of saying 'cool.'" Rob Horning, "Capitalist Value and Cool," *Marginal Utility Annex* (blog), July 16, 2012, http://marginal-utility.blogspot.com/2012/07/capitalist-value-and-cool.html.

74 Halberstam, *Gaga Feminism*, 143.

75 Winnubst, "Queer Thing," 95.

76 It's possible to make an analytical distinction between "uncool" as a judgment of aesthetic taste and "uncool" as an economic cost/benefit analysis. Aesthetically, uncool is the lack of avant-garde edginess, being "square" or, in more contemporary terms, "basic." Economically, something is uncool if it's an insufficiently risky, and thus insufficiently profitable, investment. Under a regime of real subsumption, it is practically difficult to disentangle aesthetics from economic production: something is aesthetically "uncool" if it is economically "uncool."

77 Temperance, "Birth of Uncool."

78 Temperance, "Birth of Uncool."

79 Former postpunkers who, like Joy Division, gave themselves a Nazi-chic name, Spandau Ballet come from a much different musical background than most of the rest of the artists in the yacht rock genre and are probably better classified as New Romantics. However, they're commonly understood as part of yacht rock. For example, writing in *The Independent*, Elisa Bray says, "Yacht-rock, once dominant in southern California, in a golden age of studio music purveyed by acts including Steely Dan, The Doobie Brothers, Hall and Oates, Toto, Christopher Cross, Kenny Loggins, Robert Palmer, The Eagles, Spandau Ballet and even Rumours and Mirage-era Fleetwood Mac, is back." Elisa Bray, "From HAIM to Chromeo: The New Wave of Yacht Rockers," *Independent*, June 6, 2014, http://www.independent.co.uk/arts-entertainment/music/features/from-haim-to-chromeo-the-new-wave-of-yachtrockers-9492479.html.

80   Stratton, "Why Doesn't Anybody," 16.

81   Rowe, "Rock Culture," 131.

82   Gill, "Genealogical Approach," 200.

83   Tomas et al., "Perceptibility of Aggressive Dynamics Processing," 1.

84   Tomas et al., "Perceptibility of Aggressive Dynamics Processing," 2.

85   Tomas et al., "Perceptibility of Aggressive Dynamics Processing," 1.

86   Tomas et al., "Perceptibility of Aggressive Dynamics Processing," 2.

87   Clayton, "Belfast Quartone Punks."

88   Spence, *Stare in the Darkness*, 15.

89   Foucault, *Security, Territory, Population*, 90.

90   Swift's performance in "Shake It Off" adopts the neoliberal multicultural/
     multiracial approach to pop that Tamara Roberts identifies in Michael Jack-
     son's work in the 1980s and 1990s. As Roberts argues, "Jackson was key in
     establishing a musical category that was simply POP: a late 1970s originated
     amalgam of rock, funk, disco, and R&B, Jackson pulled from these genres but
     did not perform one in particular; he borrowed from them all and mixed them
     into his own unique musical base" ("Michael Jackson's Kingdom," 20). Indi-
     vidual uniqueness, Jackson's sonic "brand," is the effect not of some pure, un-
     adulterated expression but of a distinctly balanced mix of external influences.
     This approach to pop parallels historically concurrent shifts in the texture of
     white supremacy: it was no longer a matter of white racial purity but of main-
     taining the health of a multiracial mix (Sexton, *Amalgamation Schemes*). "Pop
     and 'the mainstream' Jackson helped establish are based not on a specific sonic
     or racial category but on the tension between realizing and transcending race
     through sound" (Roberts, "Michael Jackson's Kingdom," 20). Jackson's late
     millennial pop is the ideal neoliberal racial mix: it provides a productively and
     pleasurably tuned mix in which the presence of a plurality of distinct markers
     of racial difference creates the appearance of having transcended racial hierar-
     chies. So the claim for post/multiracialism actually invokes, and must invoke,
     the racial identities and hierarchies it purports to transcend. "The ability to
     transcend racial/cultural boundaries also requires the visible — often height-
     ened — appearance of race in order to showcase this transcendence" (34–35).
     The claim performatively voids its content. Unlike Jackson, whose perfor-
     mances explicitly called on *his* blackness, both sonically and visually, Swift's
     postgenre pop never directly points to *her* specific brand of whiteness (country
     music), a tributary to her mainstream aesthetic.

91   Lipshutz, "Taylor Swift's 'Shake It Off.'"

92   Fallon, "Taylor Swift's 'Shake It Off.'"

93   Fallon, "Taylor Swift's 'Shake It Off.'"

94   Knowles, "Poll: Iowa Republicans."

95   Vargo, "Katy Perry's Boring Super Bowl Performance."

96   For example, @HonestFandom writes, "Katy Perry gave the most boring Super
     Bowl performance ever." https://twitter.com/honestfandom/status/57969358
     3797784576. For more examples, see https://twitter.com/angie_goodwood
     /status/563066213220511747; https://twitter.com/happymeme50/status/56234

195

9417408131072; https://twitter.com/DanDumlao/status/56228988895167 6928.

97 Gunderson, "Danger Mouse's Grey Album."

98 Attali, *Noise*, 142.

2. Universal Envoicement

1 Du Bois, "Sociology Hesitant," 44. My thanks to Keguro Macharia for pointing me to this passage.

2 Du Bois, "Sociology Hesitant," 44.

3 Du Bois, "Sociology Hesitant," 44; emphasis added.

4 Du Bois, "Sociology Hesitant," 44, 38, 44.

5 Du Bois, "Sociology Hesitant," 44.

6 Du Bois, "Sociology Hesitant," 44.

7 For more on Du Bois's role in founding the then-new discipline of sociology, see Dan S. Green and Robert A. Wortham, "Sociology Hesitant: The Continuing Neglect of W. E. B. Du Bois," *Sociological Spectrum* 35, no. 5 (2015): 518–33. See also Aldon D. Morris, *The Scholar Denied: W. E. B. Du Bois and the Birth of Modern Sociology* (Berkeley: University of California Press, 2015).

8 "In the red" is Tricia Rose's phrase for hip-hop aesthetics' positive valuation of technologically distorted sound: "by pushing on established boundaries of music engineering, rap producers have developed an art out of recording with the sound meters well into the distortion zone. When necessary, they deliberately work in the red" (*Black Noise*, 75). The roots of the metaphor—audio gain meters—might suggest that "in the red" is what Steve Goodman calls a "politics of amplitude" (*Sonic Warfare*, 193); gain meters measure amplitude. I'm using the metaphor in a slightly different way, to refer to the frequencies that white supremacist patriarchal property relations perceptually code out of "human" perception by quantizing everything to its rationality.

9 The slowness of "slow food" demonstrates practitioners' elite status: their refusal to adopt normative frequencies augments rather than diminishes their human capital. The slowness of slow death, however, demonstrates practitioners' exceptional status: their refusal to adopt normative frequencies compounds their low status.

10 Adeyemi, "Straight Leanin.'"

11 Babb, Sundermann, and Millard, "Lean on Me."

12 Stoever, *Sonic Color Line*.

13 There are other variations of this move that aren't constituents of the sonic episteme because they have a different definition of sound, voice, and/or resonance. For instance, see James, "Affective Resonance."

14 Rancière, *Disagreement*, 96.

15 Rancière, *Disagreement*, 101.

16 Rancière, *Disagreement*, 101.

17 Postdemocratic political ontology takes the "nature" of *Homo economicus*—patterns or rhythms that emerge from the great noisy howl as rational signal—as the (ideal-as-idealized) model for how society does and ought to work.

So his phusis is similarly irrational or contingent — it has no inherent or essential(ist) logic that follows necessarily from its nature. Instead, his phusis emerges as the outcome of choices he makes. This is the point Foucault makes about neoliberal concepts of "nature" in *Birth of Biopolitics*— "nature" is not given, as in modernity, but emergent.

18   Rancière, *Disagreement*, 106. In Plato, see *Republic* 4, 433c–e. "And in truth justice is, it seems, something of this sort. However, it isn't concerned with someone's doing his own externally, but with what is inside him, with what is truly himself and his own. One who is just does not allow any part of himself to do the work of another part or allow the various classes within him to meddle with each other. He regulates well what is really his own and rules himself. He puts himself in order, is his own friend, and harmonizes the three parts of himself like three limiting notes in a musical scale — high, low, and middle. He binds together those parts and any others there may be in between, and from having been many things he becomes entirely one, moderate and harmonious."

19   Plato, *Republic* 509d.

20   Peraino, *Listening to the Sirens*, 33.

21   Friedman and Friedman, *Capitalism and Freedom*, 15.

22   Friedman and Friedman, *Capitalism and Freedom*.

23   Cavarero, *For More Than One Voice*, 40.

24   Evans, *Multivoiced Body*, 256.

25   For example, Ryan Dohoney argues that "Cavarero's sustained reflection on voice, offered in *fmtov*, should be understood within this broader project of revising philosophical abstractions" (77). Ryan Dohoney, "An Antidote to Metaphysics: Adriana Cavarero's Vocal Philosophy," *Women and Music: A Journal of Gender and Culture* 15 (2011): 70–85.

26   This is why, as Dohoney notes, Cavarero never actually studies or cites actual sonic or musical performances, only other philosophers' accounts of voices or thought experiments (See Dohoney, "Antidote to Metaphysics," 80). She's only interested in voice as a philosophical phenomenon, not a sonic or musical one.

27   Though she thinks that "however one looks at it, logos for Plato is noetic, visual, and mute" (Cavarero, *For More Than One Voice*, 57), Plato's logos isn't mute per se; it just embodies a concept of sound and sonic harmony that Cavarero's system cannot perceive — it calculates something like resonance geometrically rather than acoustically. Ironically, Cavarero's reading of Plato ignores the role musical concepts and music theory play in his thought.

28   Cavarero, *For More Than One Voice*, 38.

29   Cavarero, *For More Than One Voice*, 176. Cavarero describes the objectifying character of the gaze: "Metaphysics not only constructs itself on the primacy of sight, but also decides to ignore the reciprocity that is inscribed, as a decisive relational factor, in the economy of the gaze. The metaphysical eye, starting with Plato, fixes as its model a gaze that allows for the isolation, distance, and noninvolvement of the observer. This in turn legitimates the reduction of whatever is seen to an object" (*For More Than One Voice*, 176).

30   Cavarero, *For More Than One Voice*, 4.

31 Al-Saji, "Phenomenology of Critical Ethical Vision," 375.

32 Al-Saji, "Phenomenology of Critical Ethical Vision," 390.

33 Al-Saji, "Phenomenology of Critical Ethical Vision," 338.

34 Al-Saji, "Phenomenology of Critical Ethical Vision," 391.

35 Al-Saji, "Phenomenology of Critical Ethical Vision," 391; emphasis added.

36 Sterne, *Audible Past*, 15.

37 Sterne, *Audible Past*, 16.

38 Peterson and Kern, "Changing Highbrow Taste," 904.

39 Cavarero, *For More Than One Voice*, 8; emphasis added.

40 Like Elizabeth Grosz, who I discuss in the next chapter, Cavarero uses Chatwin's description of Aboriginal songlines to talk about emergence: "there is no rupture between this [maternal] music and speech. The lullaby, or the song of words that rocks the baby to sleep with rhythmical movements, is perhaps the clearest example of the absence of such a rupture. In his book *The Songlines*, Bruce Chatwin notes how Aborigine women walk with their children, giving names to things while combining these names into the rhythm of a song that follows the pattern of their footsteps. In this case, therefore, the singing voice, the heartbeat, the footstep, and nomination are all one" (*For More Than One Voice*, 179–80). Their mutual reliance on Chatwin suggests a common commitment to a concept of emergence.

41 Reich, "Music as a Gradual Process."

42 Evans, *Multivoiced Body*, 143.

43 Evans uses Steve Reich and Beryl Korot's opera *The Cave* as an example of his vocal political ontology. "The multivoiced body's solidarity (the intersection of its voices), the heterogeneity of its voices, and the fecundity of the interplay between these voices give us what we have been seeking since the beginning of this book: a concrete understanding of *The Cave*'s 'unity composed of difference' and a more 'personalized' version of 'chaosmos'" (*Multivoiced Body*, 197). In this video opera, Korot's videos of Israelis, Palestinians, and Americans are projected on TV screens while an orchestra plays Reich's instrumental transcriptions of their speech patterns. Evans picks up on the interplay of simultaneously projected voices: sonic patterns do emerge from that. However, it's important to note that, at the level of composition, this work is *not* an open or process piece, at least in Reich's own understanding of compositional processes. In an interview with Bruce Duffie, Reich explains: "the music comes from the speech, and literally and exactly from the speech." He would take Korot's recordings, "listen to them in detail, choose the ones that I was going to use, find out where the speech melodies were by listening to them over and over and over again, and then writ[e] them down by playing them at the piano and putting them into my music notebook." The music is effectively some creatively fictionalized transcriptions from source material, not a musical process in the vein of "Pendulum Music" or "It's Gonna Rain." Listening to *The Cave* may mimic the metaphysics of chaosmos, but the work's composition does not itself follow those rules. Bruce Duffie, "Composer Steve Reich: Two Conversations

with Bruce Duffie," BruceDuffie.com (blog), 2010, http://www.bruceduffie
.com/reich.html.

44   Technically, resonance is a mathematical relationship among rhythmic patterns or frequencies. In effect, resonance is the meta-ratio that compares the "rhythm" or rate of two or more frequencies. Relationships that can be expressed as a fraction with integers (i.e., rational numbers) as its numerator and denominator are "rational," and those that can't be expressed that way are "irrational." Western-tuned ears hear that mathematical rationality and irrationality as consonance and dissonance, respectively. Leaving the technical behind and thinking more simply, resonance is about the interaction of patterns: do they sync up or do they clash?

45   Evans, *Multivoiced Body*, 150, 249. Evans thinks the heterogeneity of individual voices is due to something more or less like sociocultural intertextuality—lots of different things have influenced me—and not due to any philosophical aspect of the human body. "Society is a multivoiced body" because "the social history of hybrid voices and their social languages—not bodily noises—permit us to attribute uniqueness to them" (76).

46   Evans never *says* "overtones," but phrases like "the hierarchical arrangement of the voices contained in the schema of our lead voice" (*Multivoiced Body*, 193) make these secondary voices sound like overtones.

47   Cavarero, *For More Than One Voice*, 198.

48   Evans, *Multivoiced Body*, 76.

49   Cavarero, *For More Than One Voice*, 7.

50   Foucault, *History of Sexuality*, vol. 1.

51   Cavarero, *For More Than One Voice*, 209.

52   Evans, *Multivoiced Body*, 2.

53   Rancière, *Disagreement*, 20.

54   Though it may well be a type of postdemocratic consensus, German critical theorist Hartmut Rosa's concept of resonant democracy is not a constituent of the sonic episteme because it is not a theory of acoustic resonance. He has a very loose and varied definition of resonance: sometimes it means something like sympathetic resonance, sometimes it means dialogic interaction, but most often and importantly it means a pattern of social interaction that is the ideal sweet spot between poles of absolute purity and absolute pluralism. Arguing that "resonance is the in-between of consonance and dissonance" that "move[s] beyond the sterile opposition between difference-theory and identity-thinking" (Zaretsky, "Crisis of Dynamic Stabilization"), Rosa understands resonance as the healthy middle between theories of essentialist identitarianism, where there is strict agreement, and absolute pluralism, where there is no agreement. In technical musical terms, he's pointing to some midpoint between unison (all identical frequencies) and noise (no discernable pattern among frequencies). He doesn't actually mean consonance or dissonance in the musical sense. For example, he says that "if you are in complete harmony, you are not in resonance" (Zaretsky, "Crisis of Dynamic Stabilization"). This statement makes no

sense, musically; frequencies sound harmonious because their fundamentals and overtones resonate consonantly. So for Rosa, resonance describes something other than variable patterns of intensity that interact via phase relationships. Though Rosa thinks resonance "allowed me to move beyond identity and authenticity as ultimate normative yardsticks" (Zaretsky, "Crisis of Dynamic Stabilization"), his theory is not a constituent of the sonic episteme because he has a different definition of resonance. There's plenty to problematize in Rosa's theory of resonant democracy, but this book isn't the place to do it.

55 For example, Rebecca Adami describes Cavarero's political ontology as "question[ing] the dichotomy of universal/particular in raising the importance of a plurality of unique voices who create a spectrum for the universality of rights" (163). Rebecca Adami, "Human Rights for More Than One Voice: Rethinking Political Space beyond the Global/Local Divide," *Ethics and Global Politics* 7, no. 4 (2014): 163–80.

56 Evans, *Multivoiced Body*, 270, 271. Evans is very explicit that he's upgrading traditional liberalism. His principle of justice "captures the core of progressive forms of liberalism, but on a new basis: voices and their creative interaction" (255).

57 Cavarero, *For More Than One Voice*, 205.

58 Cavarero, *For More Than One Voice*, 205.

59 Rancière's description of postdemocracy sounds quite close to Cavarero's and Evans's own descriptions of their projects: "It is supposed to liberate the new community as a multiplicity of local rationalities and ethnic, sexual, religious, cultural, or aesthetic minorities, affirming their identity on the basis of the acknowledged contingency of all identity" (*Disagreement*, 104).

60 Cavarero, *For More Than One Voice*, 209.

61 Cavarero, *For More Than One Voice*, 211; emphasis added.

62 Cavarero, *For More Than One Voice*, 14.

63 Speech is rather the point of intersection, or tension, between two poles: the voice that makes up its sonorous texture and the verbal signified that it is bound to express. Thus, what gets conquered in the victory of the feminine over the masculine is not really speech but rather the videocentric pole of the signified, or the register of thought to which the metaphysical tradition subjugates speech" (Cavarero, *For More Than One Voice*, 127).

64 Cavarero, *For More Than One Voice*, 137.

65 In his review of the book, Tony Smith notes that Evans's project cannot account for systemic and institutionalized social inequities, such as capitalism. Tony Smith, "Review of *The Multivoiced Body*, by Fred Evans," *Philosophy and Social Criticism* 39, no. 6 (2013): 597–601.

66 Peterson and Kern, "Changing Highbrow Taste," 900.

67 Peterson and Kern, "Changing Highbrow Taste," 905.

68 As Peterson and Kern note, "highbrows are more omnivorous than non-highbrows" ("Changing Highbrow Taste," 904) — nonhighbrows may like lowbrow things, but not necessarily a variety of different lowbrow things or lowbrow things *and* highbrow things.

69 Appiah, "Is the Post- in Postmodernism the Post- in Postcolonial?," 341–42.

70 Evans, *Multivoiced Body*, 197.

71 Evans, *Multivoiced Body*, 17; emphasis added.

72 Lugones, "Playfulness."

73 "Oblique pivot" (Havis, "Now, How Do You Sound?"); "spark" (Lorde, *Sister Outsider*); "viscus deviance" (Weheliye, *Habeas Viscus*).

74 Havis, "Now, How Do You Sound?," 241.

75 Havis, "Now, How Do You Sound?," 241.

76 Havis, "Now, How Do You Sound?," 243, 251.

77 Du Bois, "Sociology Hesitant," 44.

78 Havis, "Now, How Do You Sound?," 248.

79 Havis, "Now, How Do You Sound?," 244.

80 Havis, "Now, How Do You Sound?," 251.

81 Havis, "Now, How Do You Sound?," 247.

82 Foucault, *History of Sexuality*, vol. 1.

83 See Hill Collins, *Black Feminist Thought*.

84 Davis, *Blues Legacies and Black Feminism*.

85 Bradley, "I Been On."

86 Bradley, "I Been On."

87 James, "Listening to Sounds."

88 Weheliye, *Habeas Viscus*, 112.

89 Weheliye, *Habeas Viscus*, 112.

90 Crawley, "Stayed/Freedom/Hallelujah."

91 Weheliye, *Habeas Viscus*, 138.

92 Nash, *Black Body in Ecstasy*, 52.

93 Nash, *Black Body in Ecstasy*, 52.

94 As Mills and Pateman have shown, white women are granted the right to nominal consent over the use of their bodies as sexual property. Marriage contracts essentially sign that right over to husbands. White women are thus required to consent to give up their right to consent. Black women aren't even accorded this paradoxical ownership of their bodies as sexual property. See Pateman, *Sexual Contract*, and Mills and Pateman, *Contract and Domination*.

95 Think of it this way: all women are targets of racialized sexual violence, but there's something particular to the racialized sexual violence black women experience (namely, misogynoir) that produces them as *black*, and thus both women and imperfectly feminine. In her classic "Visual Pleasure in Narrative Cinema," Laura Mulvey argues that the objectification and fragmentation of the white woman's body organizes both classic Hollywood narrative cinema and classically liberal patriarchy. This violence happens to white women in film and in discourse. This objectification and fragmentation—what Weheliye calls "the profitable 'atomizing' of the captive body'" (*Habeas Viscus*, 68)—actually, materially happened to black women (i.e., it's not just represented violence that happens in cinema). I'm not saying that white women aren't victims of sexual violence but rather that the specific types of violence Mulvey, "Visual Pleasure and Narrative Cinema," locates in the formal structure of narrative cinema happen in real life to black women.

96 Nash, *Black Body in Ecstasy*, 52.

97 Remember, "in the red" is Tricia Rose's term for the hip-hop aesthetic practice of pushing sounds (especially the gain) past the point of distortion.

98 Weheliye, *Habeas Viscus*, 67; emphasis added.

99 Weheliye, *Habeas Viscus*, 120.

100 Galloway and LaRiviere, "Compression in Philosophy," 143.

101 Galloway and LaRiviere, "Compression in Philosophy," 143.

102 Rihanna, "BBHMM," directed by Rihanna and Megaforce, June 28, 2015; Rihanna, "Bitch Better Have My Money," Roc Nation, March 26, 2015.

103 For more on the way Rihanna's oeuvre rejects hegemonic narratives about black women survivors of sexual violence, see Nicole R. Fleetwood, "The Case of Rihanna," *African American Review* 45, no. 3 (Fall 2012): 419–35; and Esther Jones, "On the Real," in "Hip Hop and the Literary," special issue, *African American Review* 46, no. 1 (Spring 2013): 71–86. On "BBHMM" in particular, see Debra Ferreday, "'Only the Bad Gyal Could Do This': Rihanna, Rape-Revenge Narratives and the Cultural Politics of White Feminism," *Feminist Theory* 18, no. 3 (2017): 263–80.

104 Dijana Jelača describes them as "the phallic tools frequently deployed as weapons of violence toward women in horror movies and TV shows" (454). Dijana Jelača, "Film Feminism, Post Cinema, and the Affective Turn," in *The Routledge Companion to Cinema and Gender*, ed. Kristin Lené Hole, Dijana Jelača, E. Ann Kaplan, and Patrice Petro (New York: Routledge, 2017), 446–57. Jelača argues that "BBHMM" produces a feminist excess that is difficult for postfeminism or capitalism to co-opt. My analysis points to something similar but frames it differently: not as excess but as in the red. Jelača's piece also ignores the role of sound in the video and focuses solely on its cinematic aspects.

105 St. Felix, "Prosperity Gospel of Rihanna."

106 St. Felix, "Prosperity Gospel of Rihanna." For more on the role of smell in black feminist approaches to sexuality, see Stallings, *Funk the Erotic*.

3. Vibration and Diffraction

1 Hardesty, "Extracting Audio from Visual Information."

2 Hardesty, "Extracting Audio from Visual Information."

3 "An input sound (the signal we want to recover) consists of fluctuations in air pressure at the surface of some object. These fluctuations cause the object to move, resulting in a pattern of displacement over time that we film with a camera. We then process the recorded video with our algorithm to recover an output sound." Abe Davis et al., "The Visual Microphone: Passive Recovery of Sound from Video," 2014, http://people.csail.mit.edu/mrub/papers/Visual Mic_SIGGRAPH2014.pdf.

4 "We combine these motion signals through a sequence of averaging and alignment operations to produce a single global motion signal for the object" (Davis et al., 2).

5 Bennett, *Vibrant Matter*.

6   See Coole and Frost, *New Materialisms*, and Thompson, "Whiteness and the Ontological Turn."

7   Bennett, *Vibrant Matter*, 22.

8   Grosz, *Chaos, Territory, Art*, 5; emphasis added.

9   In acoustics, a phase refers to a complete oscillation or cycle. When a higher frequency's phases are completely divisible into a lower frequency's larger phase, they are in phase. When a higher frequency's phases aren't fully divisible into the lower frequency's larger phase, they are out of phase.

10 Steve Goodman's "ontology of vibrational force" has a lot in common with vibratory new materialisms, including a reliance on acoustic resonance: "concerned primarily with the texturhythms of matter, the patterned physicality of a musical beat or pulse . . . the question of vibrational rhythm shoots right to the core of an ontology of things" (Goodman, *Sonic Warfare*, 83). However, he situates his vibrational ontology in a different position with respect to post/modern European philosophy than new materialisms do: they argue vibratory resonance surpasses traditional philosophical abstraction, but he claims vibratory ontologies are ontologically prior to those traditional philosophical tools. As I discuss later in the chapter, this claim of supersession is how new materialisms create the same relations among theories that neoliberalism creates among people. Goodman doesn't make that claim, so for my purposes in this chapter he can't be lumped in with new materialisms.

11 Briefly, I think there are similarities between Barad's ontology and Simone de Beauvoir's existentialist ontology, which I think adequately accounts for the relationship between materiality or facticity, on the one hand, and humanity's collective and individual relations with it. Both stress material dependence and interconnection, and the importance of "situation." I have no particular interest in the correlationism debate, so Beauvoir's focus on the subject isn't objectionable to me as it would be for new materialists. However, because Beauvoir's ontology begins from material and historical relations of domination, I prefer her non-ideal approach to Barad's approach. For more on the relationship between Beauvoir and new materialism, see Susan Hekman, "Simone de Beauvoir and the Beginnings of the Feminine Subject," *Feminist Theory* 16, no. 2 (2015): 137–51.

12 I'm also not interested in new materialism's critique of anthropocentrism or correlationism, because claiming to move beyond the human as a category of analysis before one interrogates the way that category is theorized and functions in white supremacist patriarchal ways just occludes and naturalizes the racial, sexual, and gendered status differences marked by "the human." See, for example, Jackson, "Outer Worlds."

13 As Silvia Federici explains, "in the 16th century, 'enclosure' was a technical term, indicating a set of strategies the English lords and rich farmers used to eliminate communal land property and expand their holdings." Federici, *Caliban and the Witch*, 69.

14 Grosz, *Chaos, Territory, Art*, 54.

15 Grosz, *Chaos, Territory, Art*, 19, 16.

16 Bennett, *Vibrant Matter*, 106, 22.

17 Bennett, *Vibrant Matter*, 57; emphasis added.

18 Bennett, *Vibrant Matter*, 57.

19 Barad, *Meeting the Universe Halfway*, 72.

20 As Barad explains, "a key piece of evidence leading to the development of quantum physics, is that under certain circumstances matter (generally thought of as being made of particles) is found to produce a diffraction pattern" (*Meeting the Universe Halfway*, 82).

21 Barad, *Meeting the Universe Halfway*, 77.

22 Grosz, *Chaos, Territory, Art*, 44.

23 Grosz uses musical terms in a generalist manner that lacks the precision and specialist meanings these terms carry in music and sound studies scholarship. So, to study the role of music and sound in her ontology, it's better to unpack the phenomenon or concept she's describing and then determine the musical or sonic term that best describes it than it is to take Grosz's stated term in its strict musicological or sound studies sense. This doesn't change her argument so much as reduce potential confusion between her particular use of a musical term and the standard technical use of that term in music scholarship.

24 Grosz, *Chaos, Territory, Art*, 3.

25 Grosz, *Nick of Time*, 21.

26 Grosz, *Chaos, Territory, Art*, 19.

27 Bennett, *Vibrant Matter*, ix.

28 Barad, *Meeting the Universe Halfway*, 77.

29 Though Shelley Trower's *Senses of Vibration: A History of the Pleasure and Pain of Sound* (New York: Continuum, 2012) does express some affinities with new materialism in general ("vibration allows me to move beyond the category of the material object and to resist its distinction from the human subject" (7) and with Bennett's project in particular, this project neither models vibration on acoustic resonance, nor does it practice ideal theory. First, she studies vibration as people begin to understand it as "moving or quivering rapidly" (9), not dynamic patterns of pressure or intensity, or frequency ratios, or rhythms of condensation and rarefaction. The kind of movement or quivering is too general and not specifically patterned oscillations. Second, Trower is not advancing an ontology so much as studying past concepts and practices of vibration. She doesn't abstract away from the texts, practices, and relations she studies, and even calls out twenty-first-century uses of vibration as an idealized model for economic success. Studying the frequent appeals to "vibrancy" in U.K. universities' marketing copy and British politicians' speeches, Trower finds that "the use of the word 'vibrant' in these and many comparable descriptions seems to belong to the discursive rather than the material, in that there is no actual vibration going on" (151). What is going on is "economic development" and "the public 'regeneration' of buildings and communities" (151).

30 Bennett, *Vibrant Matter*, 2, xiii.

31 Bennett, *Vibrant Matter*, 2.

32 Leong, "Mattering of Black Lives."

33 Grosz, *Chaos, Territory, Art*, 26, 47.

34 Grosz, *Chaos, Territory, Art*, 55.

35 Grosz, *Nick of Time*, 12.

36 And though Grosz clearly admits that there are "affinities and points of congruence between Darwin's understanding of natural selection," which is the basis of much of her thought here, and "virtually all economic models" (*Nick of Time*, 37), it matters that there are strong affinities between her ontology and neoliberal economic theory. Not because that proves that Grosz is ultimately a neoliberal, but because it proves that her ontology and neoliberal economic theory inhabit the same episteme: they appeal to the same concepts, organizing principles, values, and so on, without explicitly overlapping or having a direct causal connection. For more on the relationship between evolution and neoliberalism, see Cooper, *Family Values*.

37 Grosz, *Chaos, Territory, Art*, 62.

38 Grosz, *Chaos, Territory, Art*, 55.

39 A geometric relationship "holds object and subject at a distance as the very condition for knowledge's possibility" (Barad, *Meeting the Universe Halfway*, 87–88). For example, Velasquez uses perspective — a kind of geometry — to arrange the composition of Las Meninas so spectators can see the King and Queen's reflection in the mirror he depicts in the painting; that composition requires distance between the spectator, the painting, and the painted mirror's implied subjects. Barad doesn't say, "Hey, I'm talking about Foucault's discussion of Velasquez here," but her discussion of mirrors, reflection, and subject-object metaphysics as the condition for knowledge make it clear that her concept of "reflection" describes the same episteme Foucault does in his analysis of *Las Meninas*.

40 Ahmed, "Founding Gestures," 25.

41 Leong, "Mattering of Black Lives."

42 New materialists use "representationalism" to identify roughly the same aspects of European modernity that Attali refers to in *Noise* as "representation."

43 Sterne, *Audible Past*, 15. See also Thompson, "Whiteness and the Ontological Turn." Ethnomusicologists Kariann Goldschmitt and Ben Tausig have made similar claims in work that has, at the time of this writing, not yet been published.

44 Sterne stresses that the aim is to establish the moral and metaphysical superiority of hearing over seeing: "It is essentially a restatement of the longstanding spirit/letter distinction in Christian spiritualism. The spirit is living and life-giving — it leads to salvation. The letter is dead and inert — it leads to damnation. Spirit and letter have sensory analogues: hearing leads a soul to spirit, sight leads a soul to the letter" (Sterne, *Audible Past*, 16).

45 Sterne, *Audible Past*, 18.

46 Sterne, *Audible Past*, 16.

47 Thompson, "Whiteness and the Ontological Turn," 267.

48 Barad, *Meeting the Universe Halfway*, 87.

49 Barad, "Posthuman Performativity," 811.

50 Barad, *Meeting the Universe Halfway*, 107, 55.

51 Arguing that "the belief that words, concepts, ideas, and the like accurately reflect or mirror the things to which they refer . . . makes a finely polished surface of this whole affair" (*Meeting the Universe Halfway*, 86), Barad connects philosophical representationalism with vision.

52 Barad, "Posthuman Performativity," 812.

53 Bennett, *Vibrant Matter*, xiv. As Bennett argues, "demystification presumes that at the heart of any event or process lies a *human* agency that has illicitly been projected into things. This hermeneutics of suspicion calls for theorists to be on high alert for signs of the secret truth (a human will to power) below the false appearance of nonhuman agency" (*Vibrant Matter*, xiv).

54 Bennett, *Vibrant Matter*, 4, xv; emphasis added.

55 Grosz, *Chaos, Territory, Art*, 40.

56 European philosophy strongly associates wildness with racial non-whiteness. This begins with social contract theorists such as Locke and Rousseau, who imagine the uncolonized parts of the Americas as an actually existing state of nature. In this context, Abbate's appeal to "wildness" sounds like a thinly veiled reference to racial non-whiteness. For the problems with such appeals in aesthetics, see Gooding-Williams, *Look, A Negro!*

57 Abbate, "Music — Drastic or Gnostic?" 511.

58 Eidsheim, *Sensing Sound*, 3.

59 Eidsheim, *Sensing Sound*, 181, 2.

60 Though Eidsheim could be interpreted as rejecting conceptual research in favor of practice-based research, she's not actually abandoning concepts or conceptual abstractions. Explaining that "intermaterial vibration is only a placeholder for the thick event" (183) of an empirical sonic phenomenon, Eidsheim clarifies that she uses vibration as an abstraction: it reduces the "thick event" into a form that fits into the places set at what Sara Ahmed calls philosophy's "table." Like Abbate and Barad, she uses vibration as the abstraction that translates practice or performance into conceptual terms.

61 Ahmed, "Founding Gestures," 25. Leong describes this rhetorical move less as a gesture and more as an attitude, a "dissatisfaction with the linguistic and cultural paradigms of post-structuralism" ("Mattering of Black Lives").

62 Spence, *Stare in the Darkness*.

63 Barad, *Meeting the Universe Halfway*, 26; emphasis added.

64 Grosz, *Nick of Time*, 10.

65 Epstein, "Mirroring and Mattering," emphasis added.

66 Choreographing their turn from representationalism to vibratory resonance as a surpassing, new materialist theorists perform a different rhetorical gesture than Steve Goodman does in his ontology of vibratory resonance. Instead of superseding it with a chronologically newer, better method of abstraction, Goodman gets in behind it with an abstraction that is ontologically prior (i.e., it addresses a more fundamental part of existence, like shifting focus from atoms to subatomic particles). Vibration is "subpolitical": it works "underneath the segmentation of belief into ideological, territorial, affiliative, or gang

camps" (*Sonic Warfare*, 175) that representationalist abstractions create. As Wayne Marshall emphasizes in his review of the book, Goodman "focus[es] on sound as physical force, as something subpolitical and pre-ideological" ("How to Wreck a Nice Beach/Sonic Warfare," *Current Musicology* 90 [Fall 2010]: 98). Treating identity politics as merely ontic and rhythmic vibration as fundamental ontology, Goodman imagines himself to be taking a step back from the level of analysis common in philosophy and musicology and proceeding down an entirely different route. Rhythmanalysis "sidesteps those preoccupations of cultural studies' critical musicological approaches that tend to limit discussion around issues of representation, identity, and cultural meaning" (*Sonic Warfare*, 9). A sidestep is literally and metaphorically a different gesture than supersession or renewal: it doesn't overcome or push through the problem, it goes around it. Even though Goodman uses resonance to abstract away from what he thinks are merely "ontic" concerns like race or gender (191), his project doesn't enact a politics of exception.

67 Bennett, *Vibrant Matter*, 116.

68 Bennett, *Vibrant Matter*, 112.

69 From the perspective of a pop music studies scholar, this effectively sounds like an argument for omnivorous consumption over highbrow exclusivity: whereas one used to demonstrate one's elite status by having exclusive taste, now one does this by having diverse tastes. See Peterson and Kern, "Changing Highbrow Taste."

70 See James, "Is the Post- in Post-Identity the Post- in Post-Genre?"

71 Bennett, *Vibrant Matter*, 46.

72 Bennett, *Vibrant Matter*, 47.

73 Grosz, *Nick of Time*, 32.

74 Grosz, *Nick of Time*, 10.

75 Grosz, *Nick of Time*, 30.

76 On this point Grosz uses sexuality to moderate the effect of deregulated chance in exactly the same way neoliberal economist Friedrich Hayek does. As Melinda Cooper explains, "Hayek's political philosophy of neoliberalism could usefully be described as preemptive in the sense that its first instinct is to accommodate the future," but this "will to adapt exists side by side with an unwavering deference to historical selection—the social conventions of religion, family, and inherited wealth that are thrown up as if by chance but subsequently validated by the weight of social norms" (*Family Values*, 312). This is basically social Darwinism: new developments have to fit with patterns of living that have supposedly evolved to be most successful. The pattern Hayek is primarily concerned with is the patriarchal nuclear family. Grosz's appeal to sexual selection likewise uses heteropatriarchal gender norms to preemptively sort chance into acceptable and unacceptable variation.

77 Ahmed identifies a version of this exception-making. Surveying the authors new materialists reject as "old" and the authors they read as positive models for new theory, Ahmed argues that "what is evident here is an uneven distribution of the work of critique. . . . To be blunt, male writers (who are also usually dead

and white) are engaged with closely, while feminist writers are not" (Ahmed, "Founding Gestures," 30). Though she doesn't specifically attribute this to a logic of exception (i.e., creating an insufficiently reformable, adaptable population as a representative of the past that one has overcome), Ahmed does pick up on the same underlying politics: the exception is carved along updated versions of white supremacist patriarchy. White male writers are treated as capable of reform, but feminist writers are not.

78 Ahmed notes a similar move: "'Theory' is being constituted as anti-biological by removing from the category of 'theory' work that engages with the biological, including work within science and technology studies, which has a long genealogy, especially within feminism. Such work disappears in the very argument that we must return to the biological" (Ahmed, "Founding Gestures," 26).

79 Jackson, "Outer Worlds," 215.

80 Jackson, "Outer Worlds," 215.

81 Jackson, "Outer Worlds," 215.

82 Dotson, "How Is This Paper Philosophy?"

83 Chris Anderson, "The End of Theory: The Data Deluge Makes the Scientific Method Obsolete," *Wired*, June 23, 2008, https://www.wired.com/2008/06 /pb-theory; Nello Cristianini, "The Road to Artificial Intelligence: A Case of Data over Theory," *New Scientist*, October 16, 2016, https://www.newscientist .com/article/mg23230971-200-the-irresistible-rise-of-artificial-intelligence.

84 Writing in 2014, analytic philosopher Alex Rosenberg ties the humanities' decline to its deep investment in race and gender theory: "Cura Te Ipsum," *3:AM Magazine*, January 2, 2014, http://www.3ammagazine.com/3am/cura-te-ipsum.

85 This dynamic explains why the founding gesture "forget[s] the feminist work on the biological, including the work of feminists trained in the biological sciences" (Ahmed, "Founding Gestures," 27).

86 Braun, "New Materialisms and Neoliberal Natures," 12.

87 Braun, "New Materialisms and Neoliberal Natures."

88 As Sara Ahmed notes, with new materialism "we now have the defence of a return to biology (which is after all a highly funded discipline and a much valorized term within the general economy)" (Ahmed, "Founding Gestures," 32).

89 See, for example, this 2008 article in *Wired*: Anderson, "End of Theory." Then again in 2013 *Wired* ran an article titled "Big Data and the Death of the Theorist": Ian Steadman, "Big Data and the Death of the Theorist," *Wired*, January 25, 2013, http://www.wired.co.uk/article/big-data-end-of-theory. That same year, economist Noah Smith blogged about "The End of Theory" in economics: "The End of Theory," *Noahpinion* (blog), August 5, 2013, http:// noahpinionblog.blogspot.jp/2013/08/the-death-of-theory.html.

90 On reparative reading, see Heather Love, "Truth and Consequences: On Paranoid and Reparative Reading," *Criticism* 52, no. 2 (Spring 2010): 235–41. See also Bruno Latour, "Why Has Critique Run Out of Steam?," *Critical Inquiry* 30 (Winter 2004): 225–48; and Rita Felski, *The Limits of Critique* (Chicago: University of Chicago Press, 2015).

91 Mills, "Ideal Theory," 168. In philosophy the letters *S* and *P* are commonly used as variables to represent the "subject" and "predicate" of a logical proposition.

92 Mills, "Ideal Theory," 167.

93 Mills, "Ideal Theory," 168. Mills emphasizes that it's entirely possible to "abstract without idealizing" (168); for example, he cites patriarchy and white supremacy as conceptual abstractions that do not presuppose idealized social ontologies. Descriptive models are also abstractions, but because matter and material relations embody historical and current power relations, it is more difficult to abstract away from relations of subordination and systems of domination.

94 Zepke, "Reviewed Works," 551.

95 Thompson, "Whiteness and the Ontological Turn," 269.

96 Parikka, "New Materialism as Media Theory," 98–99.

97 My argument in this chapter shares the concern Brian Kane articulates in his analysis of "the 'ontological turn' in sound studies," which, "setting itself against the so-called 'linguistic turn' in the humanities, directly challenges the relevance of research into auditory culture, audile techniques, and the technological mediation of sound in favor of universals concerning the nature of sound, the body, and media" (3). These "universals" are what I call idealized abstractions; framing this as a matter of ideal theory highlights the fact that it's not just "culture" that gets abstracted away but institutionalized relations of domination as well. All ontologies that use acoustic resonance as an idealized model are guilty of this. Brian Kane, "Sound Studies Without Auditory Culture: A Critique of the Ontological Turn," *Sound Studies* 1, no. 1 (2015): 2–21.

98 Mills, "Ideal Theory," 172.

99 Gillespie, "Black Power as Thing Power."

100 See Stoever, *Sonic Color Line*.

101 Weheliye, *Habeas Viscus*, 10.

102 Leong makes a similar claim: "Because materiality is figured as an impersonal force of the real, it runs the risk of becoming a transcendental signified that merely replaces language or culture as an organizing principle" ("Mattering of Black Lives").

103 To the extent that the economies of funding and prestige in academia reward scholarship that overlooks and does not engage research by and about oppressed people, scholarly citational practices are a type of perceptual coding. Dominant models of epistemology and disciplinarity treat scholarship by and about oppressed people as redundant signals that nobody needs or wants to listen for, and that don't need to be transmitted (read, cited, etc.) for successful scholarly communication.

104 Whereas traditional modes of philosophical abstraction, such as Hegelian *Geist* (which means spirit or mind) or the Arendtian art of making distinctions, strive for ever-more determinate concepts, black pneumatological abstractions (*pneuma* means both "breath" and "soul" or "spirit") create intervals of *indeterminate* length and content. See Seyla Benhabib, *The Reluctant Modernism of Hannah Arendt* (New York: Rowman and Littlefield, 2000); Georg Wilhelm

209

Friedrich Hegel, *The Phenomenology of Spirit*, translated by A. V. Miller (Oxford: Oxford University Press, 1979).

105 Rihanna, "Love on the Brain," Westbury Road/Roc Nation, September 27, 2016, *YouTube*, https://www.youtube.com/watch?v=oRyInjfgNc4.

106 Crawley, *Blackpentecostal Breath*, 170. For more on the aesthetics of the cut in hip-hop, see Rose, *Black Noise*, chapter 2.

107 In *The Undercommons* (Brooklyn: Minor Compositions, 2013), Stefano Harney and Fred Moten define fugitivity as the quality of existing below the radar of capitalist enclosure—i.e., in the undercommons. "To enter this space is to inhabit the ruptural and enraptured disclosure of the commons that fugitive enlightenment enacts, the criminal, matricidal, queer, in the cistern, on the stroll of the stolen life, the life stolen by enlightenment and stolen back, where the commons give refuge, where the refuge gives commons" (28).

108 Crawley, *Blackpentecostal Breath*, 106.

109 Dotson, "How Is This Paper Philosophy?"

110 Commonly, philosophers assume the academic equivalent of terra nullius: even if there is scholarship on a topic in fields outside philosophy, philosophers are allowed if not encouraged to ignore that scholarship because the only "ownership" claims that count are ones made by capital-P Philosophy. See, for example, Olufemi Taiwo writing on citational norms in philosophy at *Philosophical Percolations*: "More on Citation Norms," April 28, 2017, http://www.philpercs.com/2017/04/more-on-citation-norms-.html.

111 The connection between philosophical abstraction and enclosure is especially clear in the German word for "concept," *Begriff*, whose root means grab, hold, or seize. Crawley alludes to this in his claim that philosophy is the capacity for "graspability, for assumption, for the literal taking objects up into the hand and placing them off and to the side" (*Blackpentecostal Breath*, 137).

112 Sharon Meagher, "Feminist Transformations," *Journal of Speculative Philosophy* 26, no. 2 (2010): 200–210.

113 On whiteness as property, see Cheryl Harris, "Whiteness as Property," *Harvard Law Review* 106, no. 8 (June 1993): 1707–91.

114 "Some definitions, phrases, and quotations (like, for example, the definitions of wake) will repeat throughout the text of *In The Wake* and will be marked by italics. I imagine these italicized repetitions as a reminder, a refrain, and more" (Sharpe, *In the Wake*, 135n1).

115 Sharpe, *In the Wake*, 51–52.

116 Sharpe, *In the Wake*, 41, citing Toni Morrison.

117 Steven Dillon, "Possessed by Death," *Radical History Review* 112 (2012): 113–25.

118 Los Angeles sound collective Ultra-Red's *4'33" (Arrest Record #1, County USC Hospital, May 22, 2004)* takes a similar approach to wake and residence time. In this project, they recorded themselves in USC Hospital on the fourteenth anniversary of a demonstration that ultimately led to the opening of an AIDS ward there. Describing their action, Ultra-Red writes, "Perhaps in that invocation I may retrieve some sort of trace echoes of that day in 1990. To do so, I would need an especially sensitive microphone. I would also need to calcu-

late the exact density of a waveform after fourteen years of decay. What conditions would require me to modify such calculations: the temperature of each day that passed between May 20, 1990 and the present? What about the conflagration that followed the trial of the officers accused of torturing Rodney King? I might need to consider the impact of vibrations from the Northridge earthquake of 1994. Then there are the daily vibrations from buses, helicopters, sirens, passing jets, construction, the nearby train tracks, passing trucks, lowriders with their booming bass, motorcycles, the daily waves of people streaming in and out of [the hospital's] doors, footsteps, voices, cries and the calls of the nearby street vendor" (cited in Terry Thaemlitz, "Utopia of Sound," *Comatonse* [blog], August 2008, http://www.comatonse.com/writings/utopiaof sound.html.) Their questions probe the residence time of historical events as they impact and form either rational or irrational relationships with present vibrations.

119 Sharpe, *In the Wake*, 56.

120 Sharpe, *In the Wake*, 21.

121 Thaemlitz also works with an idea of absent archives/archives of absence: "the sound of politics is more often than not the silence of memory?" (Thaemlitz, "Utopia of Sound"). I'm not a historian and don't have the training to do this work, but it would be worthwhile to examine the archives to ascertain the extent to which the psychoacoustic research that led to perceptual coding as an audio engineering practice either implicitly or explicitly appealed to information compression techniques developed in the slave trade, such as the "ditto ditto" Sharpe identifies.

122 Sharpe, *In the Wake*, 11. In Sharpe's work, in-the-redness isn't a feature of the physics of sound as such but an effect of the racial-sexual coding out of black people from existence as persons. In-the-red sound—irrational noise, infra- and ultra-sound—can be an effective weapon against technologies like the ship and the hold only when we account for the fact that those technologies are responsible for the coding of red and "black" sound in the first place. Because it is grounded in an analysis of the sociohistorical conditions that shape perception, Sharpe's (and Weheliye's) theorization of in-the-red sound is superior to the ultimately ambivalent uses of sonic irrationality or infra-/ultra-sound that thinkers such as Terre Thaemlitz and Steve Goodman identify in their work. See Thaemlitz, "Utopia of Sound"; and Goodman, *Sonic Warfare*, especially 24–25.

123 Cited in Sharpe, *In the Wake*, 38; emphasis added.

124 Sharpe, *In the Wake*, 38. "The dead appear in Philip's Zong!, beyond the logic of the ledger, beyond the mathematics of insurance. . . . Philip aspirates those submerged lives and brings them back to the text from which they were ejected. Likewise, in the structure of Zong! the number of names of those people underwriting the enterprise of slavery do not match the number of the thrown and jumped, and so, with that too, Philip dispenses with a particular kind of fidelity to the invention of the historical archive" (38).

125 The poem visually represents this revised mathematical relationship by echo-

ing the form of a fraction. The two long lines in the poem visually resemble the division bar in fractions. According to Sharpe, black personhood, not the property-status of slaves, "underwrite[s]" and rationalizes Philip's ratios (*In the Wake*, 38).

126 Sharpe, *In the Wake*, 142n15.

127 Sharpe, *In the Wake*, 38.

128 Beyoncé, "Hold Up," on *Lemonade*, Parkwood, 2016.

129 See James, "Robo-Diva."

130 Crawley, *Blackpentecostal Breath*, 65.

131 Crawley, *Blackpentecostal Breath*, 63–64.

132 For more on Holiday's use of accent and inflection, see Davis, *Blues Legacies and Black Feminism*.

133 In the interview, Vanilla Ice/Robert Van Winkle expresses the purported difference between the two riffs as a difference in vocal melody—the same kind of diacritical difference I discuss here. "Ding ding ding di-gi ding-ding [BREATH] Ding ding ding di-gi ding-ding" is how he characterizes Queen and Bowie's riff; "ding ding ding di-gi ding-ding CHIK ding-ding ding ding di-gi ding-ding" is how he characterizes his. Years later he retracted his defense and admitted to sampling the riff. "Vanilla Ice MTV Interview," *YouTube* (posted by Daniel Bothma, June 17, 2012), https://www.youtube.com/watch?v=bid0AbLTcco. My transcription.

134 Beyoncé doesn't always follow the practices she models. Though "Hold Up" expresses or represents aspiratory patterns and choreosonic accents, *Lemonade* as a whole is obviously a commercial artwork credited to Beyoncé, one that is her intellectual property and that made her lots of money. This is a long-standing tension in pop music: it's both inherently commercial and yet, as an artwork, has aesthetic features that function beyond and occasionally in conflict with its status as a commodity. As Angela Davis has argued in her reworking of Marcuse's theory of the aesthetic dimension, black women's music has long exploited this tension (Davis, *Blues Legacies and Black Feminism*).

135 Beyoncé, "Denial," on *Lemonade*, Parkwood, 2016.

136 Beyoncé released the video as a stand-alone work on her thirty-fifth birthday, which reinforces the interpretation that "Hold Up" is about birth and self-rebirth. Daniel Kreps, "Beyonce Posts Standalone 'Hold Up' Video on 35th Birthday," *Rolling Stone*, September 4, 2016, https://www.rollingstone.com/music/music-news/beyonce-posts-standalone-hold-up-video-on-35th-birthday-113668.

137 Other than the sound of the narrator plunging into the water, there are no percussion sounds in the underwater section of the video. This is further evidence that the percussion riffs represent the choreosonic sounds muted by submersion in denial.

138 Ending with a soar is not uncommon. For example, Ludacris featuring Usher and David Guetta's 2012 "Rest of My Life" ends with a fake-out soar, a soar that never lands on a downbeat.

139 This syllabic laughter can be heard as a sonic instance of what Sharpe calls the

asterisk. Neoliberal biopolitics uses statistics to normalize risk, to distribute it so that the costs and benefits disproportionately accumulate along entrenched lines of subordination and supremacy. In contrast to this normalized risk, Sharpe offers the theory of the "asterisk"—which, she notes, is in part homophonically related to "risk" (*In the Wake*, 29). Whereas neoliberal biopolitics uses relations of subordination and supremacy to normalize risk, that is, to make sure that risk never meaningfully harms (and often benefits) dominant groups and institutions, "the asterisk . . . functions as the wildcard" (30) by eschewing fidelity to that normalized frequency. With no obligation to refrain from distorting those frequencies, the asterisk can go into the red as far and as often as possible. Sharpe argues that the asterisk's wildcard function is related to the open-endedness the asterisk signifies in the term "trans*": "It speaks, as well, to a range of embodied experiences called gender and to Euro-Western gender's dismantling, its inability to hold in/on Black flesh" (30). Popular music scholar Francesca Royster identifies a similar "wildcard" function "in the moments when [Michael Jackson] didn't use words, 'ch ch huhs,' the 'oohs,' and the 'hee hee hee hee hees'" (Francesca Royster, *Sounding Like a No-No* [Ann Arbor: University of Michigan Press, 2012], 117). According to Royster, these vocals took binary gender into the red, presenting Jackson "to be neither/nor or both" (117), which is how Royster defines trans. Thus, she argues, "through his cries, whispers, groans, whines, and grunts, Jackson occupies a third space of gender, one that often undercuts his audience's expectations of erotic identification" (119). Beyoncé often makes her inheritance from Jackson explicit (her 2016 Super Bowl halftime costume is a widely acknowledged riff on a famous Jackson outfit: Gaby Wilson, "You Probably Missed Beyonce's Super Bowl Tribute to Michael Jackson," MTV, February 7, 2016, http://www.mtv.com /news/2736806/Beyoncé-super-bowl-michael-jackson), so we have good reason to hear the laughter on "Hold Up" as echoing Jackson's. As such, Beyoncé's laughter here calls on the trans-ness in Jackson's vocals; at the very end of the song, it's easy to hear these laughs as an asterisk in the vein of the asterisk at the end of trans*.

140   Robinson, "How Beyonce's 'Lemonade.'"

141   In fact, "Hold Up" may break conventional logics of enclosure only so they can be remade at another level. *Lemonade* gestures toward different types of private property and property-in-person: there's the closing of "Formation," which argues that the best revenge is "paper," like money or "receipts" (i.e., proof of another person's bad behavior), and there's the fact that Beyoncé Knowles-Carter—and lots of other people—made a good amount of money off this project. As *Newsweek* reports, *Lemonade* was the best-selling album of 2016. Tufayel Ahmed, "Beyoncé's 'Lemonade' Was the Best-Selling Album of 2016," *Newsweek*, April 26, 2017, https://www.newsweek.com/beyonces-lemonade -was-best-selling-album-2016-590147.

142   Tracking diacritical patterns without also accounting for their antiphonal character (that they call to and recall existing practices and traditions) is just plain old Deleuzo-Goodmanian rhythmanalysis. It's not just the rhythm of, say, cita-

213

tion that is important: it's who those rhythms call out to, who is cited, and with what kind of emphasis—i.e., accent and inflection. Attention to antiphonal oscillation allows us to consider who we are calling out to and to whose calls we listen and to ask questions such as: Are women of color cited only superficially, their critiques acknowledged but then largely ignored? Does scholarship on race cite only white authors? What is the texture and effect of our response(s) to those on whom our research calls: Do they allow for further response (and from whom), or do they appropriate those on whom we call to our own practices of enclosure?

4. Neoliberal Sophrosyne

My thanks to Barry Shank for his ongoing feedback on this chapter, both at conferences and reading drafts.

Epigraph: Cooper, *Family Values*, 60.

1 See James, *Resilience and Melancholy*, for more on this.
2 *Huffpost*, "Molly Is a Drug."
3 Ishler, "Chill Pop."
4 *Billboard* Staff, "15 Best."
5 Kupperman, "Chainsmokers."
6 Molanphy, "Why Is the Chainsmokers."
7 Davies, "Thoughts on the Sociology."

8 Jenny Gold, "'Post-Election Stress Disorder' Sweeps the Nation," PBS *Newshour*, February 23, 2017, http://www.pbs.org/newshour/rundown/post-election-stress-disorder-sweeps-nation.
9 Hatewatch Staff, "Post-Election Bias Incidents Up to 1,372," *Hatewatch*, Southern Poverty Law Center, February 10, 2017, https://www.splcenter.org/hatewatch/2017/02/10/post-election-bias-incidents-1372-new-collaboration-propublica.
10 James Griffiths and Barbara Starr, "North Korea Accuses US of Provocation after Bomber Drills," CNN, May 4, 2017, http://www.cnn.com/2017/05/02/asia/thaad-south-north-korea.
11 Richards, "Soft, Smooth, and Steady."
12 Richards, "Soft, Smooth, and Steady."
13 Richards, "Soft, Smooth, and Steady."
14 Richards, "Soft, Smooth, and Steady."
15 Keenan, "Harry Styles."
16 SammyJiss, "Question about English (US): What Does 'He Got No Chill' Mean?," *HiNative.com*, February 23, 2017, https://hinative.com/en-US/questions/1870056.
17 Urbandictionary.com, s.v. "No Chill" (6), https://www.urbandictionary.com/define.php?term=No+Chill&defid=7020609.
18 Massey, "Against Chill."
19 Stevenson, "Why Women."
20 Harry Styles, "Sign of the Times," on *Harry Styles*, Erskine/Columbia, April 7, 2017.

21 Andy Cush writes in *Spin*, "It's clear that this is Styles's attempt to distinguish himself as an artist with real depth." "Harry Styles' 'Sign of the Times' Is
Pompous, Overblown, and Too Long, and His Fans Are Gonna Love It," *Spin*,
April 7, 2017, http://www.spin.com/2017/04/harry-styles-sign-of-the-times
-review.

22 Crowe, "Harry Styles."

23 Crowe, "Harry Styles." The Rapture's 2006 single "WAYUH" characterizes and
mocks hipsters' stereotypical skepticism and emotional restraint: "They cross
their arms and stare you down / And drink and moan and diss." The Rapture,
"WAYUH," on *Pieces of People We Love*, Universal Motown, 2006.

24 "Loud-quiet-loud" is a song form associated with the modern rock band the
Pixies (there is a group biopic titled *LoudQuietLoud*) and popularized by 1990s
grunge artists like Nirvana and the Smashing Pumpkins. The term comes from
Kurt Cobain's 1994 interview with *Rolling Stone*, where he described the Pixies'
influence on Nirvana's songwriting: "We used their sense of dynamics, being
soft and quiet and then loud and hard." "Sign" flips around the order of the
dynamics—quiet-loud-quiet rather than loud-quiet-loud. David Fricke, "Kurt
Cobain, The Rolling Stone Interview: Success Doesn't Suck," *Rolling Stone*,
January 27, 1994, http://www.rollingstone.com/music/news/kurt-cobain-the
-rolling-stone-interview-19940127.

25 Paul Sexton, "Harry Styles Ends Ed Sheeran's Reign atop U.K. Singles Chart,"
Billboard, April 14, 2017, http://www.billboard.com/articles/columns/chart
-beat/7760411/harry-styles-tops-ed-sheeran-uk-singles-chart.

26 The Chainsmokers, "Closer," on *Collage*. Disruptor/Columbia, 2016; Ed
Sheeran, "Shape of You," Rokstone Studios, January 6, 2017. Readers familiar
with my previous book, *Resilience and Melancholy*, may notice that these chill
songs treat their soars similarly to the way melancholic songs do (they tone
down their intensity). The difference between chill and melancholy lies in two
related features: (1) their differing approaches to hegemonic relations of subordination and (2) their perceived economic rationality. First, chill supports
and syncs up with large-scale patterns of domination and relations of subordination, whereas melancholy does not rationally sync up with them. Whether a
behavior counts as chill or melancholy depends on the body and the identity of
the person performing that behavior. As I argued in *Resilience and Melancholy*,
the same behavior will appear to be resilient when attributed to white women
but melancholic when attributed to black women. Second, as I have argued in
both my analysis of Taylor Swift in chapter 1 and in a post about Sia's "Cheap
Thrills" in *SoundingOut!*, chill is perceived to be economically rational even in
its defiance of no-holds-barred entrepreneurialism. Melancholy, on the other
hand, always appears economically irrational, even when it's the most economically rational decision possible given the subject's social location.

27 Cush, "Harry Styles."

28 Jonze, "Harry Styles Debuts."

29 Carson, "Gender of Sound."

30 I'm using "personhood" in the sense that political philosophers do to indicate

the status of full membership in society. Persons are both obligated to follow social rules and norms and recognized as deserving of those rules' and norms' protections; non- or subpersons are obligated to the former but seen as undeserving of the latter.

31 North, *From Myth to Icon*, 89.

32 *Phaedo* 84a, 68c, 69c.

33 *Phaedo* 62e.

34 Independence and autonomy are not ideals for Plato. Even the person free from the authority of other people is deserving of such freedom because he submits to the authority of the logos/good/true. As he writes in *Republic* 590c-d, "Therefore, to insure that someone like that is ruled by something similar to what rules the best person, we say that he ought to be the slave of that best person who has a divine ruler within himself. It isn't to harm the slave that we say he must be ruled, which is what Thrasymachus thought to be true of all subjects, but because it is better for everyone to be ruled by divine reason, preferably within himself and his own, otherwise imposed from without, so that as far as possible all will be alike and friends, governed by the same thing."

35 *Phaedo* 66b-e.

36 "Well, I think that when a moderate man comes upon the words or actions of a good man in his narrative, he'll be willing to report them as if he were that man himself, and he won't be ashamed of that kind of imitation" (*Republic* 396c).

37 North, *Sophrosyne*, 174.

38 Foucault, *History of Sexuality*, vol. 2, 87; emphasis added.

39 Jorgensen, "Takin' It to the Streets," 140.

40 North, *From Myth to Icon*, 106.

41 Foucault, *History of Sexuality*, vol. 1, 83.

42 *Republic* 591d. "ἁρμονίᾳ τινὶ ἡ σωφροσύνη ὡμοίωται" (*Republic* 431e). See also "καὶ τοῦ μὲν ἡρμοσμένου σώφρων τε καὶ ἀνδρεία" (*Republic* 410e).

43 North, *Sophrosyne*, 164. For more on Plato's debt to Pythagorean notions of musical proportion, especially with respect to the concept of sophrosyne, see J. S. Morrison, "The Origin of Plato's Philosopher-Statesman," *Classical Quarterly* 8 (1958): 198-218.

44 Philosopher Christopher Long argues that the *Republic* itself is organized as a "proaulion" or "'prelude to the song [nomos] that must be learned' (531d)" (74). In other words, the *Republic* itself is structured like a well-ordered, consonant song and thus exhibits sophrosyne because the part that should rule—the True—does in fact rule the composition of the dialogue. As Long explains, it is "a central trope of the Republic in which musical vocabulary lends compositional order to the discussion" (70) and to the concept of politics Socrates develops therein. Christopher P. Long, "Socrates and the Politics of Music: Preludes of the Republic," *Polis* 24, no. 1 (2007): 70-90.

45 Stalley argues that "Sōphrosunē will consist in an agreement and harmony among the parts, whereby appetite and spirit willingly accept the rule of reason (442c-d). There is an important link between the order and harmony of the soul and that of music, but it is not to be understood, in Eryximachus's way, as

a balance between opposites. The key point is that reason must be in control. Only then can the soul as a whole and its individual parts achieve their good" (203). Richard Stalley, "Sophrosyne in Symposium," in *Proceedings I of X Symposium Platonicum* of the International Plato Society (Pisa, July 15–20, 2013), 201–7; A. Domanski, "The Heart of a Healthy Constitution," *Phronimon* 1 (2003): 1–17, http://repository.up.ac.za/bitstream/handle/2263/11519/Domanski_Platonic.pdf?sequence=1; and G. M. A. Grube, "Plato's Theory of Beauty," *Monist* 37, no. 2 (April 1927): 269–88.

46   Mathiesen, "Greek Music Theory," 116.

47   This is consistent with what Rancière says about Plato's political philosophy: "Philosophy's atomic project, as summed up in Plato, is to replace the arithmetical order, the order of more or less that regulates the exchange of perishable goods and human woes, with the divine order of *geometric proportion* that regulates the real good, the common good that is virtually each person's advantage without being to anyone's disadvantage.... In the city and in the soul, as in the science of surfaces, volumes, and stars, philosophy strives to replace arithmetical equality with geometric equality" (*Disagreement*, 15; emphasis added).

48   This is why he disagrees with Pythagoras's theory of harmony, which reverses the proper order between material structure and audible output. Thomas Mathiesen, an expert in ancient Greek music theory, writes that "in the Republic, the Laws, and the Timaeus, Plato was especially influenced by the Pythagorean tradition in his treatments of music" ("Greek Music Theory," 115). According to Plato, Pythagoras "put[s] ears before the intelligence" (*Republic* 531a), placing disproportionate emphasis on auditory perception and insufficient emphasis on mathematical proportion (or, "consideration of . . . numbers" [531c]). So Plato is basically arguing that Pythagoras got it right, except in this one detail, taking the sound before the number.

49   This informs the distinction Plato draws between philosophy and sophistry in *Symposium*. What comes out of the mouth of sophists may sound identical to what comes out of the mouth of philosophers — the difference is in the relationship between the body/soul of the speaker and the sounds that come out of his mouth. A sophist is immoderate because the "wisdom" of his words does not correspond to a proportionately ordered body — he can produce words that sound wise, but only through immoderate bodily practices (i.e., bodily practices that don't reflect the proportions expressed in the Good as represented on the divided line). In this way, the sophist is like the aulos (αυλους) player, a figure who appears a lot in the *Symposium* (see 215b, 212c, 176e).

50   Shannon Winnubst reminds us that "neoliberals are not ancient Greeks" because "neoliberal practices of pleasure, freedom, and truth . . . diverge widely from those of the ancient Greeks" (Winnubst, "Queer Thing," 88, 91). Both neoliberals and ancient Greeks (in this case, Plato) focus pleasure, freedom, and truth around practices of harmonious sophrosyne — but "harmonious" means something entirely different in each context. So neoliberals both are and are not ancient Greeks.

51   See Winnubst, *Way Too Cool*.

217

52   Dilts, "From Entrepreneur of the Self."

53   Hull, "Kant on Big Data?"

54   Stanisevski, "Agonistic Moderation," 16.

55   Guest Contributor, "Risk in Moderation."

56   As some scholars of neoliberalism have argued, "blackness" comes to be identified with and as risk. Given the general criminalization of blackness, being black is generally risky enough in itself, and it intensifies the risk of other transgressions. For example, in their May 30, 2015, report, the *Washington Post* found that in the first six months of 2015, of the 385 fatal shootings by police, about half the victims were white, half minority. But the demographics shifted sharply among the unarmed victims, two-thirds of whom were black or Hispanic. Overall, blacks were killed at three times the rate of whites or other minorities when adjusting by the population of the census tracts where the shootings occurred. It's three times as risky to be black than it is to be any other race. As cases like Jonathan Ferrell's demonstrate (he was killed by a Charlotte, North Carolina, police officer after requesting assistance because he was in a car accident), black people don't have to do anything illegal, or even questionable, to be treated as an unacceptable risk in need of quarantine. In fact, even entrepreneurial risk is disproportionately risky for black people: police officers thought Eric Garner's small business selling cigarettes was such an imminent threat to their safety that it justified the use of deadly force. Similarly, Lester Spence argues that "although the drug gangs that quickly fill the vacuum left by manufacturers do generate a certain type of 'entrepreneur'—the hustler represented by Ace Hood—that particular entrepreneur is routinely victimized and punished by government" (Spence, *Knocking the Hustle*, 38). Blackness may be so risky that it can make neoliberal cost/benefit calculus an impossible venture. Especially when combined with other risks like low socioeconomic status or nonbinary gender, the cost of insuring against or moderating the risks of blackness may never outweigh the benefits.

57   Foucault, *Birth of Biopolitics*, 118.

58   Stanisevski, "Agonistic Moderation," 6–7.

59   Schatman and Lebovits, "Transformation of the 'Profession' of Pain Medicine," 453.

60   Giordano and Schatman, "Ethical Insights to Rapprochement," E266; emphasis added.

61   Stanisevski, "Agonistic Moderation," 15; emphasis added.

62   Pan, "New Yuppies."

63   For example, Mills and Pateman argue that we ought "to recognize gender itself as a political system established by the contract" (*Contract and Domination*, 90).

64   Spence, *Knocking the Hustle*, 139.

65   Browne, *Dark Matters*, 140.

66   Browne, *Dark Matters*, 147.

67   "The successful card applicant must strategize as an economic, rational actor, for example, by venturing outside of the state only for travel that is state sanc-

tioned and calculating the probable consequences for travel that does not fall under that category" (Browne, *Dark Matters*, 147).

68 Browne, *Dark Matters*, 144.

69 Carson, "Gender of Sound," 126.

70 Carson, "Gender of Sound," 130.

71 "High vocal pitch goes together with talkativeness to characterize a person who is deviant from or deficient in the masculine ideal of self-control" (Carson, "Gender of Sound," 119).

72 Carson, "Gender of Sound," 126.

73 As Judith Peraino puts it, moderation "tunes the soul to the cosmic scale (rather than the physical body)" (*Listening to the Sirens*, 33).

74 Carson, "Gender of Sound," 120.

75 Mathiesen, *Apollo's Lyre*, 209.

76 Carson, "Gender of Sound," 126.

77 X-Ray Spex, "Oh Bondage, Up Yours!," Virgin, September 30, 1977.

78 Rebecca Solnit, *Men Explain Things to Me* (Chicago: Haymarket, 2014).

79 Solnit, "Listen Up."

80 Caplan-Bricker, "Louder Than Trolls."

81 Anne Helen Peterson, *Too Fat, Too Slutty, Too Loud: The Rise and Reign of the Unruly Woman* (New York: Penguin, 2017).

82 Hess, "Why Old Men."

83 Journalist Emma Barnett argues that these videos create the perception that "it's OK to be strong, brave, and loud." Emma Barnett, "I'm a 'Loud,' 'Feisty,' and 'Childless' Woman. Hate Me Already?," *Telegraph*, July 9, 2015, http://www.telegraph.co.uk/women/womens-life/11726748/Im-a-loud-feisty-and-childless-woman-Hate-me-already.html.

84 I'm using the terms "woman" and "women" because nonbinary people aren't as consistently and intensely praised for speaking up about cissexism. These post-feminist narratives about women's envoicement generally recenter cisbinary notions of gender difference and sexism (e.g., as something that men perpetrate against women, on the assumption that these are two clearly different categories) and end up further marginalizing nonbinary people.

85 Heath, Flynn, and Holt, "Women, Find Your Voice."

86 Goldberg, "Feminism's Toxic Twitter Wars."

87 "Masking" is the audio engineering term for frequencies that cancel each other out. This happens when frequencies have exactly opposite phase patterns: frequency A is at a peak when frequency B is at a valley, and vice versa.

88 Beyoncé, "Solange."

89 You could call variability something like dynamism, but, given the focus of this chapter on musical dynamics (loudness and softness), I thought that term would be too confusing.

90 Loud mixes compress audio files so that the amplitude of all the frequencies is (more or less) uniform. Or, as Sreedhar puts it, compression "reduc[es] the dynamic range of a song so that the entire song could be amplified to a greater extent before it pushed the physical limits of the medium. . . . Peak levels were

brought down . . . [and] the entire waveform was amplified." Sreedhar, "Future of Music."

91 "About," *Dynamic Range Day*, http://dynamicrangeday.co.uk/about, accessed January 14, 2015.

92 Sreedhar, "Future of Music."

93 See Goldberg, "Feminism's Toxic Twitter Wars"; Mark Fisher, "Exiting the Vampire Castle," *Open Democracy UK*, November 24, 2013, https://www .opendemocracy.net/ourkingdom/mark-fisher/exiting-vampire-castle, accessed January 16, 2015; and Trudy, "Mainstream White Feminism, Racism, and Claims of Black 'Toxicity,'" *Gradient Lair* (blog), January 31, 2014, http://www .gradientlair.com/post/75148751381/bigotry-not-twitter-makes-feminism-toxic.

94 Sreedhar, "Future of Music."

95 Beltran, "Racial Presence versus Racial Justice," 141.

96 Beltran, "Racial Presence versus Racial Justice," 143.

97 Wilson, "Our Final Answer on 'Too Many Women.'"

98 See, for example, Lencore's office sound masking products: http://www.lencore .com/ResourceCenter/CommonResources/PopularResources/BasicsofSound Masking.aspx.

99 McKittrick, "Black Sense of Place."

100 McKittrick, *Demonic Grounds*.

101 For more on parrhesia, see Michel Foucault, *Fearless Speech*, ed. Joseph Pearson (Los Angeles: Semiotext(e), 2001).

102 McKittrick, "On Algorithms," 11:37–43.

103 See Safiya Noble, *Algorithms of Oppression* (New York: New York University Press, 2018).

104 McKittrick, "Mathematics Black Life," 24–25.

105 McKittrick, "Mathematics Black Life," 25.

106 Echoing Silvia Federici's work in *Caliban and the Witch*, which argues that European persecution of devil-worship and witchcraft were central to early capitalism's enclosure of the commons, the "demonic" in demonic calculus em- phasizes its relationship to perceptual coding, which was invented as a way to efficiently enclose bandwidth. The "demonic" is what must get coded out to allow for the efficient reproduction of white supremacist patriarchal distribu- tions of personhood-as-property.

107 Harris-Perry, "Call and Response."

108 Gaunt, "Beyonce's Lemonade"

109 Beyoncé, "6 Inch," on *Lemonade*, Parkwood, 2016; Beyoncé, "Formation," on *Lemonade*, Parkwood, 2016.

110 Lordi, "Beyoncé's Other Women."

111 Lordi, "Beyoncé's Other Women."

112 Lordi, "Beyoncé's Other Women."

113 See James, *Resilience and Melancholy*, 43–47, for the argument about soars rep- resenting entrepreneurial risk.

114 Robinson, "How Beyonce's 'Lemonade.'"

115 For more on the aesthetics of black women's strip club dancing, see Stallings, *Funk the Erotic*.

116 Like most of Beyoncé's songs, "Formation" is a complicated track with possibly contradictory messages, some more progressive and some less so. My analysis here focuses only on one specific component of the song: its use of repetition in the lyrics and the large-scale form of the song.

117 Morgan, "Beyoncé, Black Feminist Art."

118 Julious, "Beyoncé: Formation."

119 Robinson, "We Slay."

120 Keleta-Mae, "Get What's Mine."

121 Keleta-Mae reinforces a similar reading of "Formation": "In 'Formation,' black women's bodies are literally choreographed into lines and borders that permit them to physically be both inside and outside of a multitude of vantage points. And what that choreography reveals is the embodiment of a particular kind of 21st Century black feminist freedom in the United States of America; one that is ambitious, spiritual, decisive, sexual, capitalist, loving, and communal."

122 Thurman, "Beyoncé Steps into the Black Feminist Cypher."

123 Carson, "Gender of Sound," 126.

124 Robinson, "How Beyonce's 'Lemonade.'"

125 Robinson, "How Beyonce's 'Lemonade.'"

126 Ray-Harris "Beyoncé's *Lemonade*."

127 McKittrick and Weheliye, "808s and Heartbreak."

5. Social Physics and Quantum Physics

1 Mader, *Sleights of Reason*, 52–53.

2 Hacking, *Taming of Chance*, 110. See also Gustav Jahoda, "Quetelet and the Emergence of the Behavioral Sciences," *SpringerPlus* 4 (2015): 473, https://doi.org/10.1186/s40064-015-1261-7.

3 Pentland, *Social Physics*, 193. In the academic discipline of data science, "harmonization" refers to the compatibility of different data sets. For example, the Data Sharing for Demographic Research project at the University of Michigan defines data harmonization as "all efforts to combine data from different sources and provide users with a comparable view of data from different studies" (https://www.icpsr.umich.edu/icpsrweb/content/DSDR/harmonization.html). Harmonization can include something like modulating in the music theory sense (i.e., changing key): "In harmonization, this means moving from source variables — the original variables in the datasets of particular surveys — to target variables, i.e. the harmonized, common variable produced from the source variables" (http://link.springer.librarylink.uncc.edu/article/10.1007%2Fs11135-015-0215-z, membership required). This type of harmonization redefines variables from different studies so they are consistent with one another. Another type of harmonization refers to the compatibility of metadata across diverse datasets. This metaphor uses the relationships among the overtones of a chord's primary frequencies as a model for the relation-

ships among metadata using different datasets. Like overtones, this metadata can fall into either rational or irrational relationships. See Eugene Kolker et al., "Toward More Transparent and Reproducible Omics Studies through a Common Metadata Checklist and Data Publications," *Big Data* 1, no. 4 (December 2013): 196–201, https://doi.org.10.1089/big.2013.0039.

4   In his review of Pentland's book, Nicholas Carr calls this Pentland's "statistical model of society." "The Limits of Social Engineering," *MIT Technology Review*, April 16, 2014, https://www.technologyreview.com/s/526561/the-limits-of-social-engineering.

5   Halford and Savage, "Speaking Sociologically with Big Data," 1145.

6   James, *Resilience and Melancholy.*

7   *Masschallenge*, "Resonance."

8   Pentland even makes *biological* claims about consonant idea flow. First, he uses primate vocal communications as an example (*Social Physics*, 62–63), suggesting that such consonance is evolutionary rather than artificial. Second, arguing that "doing the same thing in synchrony with others . . . our bodies release endorphins" (64), he suggests that our ability to perceive rational, consonant harmony is somehow "natural" and not, as Steve Reich emphasizes, something we learn to recognize — which is odd, given that Pentland's focus is on how individuals learn and adopt new rhythmic patterns.

9   Newman, "Power Laws," 1.

10 See New England Complex Systems Institute, "Power Laws," 2011, http://www.necsi.edu/guide/concepts/powerlaw.html.

11 See Eric W. Weisstein, "Zipf's Law," *Wolfram Math World*, http://mathworld.wolfram.com/ZipfsLaw.html, accessed December 15, 2017. See also J. B. Carroll, "Diversity of Vocabulary and the Harmonic Series Law of Word-Frequency Distribution," *Psychological Record* 2 (1938): 379–86.

12 Pentland's concept of influence appeals to older, pre-acoustic theories of resonance as mutual affection. According to Pentland, "the basic idea of influence is that an outcome in one entity can cause an outcome in another" (*Social Physics*, 241); more specifically, influence is the principle that "an entity's state is affected by its network neighbors' states and changes accordingly. Each entity in the network has a specifically defined strength of influence over every other entity and, equivalently, each relationship can be weighted according to this strength" (243).

13 Even though social physics focuses lots of attention on human speech and verbal interaction, "it was engagement that mattered, not what they said" (Pentland, *Social Physics*, 110); social physics works "without listening to the words" (133).

14 Mills and Pateman, *Contract and Domination*, 17.

15 Locke, *Two Treatises of Government.*

16 Pateman, *Sexual Contract*, 55.

17 See Foucault, *Birth of Biopolitics*, 223–24.

18 Pentland, *Social Physics*, 180; emphasis added.

19 Pentland, *Social Physics*, 129.

20 Pentland, *Social Physics*, 226; emphasis added.

21 Pentland distinguishes between rational free will and rationally patterned behavior as follows: traditional concepts of rational free will are concepts of "rational reflection based directly on our individual biological drives or inborn morals," whereas rational idea flow is a matter of "what our peer community agrees is valuable" (*Social Physics*, 60)—i.e., normalization.

22 Pateman, *Sexual Contract*, 149.

23 Pateman, *Sexual Contract*, 150.

24 Pentland, *Social Physics*, 229.

25 Mills and Pateman, *Contract and Domination*, 20.

26 Marx, "On the Jewish Question"; Mills and Pateman, *Contract and Domination*.

27 Mill, *On Liberty*, 76.

28 Pentland, *Social Physics*, 141; emphasis added.

29 As Nicholas Carr points out in his critique of Pentland's book, social physics "ignores the deep, structural sources of social ills." It replaces the old model of abstraction—stereotypes—with a new model of abstraction; like the old one, this new model of abstraction is an idealized model that abstracts away ongoing relations of systemic subordination and domination. Pentland's claim to surpass obsolete social identities and perceive more fine-grained phenomena is, in effect, an upgrade on "colorblind"-style racism. "Limits of Social Engineering."

30 This range has a lot more exploration relative to engagement. As Pentland puts it, "one reason human culture grows while ape culture remains stagnant may be that, unlike apes, we occasionally choose to row against the flow of ideas that surround us and dip into another stream" (*Social Physics*, 45).

31 Pesic and Volmar, "Pythagorean Longings"; emphasis added.

32 Pesic and Volmar, "Pythagorean Longings."

33 Greene, *Elegant Universe*, 7.

34 Greene, *Elegant Universe*, 82.

35 Alexander, *Jazz of Physics*, 89. Emphasis added.

36 Alexander, *Jazz of Physics*, 2–3.

37 Alexander, *Jazz of Physics*, 89, 147.

38 Greene, *Elegant Universe*, 101.

39 Greene, *Elegant Universe*, 101–2.

40 Greene, *Elegant Universe*, 102.

41 Alexander, *Jazz of Physics*, 92. These descriptions of a "symphonic orchestra" of "harmonious vibrations" (120) that "resonat[e] with, or vibrat[e] in sync with" (71) one another use notions of musical harmony as rational phase relationships to translate the mathematical function known as the Fourier Transform into nonmathematical terms. The Fourier Transform is an operation for combining different frequencies or waveforms to create a new waveform. Because audio engineers apply the Fourier Transform to actual, not metaphorical, soundwaves, it makes sense for Alexander to use sonic harmony as a metaphor for this mathematical function (111–13).

42 Greene, *Elegant Universe*, 20.

43 Alexander, *Jazz of Physics*, 166; emphasis added.

44 George Gibson, "Pythagorean Intervals," UConn Physics website, http://www
.phys.uconn.edu/~gibson/Notes/Section3_2/Sec3_2.htm, accessed February
14, 2019; emphasis added.

45 Greene, *Elegant Universe*, 79.

46 Alexander, *Jazz of Physics*, 7.

47 For more on the role of Pythagorean analogies in early string theory, see Pesic,
Music and the Making of Modern Science, 270–80.

48 Mader, *Sleights of Reason*, 3.

49 Mader, *Sleights of Reason*, 5.

50 Milli Vanilli was an Afro-German pop duo that infamously had to return their
1990 Best New Artist Grammy after it was revealed that Fab Morvan and Rob
Pilatus didn't actually sing on their album despite being credited in the liner
notes. Music critics tend to believe that their manager, Frank Farian, used Morvan and Pilatus as figureheads to market the sounds of less-photogenic backup
singers. (See, for example, Chuck Philips, "It's True: Milli Vanilli Didn't Sing,"
Los Angeles Times, November 16, 1990, http://articles.latimes.com/1990-11-16
/entertainment/ca-4894_1_milli-vanilli/2.)

51 Mader, *Sleights of Reason*, 8.

52 Alexander, *Jazz of Physics*, 71.

53 Mader, *Sleights of Reason*, 48.

54 As Pesic explains, "The experimental detection of a high-energy particle requires the observation of what is still called resonance, namely finding in particle data the same bell-shaped response curve first derived from a glass reso-
nating at its natural frequency" (*Music and the Making of Modern Science*, 280).

55 Physicists might argue that this kind of abstraction actually describes reality
itself. I'm a philosopher, however, and I know that abstractions are historical
and local: what Westerners understand as "math" is just one type of quantitative abstraction, and its different types of quantitative abstraction—geometric,
algebraic, probabilistic, etc.—each arose in the context of specific epistemic
frameworks. Math is just one type of abstraction we can use to understand the
physical world. The question is why we use it and what it does for us when we
do. So if your objection to this part of my project is that I'm doing philosophy
instead of physics, well—yes, I am. This may just be reducible to the stereotypical philosophy/physics beef about who really understands how the universe
works.

56 Arguing that "my vision of a musical universe was more than an analogy" (*Jazz
of Physics*, 156–57) because "the structures in the universe started out as sound
waves" (154), Alexander explains how some physicists think "the universe is
musical" (207), at least in its origins. From this perspective, order emerged
from nonordered plasma as the force of particle interaction (photons) created
expansions in matter, which were then countered by gravitational compression (151); these patterns of condensation and rarefaction were the "original
quantum sound" (154) whose echoes we can find in cosmic background radi-
ation (152).

57 See, for example, Stoever, *Sonic Color Line*, on the listening ear.
58 McKittrick and Weheliye, "808s and Heartbreak," 13.
59 McKittrick and Weheliye, "808s and Heartbreak," 13.
60 In this respect, normalized statistical distributions are just another capitalist/consumer technology that black people have repurposed in ways that express black cultural and aesthetic values. As Weheliye and McKittrick put it, "one way to understand Black culture's relationship to technology is through the way that especially Black music/sound humanizes by enfleshing supposedly discrete, abstract, rigid, inhuman machines by making them usable in heretofore nonexistent modalities, whether this is the turntable, the player piano, or the 808" ("808s and Heartbreak," 26).
61 McKittrick and Weheliye, "808s and Heartbreak," 15.
62 McKittrick and Weheliye, "808s and Heartbreak," 27.
63 Timbaland feat. Brandy, "808," on *Timbaland Thursdays*, Interscope 2011.
64 McKittrick and Weheliye, "808s and Heartbreak," 14.
65 McKittrick and Weheliye, "808s and Heartbreak," 14.
66 McKittrick and Weheliye, "808s and Heartbreak," 33.
67 "Intonation is not just the enunciation and performance of 'look!'; intonation ('look!') is reflexly felt (heartbreak) (which is not exactly affect, is it, but can be studied as such?)" (McKittrick and Weheliye, "808s and Heartbreak," 30).
68 Davis, *Women, Race, and Class*, 1981.
69 McKittrick and Weheliye, "808s and Heartbreak," 18.
70 Harvey, "Neoliberalism as Creative Destruction."
71 Harvey, "Neoliberalism as Creative Destruction"
72 McKittrick and Weheliye, "808s and Heartbreak," 23.
73 McKittrick and Weheliye, "808s and Heartbreak," 23.
74 James, "Cloudy Logic," 157.
75 James, "Cloudy Logic," 159.
76 Gilmore, *Golden Gulag*.
77 McKittrick and Weheliye, "808s and Heartbreak," 34.
78 Theorists from Orlando Patterson to Lisa Guenther argue that the prohibition and prevention of social relations among black people is a key feature of white supremacy.

Conclusion

1 See Pateman, *Sexual Contract*; Mills and Pateman, *Contract and Domination*.
2 See Erlmann, *Reason and Resonance*.

BIBLIOGRAPHY

Abbate, Carolyn. "Music—Drastic or Gnostic?" *Critical Inquiry* 30, no. 3 (Spring 2004): 505–36.

Acoustical Society of America. "About Acoustics." https://web.archive.org/web /20151210165950/http://acousticalsociety.org/about_acoustics.

Adeyemi, Kemi. "Straight Leanin': Sounding Black Life at the Intersection of Hip-Hop and Big Pharma." *SoundingOut!*, September 21, 2015. https://soundstudies blog.com/2015/09/21/hip-hop-and-big-pharma/.

Ahmed, Sara. "Some Preliminary Remarks on the Founding Gestures of the 'New Materialism.'" *European Journal of Women's Studies* 15, no. 1 (2008): 23–39. https://doi.org/10.1177/1350506807084854.

Alexander, Stephon. *The Jazz of Physics.* New York: Basic, 2016.

Al-Saji, Alia. "A Phenomenology of Critical Ethical Vision." *Chiasmi International* 11 (2009): 375–98.

Appiah, Kwame Anthony. "Is the Post- in Postmodernism the Post- in Postcolonial?" *Critical Inquiry* 17, no. 2 (Winter 1991): 336–57.

Attali, Jacques. "An Interview with Jacques Attali." Edited by Fredric Jameson and Brian Massumi. *Social Text* 7 (Spring–Summer 1983): 3–18.

Attali, Jacques. "Music as a Predictive Science." *Hearing Modernity*, n.d. http:// hearingmodernity.org/papers/music-as-a-predictive-science/. Accessed February 14, 2019.

Attali, Jacques. "Music as a Predictive Science." Lecture given at Harvard University, April 21, 2014. YouTube. https://www.youtube.com/watch?v=_evJY-GZ7yc.

Attali, Jacques. *Noise: The Political Economy of Music.* Translated by Brian Massumi. Minneapolis: University of Minnesota Press, 1984.

Babb, Fletcher, Eric Sundermann, and Drew Millard. "Lean on Me." *Noisey*, October 24, 2013. https://noisey.vice.com/en_us/article/6anpbr/lean-on-me.

Barad, Karen. *Meeting the Universe Halfway: Quantum Physics and the Entanglement of Matter and Meaning.* Durham, NC: Duke University Press, 2007.

Barad, Karen. "Posthuman Performativity: Toward an Understanding of How Matter Comes to Matter." *Signs: Journal of Women in Culture and Society* 28, no. 3 (Spring 2003): 801–31.

Beltran, Cristina. "Racial Presence versus Racial Justice: The Affective Power of an Aesthetic Condition." *Du Bois Review* 11, no. 1 (2014): 137–58.

Bennett, Jane. *Vibrant Matter: A Political Ecology of Things.* Durham, NC: Duke University Press, 2009.

Berlant, Lauren. *Cruel Optimism*. Durham, NC: Duke University Press, 2011.

Beyoncé. "Solange." *Interview Magazine*, January 10, 2017. http://www.interview magazine.com/music/solange.

Billboard Staff. "The 15 Best Chainsmokers Songs." *Billboard*, September 27, 2016. https://www.billboard.com/articles/news/dance/7525578/chainsmokers-songs -best-hits-list.

Bradley, Regina N. "I Been On: BaddieBey and Beyoncé's Sonic Masculinity." *SoundingOut!*, September 22, 2014. http://soundstudiesblog.com/2014/09/22 /i-been-on-baddiebey-and-beyonces-sonic-masculinity.

Braun, Bruce. "New Materialisms and Neoliberal Natures." *Antipode* 47, no. 1 (2015): 1–14.

Browne, Simone. *Dark Matters: On the Surveillance of Blackness*. Durham, NC: Duke University Press, 2015.

Caplan-Bricker, Nora. "Louder Than Trolls." *Slate*, May 17, 2016. http://www.slate .com/articles/double_x/doublex/2016/05/lindy_west_s_shrill_reviewed.html.

Carson, Anne. "The Gender of Sound." In *Glass, Irony, and God*, 119–42. New York: New Directions, 1992.

Cavarero, Adriana. *For More Than One Voice: Toward a Philosophy of Vocal Expression*. Translated by Paul Kottman. Stanford, CA: Stanford University Press, 2005.

Chapman, Dale. *The Jazz Bubble: Neoclassical Jazz in Neoliberal Culture*. Berkeley: University of California Press, 2018.

Chow, Kat. "Video Calls Out Catcallers, but Cuts Out White Men." NPR *Code Switch*, November 1, 2014. https://www.npr.org/sections/codeswitch/2014/11 /01/360422087/hollaback-video-calls-out-catcallers-but-cuts-out-white-men.

Clayton, Jace. "Belfast Quartone Punks." *Negrophonic*, December 10, 2004. https:// web.archive.org/web/20140202092403/http://negrophonic.com/words /archives/archive_2004-w50.php.

Coole, Diana, and Samantha Frost. *New Materialisms: Ontology, Agency, and Politics*. Durham, NC: Duke University Press, 2010.

Cooper, Melinda. *Family Values*. Cambridge, MA: MIT Press, 2017.

Crawley, Ashon. *Blackpentecostal Breath: The Aesthetics of Possibility*. New York: Fordham University Press, 2016.

Crawley, Ashon. "Stayed/Freedom/Hallelujah." *LA Review of Books*, May 10, 2015. https://lareviewofbooks.org/article/stayed-freedom-hallelujah/.

Crowe, Cameron. "Harry Styles' New Direction." *Rolling Stone*, April 18, 2017. https://www.rollingstone.com/music/features/harry-styles-opens-up-about -famous-flings-honest-new-lp-w476928.

Darling-Hammond, Linda. "Race, Inequality and Educational Accountability: The Irony of 'No Child Left Behind.'" *Race Ethnicity and Education* 10, no. 3 (September 2007): 245–60.

Davies, Will. "Thoughts on the Sociology of Brexit." Political Economy Research Center, June 24, 2016. http://www.perc.org.uk/project_posts/thoughts-on-the -sociology-of-brexit.

Davis, Angela. *Blues Legacies and Black Feminism*. New York: Vintage, 1998.

Davis, Angela. *Women, Race, and Class*. New York: Vintage, 1983.

Deleuze, Gilles, and Félix Guattari. *A Thousand Plateaus*. Translated by Brian Massumi. Minneapolis: University of Minnesota Press, 1987.

Dilts, Andrew. "From Entrepreneur of the Self to Care of the Self." *Foucault Studies* 12 (October 2011): 130–46.

Dotson, Kristie. "How Is This Paper Philosophy?" *Comparative Philosophy* 3, no. 1 (2012): 3–29.

Drott, Eric. "Rereading Jacques Attali's *Bruits*." *Critical Inquiry* 41, no. 4 (Summer 2015): 721–56.

Du Bois, W. E. B. "Sociology Hesitant." *boundary 2* 27, no. 3 (Fall 2000): 37–44.

Eidsheim, Nina Sun. *Sensing Sound*. Durham, NC: Duke University Press, 2017.

Epstein, Steven. "Mirroring and Mattering: Science, Politics, and the New Feminist Materialism." *LA Review of Books*, October 5, 2016. https://lareviewofbooks .org/article/mirroring-and-mattering-science-politics-and-the-new-feminist -materialism.

Erlmann, Veit. *Reason and Resonance: A History of Modern Aurality*. Cambridge, MA: MIT Press, 2011.

Evans, Fred. *The Multivoiced Body: Society and Communication in the Age of Diversity*. New York: Columbia University Press, 2011.

Fallon, Kevin. "Taylor Swift's 'Shake It Off' Is Disappointing." *Daily Beast*, August 18, 2014. http://www.thedailybeast.com/articles/2014/08/18/taylor-swift-s-shake -it-off-is-disappointing.html.

Federici, Sylvia. *Caliban and the Witch*. Chico, CA: AK, 2004.

Foucault, Michel. *The Birth of Biopolitics*. Translated by Graham Burchell. New York: Picador, 2004.

Foucault, Michel. *The History of Sexuality*. Vol. 1. Translated by Robert Hurley. New York: Vintage, 1990.

Foucault, Michel. *The History of Sexuality*. Vol. 2. Translated by Robert Hurley. New York: Vintage, 1991.

Foucault, Michel. *The Order of Things*. New York: Vintage, 1994.

Foucault, Michel. *Security, Territory, Population*. Translated by Graham Burchell. New York: Picador, 2007.

Foucault, Michel. *Society Must Be Defended*. Translated by David Macey. New York: Picador, 2003.

Friedman, Milton, and Rose Friedman. *Capitalism and Freedom*. Chicago: University of Chicago Press, 1962.

Galloway, Alexander, and Jason LaRiviere. "Compression in Philosophy." *boundary 2* 44, no. 1 (2017): 125–47.

Gaunt, Kyra. "Beyoncé's Lemonade Is Smashing." *TedFellows* (blog), May 12, 2016. https://fellowsblog.ted.com/beyonc%C3%A9s-lemonade-is-smashing-1cc70b da2197.

Gill, Rosalind. "A Genealogical Approach to Idealized Male Body Imagery." *Paragraph* 26 (2003): 187–97.

Gillespie, John Jr. "Black Power as Thing Power: The Limits of Bennet's Eco-

Philosophy." *So Solid Philosophy*, March 6, 2017. https://solidphilosophy.word press.com/2017/03/06/black-power-as-thing-power-the-limits-of-bennets-eco -philosophy/.

Gilmore, Ruth Wilson. *Golden Gulag: Prisons, Surplus, Crisis, and Opposition in Globalizing California*. Berkeley: University of California Press, 2007.

Giordano, James, and Michael Schatman. "Ethical Insights to Rapprochement in Pain Care: Bringing Stakeholders Together in the Best Interest(s) of the Patient." *Pain Physician* 12 (2009): E265–E275.

Grosz, Elizabeth. *Chaos, Territory, Art: Deleuze and the Framing of the Earth*. New York: Columbia University Press, 2008.

Grosz, Elizabeth. *Nick of Time: Politics, Evolution, and the Untimely*. Durham, NC: Duke University Press, 2004.

Goldberg, Michelle. "Feminism's Toxic Twitter Wars." *The Nation*, February 17, 2014. http://www.thenation.com/article/feminisms-toxic-twitter-wars.

Gooding-Williams, Robert. *Look, A Negro!* London: Routledge, 2006.

Goodman, Steve. *Sonic Warfare*. Cambridge, MA: MIT Press, 2012.

Guest Contributor. "Risk in Moderation." *Experian Insights*, November 13, 2008. http://www.experian.com/blogs/insights/2008/11/risk-in-moderation.

Gunderson, Philip A. "Danger Mouse's Grey Album, Mash-Ups, and the Age of Composition." *Postmodern Culture* 15, no. 1 (2004). https://instruct.uwo.ca/mit /3771-001/MashUP_Danger%20Mouse_Gunderson.pdf.

Hacking, Ian. *The Taming of Chance*. Cambridge: Cambridge University Press, 1990.

Halberstam, J. Jack. *Gaga Feminism: Sex, Gender, and the End of Normal*. Boston: Beacon, 2012.

Halford, Susan, and Mike Savage. "Speaking Sociologically with Big Data: Symphonic Social Science and the Future for Big Data Research." *Sociology* 51, no. 6 (2017): 1132–48.

Hardesty, Larry. "Extracting Audio from Visual Information." MIT News, August 4, 2014. http://newsoffice.mit.edu/2014/algorithm-recovers-speech-from -vibrations-0804.

Harris-Perry, Melissa. "A Call and Response with Melissa Harris-Perry: The Pain and the Power of 'Lemonade.'" *Elle*, April 26, 2016. https://www.elle.com/culture /music/a35903/lemonade-call-and-response.

Harvey, David. "Neoliberalism as Creative Destruction." In *Annals of the American Academy of Political and Social Science*, vol. 610, *NAFTA and Beyond: Alternative Perspectives in the Study of Global Trade and Development*, 22–44. Thousand Oaks, CA: SAGE, 2007.

Harvey, Eric. "Station to Station: The Past, Present, and Future of Streaming Music." *Pitchfork*, April 16, 2014. http://pitchfork.com/features/cover-story/9383 -station-to-station-the-past-present-and-future-of-streaming-music/3.

Havis, Devonya. "'Now, How Do You Sound?': Considering a Different Philosophical Praxis." *Hypatia* 29, no. 1 (Winter 2014): 237–52.

Heath, Kathryn, Jill Flynn, and Mary Davis Holt. "Women, Find Your Voice." *Harvard Business Review*, June 2014. https://hbr.org/2014/06/women-find-your -voice.

Helmholtz, Hermann von. *On the Sensation of Tone.* Translated by Alexander J. Ellis. London: Longmans, Green, 1912.

Hess, Amanda. "Why Old Men Find Young Women's Voices So Annoying." *Slate,* January 7, 2013. http://www.slate.com/blogs/xx_factor/2013/01/07/vocal_fry _and_valley_girls_why_old_men_find_young_women_s_voices_so_annoying .html.

Hicks, Mason. "Audio Compression Basics." *Universal Audio* (blog), November 24, 2009. https://www.uaudio.com/blog/audio-compression-basics.

Horning, Rob. "The Primitive Accumulation of Cool." *New Inquiry: Marginal Utility* (blog), June 4, 2013. https://thenewinquiry.com/blog/the-primitive -accumulation-of-cool.

Huffpost. "Molly Is a Drug & There Are a Lot of Songs about Molly." *Huffpost,* September 8, 2013. https://www.huffingtonpost.com/2013/09/05/molly-drug -songs_n_3874047.html.

Hull, Gordon. "Kant on Big Data?" *New apps* (blog), May 19, 2017. http://www.new appsblog.com/2017/05/kant-on-big-data.html#more.

Irigaray, Luce. *Speculum of the Other Woman.* Translated by Gillian C. Gill. Ithaca, NY: Cornell University Press, 1985.

Ishler, Julianne. "Chill Pop Is the New Music Trend That Isn't Going Anywhere." *Dose,* August 31, 2016.

Jackson, Zakiyyah Iman. "Outer Worlds: The Persistence of Race in Movement 'Beyond the Human.'" *GLQ: A Journal of Lesbian and Gay Studies* 21, nos. 2–3 (June 2015): 215–18.

Jacobsen, Finn. "An Elementary Introduction to Acoustics." Technical University of Denmark, November 2011. https://web.archive.org/web/20170809234543 /http://web-files.ait.dtu.dk/fjac/p_home_page/notes/Introduction_to _acoustics.pdf.

James, Robin. "Affective Resonance: On the Uses and Abuses of Music in and for Philosophy." *PhaenEx* 7, no. 2 (Fall–Winter 2012): 59–95.

James, Robin. "Cloudy Logic." *New Inquiry,* January 27, 2015. https://thenewinquiry .com/cloudy-logic.

James, Robin. "Is the Post- in Post-Identity the Post- in Post-Genre?" *Popular Music* 36, special issue no. 1, *The Critical Imperative* (January 2017): 21–32.

James, Robin. "Listening to Sounds in Post-Feminist Pop." *SoundingOut!,* February 15, 2016. https://soundstudiesblog.com/2016/02/15/listening-to-sounds-in-post -feminist-pop-music.

James, Robin. *Resilience and Melancholy: Pop Music, Feminism, Neoliberalism.* Winchester, UK: Zero, 2015.

James, Robin. "Robo-Diva R&B." *Journal of Popular Music Studies* 20, no. 4 (December 2008): 402–23.

Jonze, Tim. "Harry Styles Debuts Sign of the Times: Is He Really the New Bowie?" *Guardian,* April 7, 2017. https://www.theguardian.com/music/musicblog/2017 /apr/07/harry-styles-sign-of-the-times.

Julious, Britt. "Beyoncé: 'Formation.'" *Pitchfork: Best New Track,* February 7, 2016. https://pitchfork.com/reviews/tracks/17969-beyonce-formation.

Jorgensen, Beth. "Takin' It to the Streets: Culture War, Rhetorical Education, and Democratic Virtue." PhD diss., Iowa State University, 2002. https://lib.dr.iastate.edu/rtd/969/.

Keenan, Elizabeth. "Harry Styles, Teen Girls, and Critical Reception." *Bad Cover Version* (blog), April 21, 2017. https://badcoverversion.wordpress.com/2017/04/21/harry-styles-teen-girls-and-critical-reception.

Keleta-Mae, Naila. "Get What's Mine: 'Formation' Changes the Way We Listen to Beyonce Forever." *Noisey*, February 8, 2016. https://noisey.vice.com/en_us/article/6e48wm/beyonce-formation-op-ed-super-bowl-performance-2016.

Kennedy, Steve. "A Sonic Economy." *CTheory.net*, May 20, 2010. http://www.ctheory.net/articles.aspx?id=649.

Keohane, Robert. "Neoliberal Institutionalism." In *Security Studies: A Reader*, edited by Christopher W. Hughes and Lai Yew Meng, 157–64. New York: Routledge, 2011.

Kerr, Robert. "Compression and Oppression." *CTheory.net*, 2013. https://journals.uvic.ca/index.php/ctheory/article/view/14795/5669.

K-Hole. "Youth Mode: A Report on Freedom." 2013. http://khole.net/issues/youth-mode/.

Knouf, N. Adriana. *How Noise Matters to Finance*. Minneapolis: University of Minnesota Press, 2016.

Knowles, David. "Poll: Iowa Republicans Side with Obamas after Huckabee's Beyoncé Attack." *Bloomberg*, February 3, 2015. https://www.bloomberg.com/news/articles/2015-02-03/poll-iowa-republicans-side-with-obamas-after-huckabee-s-beyonc-attack.

Kupperman, Jacob. "The Chainsmokers Are the Boring Sort of Bad." *Stanford Daily*, April 13, 2017. https://www.stanforddaily.com/2017/04/13/the-chainsmokers-are-bad.

Leong, Diana. "The Mattering of Black Lives: Octavia Butler's Hyperempathy and the Promise of the New Materialisms." *Catalyst: Feminism, Theory, Technoscience* 2, no. 2 (2006): 1–35.

Lindsey, R. Bruce. "Report to the National Science Foundation on Conference on Education in Acoustics." *Journal of the Acoustic Society of America* 36 (1964): 2241–43.

Lipshutz, Jason. "Taylor Swift's 'Shake It Off' Single Review: The Country Superstar Goes Full Pop." *Billboard*, August 18, 2014. http://www.billboard.com/articles/review/track-review/6221814/taylor-swift-shake-it-off-single-review.

Locke, John. *Two Treatises of Government*. Cambridge: Cambridge University Press, 1988.

Lorde, Audre. *Sister Outsider: Essays and Speeches*. Berkeley: Ten Speed, 1984.

Lordi, Emily J. "Beyoncé's Other Women: Considering the Soul Muses of *Lemonade*." *Fader*, May 6, 2016. http://www.thefader.com/2016/05/06/beyonce-lemonade-women-soul-muses.

Lugones, María. "Playfulness, 'World'-Travelling, and Loving Perception." *Hypatia* 2, no. 2 (Summer 1987): 3–19.

Mader, Mary Beth. *Sleights of Reason: Norm, Bisexuality, Development*. Albany: SUNY Press, 2011.

Marx, Karl. *Capital*, vol. 1. In *Marx-Engels Reader*, 2nd ed., edited by Robert C. Trucker. New York: Norton, 1978.

Marx, Karl. "On the Jewish Question." In *Marx-Engels Reader*, 2nd ed., edited by Robert C. Trucker. New York: Norton, 1978.

Masschallenge. "Resonance." *Masschallenge*. https://web.archive.org/web/20180319 065810/https://masschallenge.org/startup/resonance.

Massey, Alana. "Against Chill." *Matter*, April 1, 2015. https://medium.com/matter /against-chill-930dfb60a577.

Mathiesen, Thomas. *Apollo's Lyre: Greek Music and Music Theory in Antiquity and the Middle Ages*. Lincoln: University of Nebraska Press, 2000.

Mathiesen, Thomas. "Greek Music Theory." In *The Cambridge History of Western Music Theory*, edited by Thomas Christensen, 107–35. Cambridge: Cambridge University Press, 2008.

McKittrick, Katherine. Abstract for "A Black Sense of Place: On Algorithms and Curiosities." Institute of Advanced Studies, Talking Points Seminar, April 24, 2017. http://www.ucl.ac.uk/institute-of-advanced-studies/ias-events/ias _talking_points_seminar_a_black_sense_of_place_on_algorithms_and _curiosities.

McKittrick, Katherine. *Demonic Grounds*. Minneapolis: University of Minnesota Press 2006.

McKittrick, Katherine. "Mathematics Black Life." *Black Scholar* 44, no. 2 (Summer 2014): 16–28. https://doi.org/10.1080/00064246.2014.11413684.

McKittrick, Katherine. "On Algorithms and Curiosities." Lecture at Duke Feminist Theory Seminar 2017. YouTube, May 8, 2017. https://www.youtube.com/watch?v =ggB3ynMjB34.

McKittrick, Katherine, and Alexander Weheliye. "808s and Heartbreak." *Propter Nos* 2, no. 1 (Fall 2017): 13–42.

McRobbie, Angela. "Post-Feminism and Popular Culture." *Feminist Media Studies* 4, no. 3 (2004): 255–64.

Mill, J. S. *On Liberty*. Indianapolis: Hackett, 1978.

Mills, Charles W. "Ideal Theory as Ideology." *Hypatia* 20, no. 3 (August 2005): 165–83.

Mills, Charles W. *The Racial Contract*. Ithaca, NY: Cornell University Press, 1997.

Mills, Charles W., and Carole Pateman. *Contract and Domination*. Cambridge: Polity, 2005.

Mitchell, Katharyne. *Crossing the Neoliberal Line: Pacific Rim Migration and the Metropolis*. Philadelphia: Temple University Press, 2004.

Molanphy, Chris. "Why Is the Chainsmokers' 'Closer' the Biggest Song in the Country?" *Slate*, August 26, 2016. http://www.slate.com/blogs/browbeat/2016 /08/26/why_the_chainsmokers_closer_featuring_halsey_is_no_1_on_the_hot _100.html.

Morgan, Joan. "Beyoncé, Black Feminist Art, and This Oshun Bidness." *Genius*,

April 30, 2016. https://genius.com/a/beyonce-black-feminist-art-and-this-oshun -bidness.

Mulvey, Laura. "Visual Pleasure and Narrative Cinema." *Screen* 16, no. 3 (Autumn 1975): 6–18.

Nash, Jennifer C. *The Black Body in Ecstasy*. Durham, NC: Duke University Press, 2014.

Nealon, Jeffrey. "Empire of the Intensities." *parallax* 8, no. 1 (2002): 78–91.

Newman, Mark E. J. "Power Laws, Pareto Distributions and Zipf's Law." *Contemporary Physics* 46, no. 5 (2005): 323–51.

North, Helen. *From Myth to Icon: Reflections of Greek Ethical Doctrine in Literature and Art*. Ithaca, NY: Cornell University Press, 1979.

North, Helen. *Sophrosyne: Self-Knowledge and Self-Restraint in Greek Literature*. Ithaca, NY: Cornell University Press, 1966.

Olson, Harry F. *Music, Physics, and Engineering*. New York: Dover, 1967.

Pan, J. C. "The New Yuppies." *New Republic*, August 1, 2017. https://newrepublic .com/article/143609/new-yuppies-how-aspirational-class-expresses-status-age -inequality.

Parikka, Jussi. "New Materialism as Media Theory: Medianatures and Dirty Matter." *Communication and Critical/Cultural Studies* 9, no. 1 (2012): 95–100.

Pateman, Carole. *The Sexual Contract*. Stanford, CA: Stanford University Press, 1988.

Pentland, Alex. *Social Physics: How Social Networks Can Make Us Smarter*. New York: Penguin, 2015.

Peraino, Judith A. *Listening to the Sirens: Musical Technologies of Queer Identity from Homer to Hedwig*. Berkeley: University of California Press, 2005.

Pesic, Peter. *Music and the Making of Modern Science*. Cambridge, MA: MIT Press, 2014.

Pesic, Peter, and Axel Volmar. "Pythagorean Longings and Cosmic Symphonies: The Musical Rhetoric of String Theory and the Sonification of Particle Physics." *Journal of Sonic Studies* 8 (2014). https://www.researchcatalogue.net/view/109371 /109372/0/53.

Peterson, Richard, and Rodger Kern. "Changing Highbrow Taste: From Snob to Omnivore." *American Sociological Review* 61, no. 5 (October 1996): 900–907.

Plato. *Phaedo*. In *The Complete Works of Plato*. Edited by John M. Cooper. Indianapolis: Hackett, 1997.

Plato. *Philebus*. In *The Complete Works of Plato*. Edited by John M. Cooper. Indianapolis: Hackett, 1997.

Plato. *Republic*. In *The Complete Works of Plato*. Edited by John M. Cooper. Indianapolis: Hackett, 1997.

Plato. *Republic*. (Greek.) Project Perseus. http://www.perseus.tufts.edu/hopper/text ?doc=Perseus%3atext%3a1999.01.0167.

Plato. *Symposium*. In *The Complete Works of Plato*. Edited by John M. Cooper. Indianapolis: Hackett, 1997.

Plato. *Timaeus*. In *The Complete Works of Plato*. Edited by John M. Cooper. Indianapolis: Hackett, 1997.

Rachiel, Daniel R. *The Science and Applications of Acoustics*. New York: Springer, 2006.

Rancière, Jacques. *Disagreement: Politics and Philosophy*. Translated by Jacqueline Rose. Minneapolis: University of Minnesota Press, 2004.

Ray-Harris, Ashley. "Beyoncé's *Lemonade* Isn't a Breakup Album, It's a Black Album." *av Club*, April 28, 2016. https://music.avclub.com/beyonce-s-lemonade -isn-t-a-breakup-album-it-s-a-black-1798246931.

Reich, Steve. "Music as a Gradual Process." Columbia Center for Teaching and Learning, n.d. http://ccnmtl.columbia.edu/draft/ben/feld/mod1/readings/reich .html, accessed November 22, 2013.

Richards, Chris. "Soft, Smooth, and Steady: How Xanax Turned American Music into Pill-Pop." *Washington Post*, April 20, 2017. https://www.washingtonpost .com/lifestyle/style/soft-smooth-and-steady-how-xanax-turned-american-music -into-pill-pop/2017/04/19/535a44de-1955-11e7-bcc2-7d1a0973e7b2_story .html.

Roberts, Tamara. "Michael Jackson's Kingdom: Music, Race, and the Sound of the Mainstream." *Journal of Popular Music Studies* 23, no. 1 (2011): 19–39.

Robinson, Zandria. "How Beyonce's 'Lemonade' Exposes Inner Lives of Black Women." *Rolling Stone*, April 28, 2016. https://www.rollingstone.com/music /music-news/how-beyonces-lemonade-exposes-inner-lives-of-black-women -36868.

Robinson, Zandria. "We Slay, Part I." *New South Negress*, February 7, 2016. http:// newsouthnegress.com/southernslayings/.

Rose, Tricia. *Black Noise*. Middletown, CT: Wesleyan University Press, 1994.

Rowe, David. "Rock Culture: The Dialectics of Life and Death." *Australian Journal of Cultural Studies* 3, no. 2 (1985): 127–37.

Schatman, Michael, and Allen Lebovits. "On the Transformation of the 'Profession' of Pain Medicine to the 'Business' of Pain Medicine: An Introduction to a Special Series." *Pain Medicine* 12, no. 3 (March 2011): 403–5.

Sexton, Jared. *Amalgamation Schemes: Antiblackness and the Critique of Multiracialism*. Minneapolis: University of Minnesota Press, 2011.

Sharpe, Christina. *In the Wake: On Blackness and Being*. Durham, NC: Duke University Press, 2016.

Shaviro, Steven. "Accelerationist Aesthetics: Necessary Inefficiency in Times of Real Subsumption." *e-flux* 46 (June 2013). http://www.e-flux.com/journal /accelerationist-aesthetics-necessary-inefficiency-in-times-of-real-subsumption.

Shaviro, Steven. *Post-Cinematic Affect*. London: Zero Books, 2011.

Solnit, Rebecca. "Listen Up, Women Are Telling Their Story Now." *Guardian*, December 30, 2014. http://www.theguardian.com/news/2014/dec/30/-sp -rebecca-solnit-listen-up-women-arc-telling-their-story-now.

Spence, Lester K. *Knocking the Hustle: Against the Neoliberal Turn in Black Politics*. New York: Punctum, 2015.

Spence, Lester K. *Stare in the Darkness: The Limits of Hip-Hop and Black Politics*. Minneapolis: University of Minnesota Press, 2011.

Sreedhar, Suhas. "The Future of Music: Part 1, Tearing Down the Wall of Noise."

235

IEEE Spectrum, August 1, 2007. http://spectrum.ieee.org/computing/software/the-future-of-music.

St. Felix, Doreen. "The Prosperity Gospel of Rihanna." *Pitchfork*, April 1, 2015. https://pitchfork.com/thepitch/724-the-prosperity-gospel-of-rihanna.

Stahl, Saul. "The Evolution of the Normal Distribution." *Mathematics Magazine* 79, no. 2 (April 2006): 97–113.

Stallings, L. H. *Funk the Erotic: Transaesthetics and Black Sexual Cultures*. Urbana: University of Illinois Press, 2015.

Stanisevski, Dragan. "Agonistic Moderation: Administrating with the Wisdom of Sophrosyne." *Administration and Society* 47, no. 1 (2015): 5–23.

Sterne, Jonathan. *The Audible Past: Cultural Origins of Sound Reproduction*. Durham, NC: Duke University Press, 2003.

Sterne, Jonathan. *MP3: The Meaning of a Format*. Durham, NC: Duke University Press, 2012. Kindle Ebook.

Stevenson, Alison. "Why Women Need to Drop the 'Chill' Act and Embrace the Hysterical." *Vice*, April 22, 2016. https://www.vice.com/en_us/article/5gj7mq/why-women-need-to-drop-the-chill-act-and-embrace-the-hysterical.

Stoever, Jennifer Lynn. *The Sonic Color Line: Race and the Cultural Politics of Listening*. New York: New York University Press, 2016.

Stratton, J. "Why Doesn't Anybody Write Anything About Glam Rock?" *Australian Journal of Cultural Studies* 4, no. 1 (1986): 15–38.

Temperance, J. "The Birth of Uncool: Yacht Rock and Libidinal Subversion." *New Inquiry*, September 4, 2012. https://thenewinquiry.com/blog/the-birth-of-the-uncool-yacht-rock-and-libidinal-subversion.

Thompson, Marie. "Whiteness and the Ontological Turn in Sound Studies." *Parallax* 23 (2017): 266–82.

Thurman, Erica. "Beyoncé Steps into the Black Feminist Cypher and Promptly Drops the Mic." *Life Behind the Veil*, 2016. http://ericathurman.com/beyonce-steps-into-the-black-feminist-cypher-and-promptly-drops-the-mic/, accessed February 21, 2018.

Tomas, Goran, Marija Furdek, Sinisa Fajt, Vladimir Olujic, and Karlo Bruci. "Perceptibility of Aggressive Dynamics Processing in Digital Audio Broadcasting." Paper presented at 3rd Congress of the Alps Adria Acoustics Association, Graz, Austria, September 27–28, 2007. http://www.gorantomas.com/perceptibility-of-aggressive-dynamics-processing-in-digital-audio-broadcasting.

Vargo, Erin. "Katy Perry's Boring Super Bowl Performance." *Acculturated*, February 2, 2015. http://acculturated.com/katy-perrys-boring-super-bowl-performance.

Waltham-Smith, Naomi. *The Sound of Biopolitics*. New York: Fordham University Press, forthcoming.

Weheliye, Alexander G. *Habeas Viscus: Racializing Assemblages, Biopolitics, and Black Feminist Theories of the Human*. Durham, NC: Duke University Press, 2014.

Weheliye, Alexander G. *Phonographies: Grooves in Sonic Afro-Modernity*. Durham, NC: Duke University Press, 2005.

White, Paul. "Advanced Compression Techniques, Pt. 1." *Sound on Sound*, December 2000. https://web.archive.org/web/20150924122828/http://www.soundonsound.com/sos/deco0/articles/adcompression.htm.

Wilson, Tracy. "Our Final Answer on 'Too Many Women.'" *Stuff You Missed in History Class* (blog), June 2, 2016. http://www.missedinhistory.com/blog/our-final-answer-on-too-many-women.

Winnubst, Shannon. "The Queer Thing About Neoliberal Pleasure." *Foucault Studies* 14 (September 2012): 79–97.

Winnubst, Shannon. *Way Too Cool: Selling Out Race and Ethics*. New York: Columbia University Press, 2015.

Zaretsky, Eli. "The Crisis of Dynamic Stabilization and the Sociology of Resonance: An Interview with Hartmut Rosa." *Public Seminar*, January 18, 2017. http://www.publicseminar.org/2017/01/the-crisis-of-dynamic-stabilization-and-the-sociology-of-resonance/#.WOzEk1MrIWr.

Zepke, Stephen. "Reviewed Works: *Chaos, Territory, Art* by Elizabeth Grosz." *Comparative Literature Studies* 47, no. 4 (2010): 549–51.

INDEX

Acoustic resonance, 49, 55, 69, 86, 124, 136, 157, 179, 181–82; Attali and, 19, 36–37, 49; and data science, 1, 160, 162, 167; defined, 7–8, 63; and episteme, 2–5, 16, 18; and frequency, 2, 4, 8, 10, 36; and harmony, 158–59; and ideal theory, 108–9; and inequality, 3, 55, 88–90, 94–95; and math, 2–3, 5, 10, 16, 20–22, 27; and modernity, 27, 92–93, 98; and new materialism, 20, 88–92; as ontology, 19–20, 55, 60, 92, 107; and phase patterns, 7; and phenomenology, 19; and phonography, 6, 74, 82, 86; and physics, 158, 168, 170; and politics of exception, 67–68, 100, 104–6; and probability, 5, 58, 93, 106, 168; Pythagoras and, 22, 169–71; Rancière and, 58, 60; and sophrosyne, 5, 136; and statistical normalization, 36, 105; and voice, 19, 64–66. See also Resonance

Acoustics, 7, 19, 76, 160–62, 192n17, 203n9; Attali and, 4–5, 19, 27–28, 31, 33, 36–37, 49; and Lindsay's wheel, 99; Rancière and, 56; and voice, 63–65

Ahmed, Sarah, 73, 206n60, 208n88; and new materialism, 20, 89, 100, 105–6, 207–8nn77–78, 208n85

Alexander, Stefon, 5, 22, 159, 168–73, 223n41, 224n56

Algorithm(s), 88, 191n6, 202n3; and data science, 2, 105, 147–48; and music, 26, 31, 37, 128; and political economy, 28

Attali, Jacques, 51, 188n37; and acoustics, 4–5, 56, 65; and composition, 38–40, 48; and financialization, 34–35; and Foucault, 28–30, 32; and human capital, 35–36; and life/biopolitics, 31–32; and math, 26, 28–33; and music, 24–25, 31–32, 36–37, 40; and neoliberalism, 8, 18–19, 24, 26–27, 33; and repetition, 28, 33; and sonic episteme, 36–37, 49–50

Audiovisual litany, 3, 62, 89, 95–98, 105, 169, 186n12

Barad, Karen, 5, 20, 95, 203n11; and acoustic resonance, 88–94; and audiovisual litany, 96–97; and ideal theory, 108–9; and math, 94, 105, 168, 205n39; and musicology, 98–99; and phonography, 112, 117; and politics of exception, 100–101, 105, 107

"BBHMM" (Rihanna) 82–86, 119

Bennett, Jane, 20, 88–103, 107–9

Berlant, Lauren, 53–54

Beyoncé, 17, 47, 143, 213n139; and capitalism, 212n134, 213n141; and choreosonics, 120, 122–24; and demonic calculus, 147, 150–56; and feigned conformity, 77–78; "Formation," 54, 152–55, 221n116; "Hold Up," 20, 90, 110, 120–24, 155; *Lemonade*, 21, 120, 131, 147, 154–56; "6 Inch," 151–52; and sound, 77–78

Biopolitics, 3, 6–7, 22, 86, 125, 150, 156–57; Attali and, 31–32, 36, 38, 40; of cool, 27–28, 38–42, 48; and big

ist, 86–87, 100, 105, 190n79, 207n77, 208n85; popular, 12–14, 21, 41, 66, 130–31, 141–43; postfeminism, 15, 21, 41, 130, 202n104, 219n84; theory and, 18–21, 52, 73, 78, 86, 90, 100, 105, 148; white, 14, 66, 144–46, 207n77; women of color, 73, 105
"Formation" (Beyoncé), 54, 152–55, 221n116
Foucault, Michel, 5, 77, 189n59, 196n17, 205n39; and biopolitics, 16; and episteme, 3–4, 18; and neoliberalism, 9, 27–38, 137, 187–88nn36–37, 192n25; and normalization, 10–11, 52, 188n38; and sophrosyne, 132, 137
Fourier Transform, 223n41

Gaga feminism, 41
Gauss, Carl Friedrich, 25–26
Gaussian distribution, 8, 25, 52–53, 156, 158–59, 162, 172, 188n37
Goodman, Steve, 196n8, 203n10, 206n66, 211n122
Greece, ancient, 1, 21, 137, 146–47, 156; and music, 5, 59, 133, 140–41, 185n2, 217n48; and philosophy, 59, 130–33, 168–69, 187n28
Greene, Brian, 5, 22, 159, 168–73
Grosz, Elizabeth, 5, 20, 88–109, 204n23, 205n36, 207n76

Halberstam, Jack, 41
Harmonics: and inharmonics, 8, 88, 112, 117
Harmony, 1, 15, 24–26, 85, 130, 162, 167, 178, 199n54, 217n50; and acoustic resonance, 60, 91–92; cosmic, 21–22, 169–71; and data science, 221n3; and Fourier Transform, 223n41; and geometric proportion, 5, 59; and new materialism, 91–92; Plato and, 59, 130–34, 197n18, 197n27, 217n48; social, 57, 140, 146, 158–60; and sophrosyne, 19, 56, 59–60, 131–36,

140–41, 216n45; tonal, 25, 85. *See also* Resonance
Havis, Devonya, 6, 20, 75–82, 176, 182
"Hold Up" (Beyoncé), 20, 90, 110, 120–24, 155
Holiday, Billie, 77, 120, 123

Ideal theory, 17, 89, 108–9, 124, 204n29, 209n93, 209n97. *See also* Nonideal theory
Identity, 40, 58, 72–73, 108, 200n59, 215n26; and inequality, 4, 12, 14–15, 20, 55, 66–70, 95, 107–8, 167, 181; intersectional, 66; politics, 172, 199n54, 207n66; racial, 15, 47, 68–69, 195n90; social, 12, 19, 56, 69–70, 130, 223n29. *See also* Postidentity
Inharmonics: and harmonics, 8, 88, 112, 117

Jackson, Michael, 195n90, 213n93
Jackson, Zakkiyah Iman, 20, 104–5, 114, 203n13
Jazz, 171, 185n5

Kane, Brian, 209n97
K-Hole, 41–42
Knouf, N. Adriana, 26, 191n4, 191n6, 192n17

Lemonade (Beyoncé), 21, 120, 131, 147, 154–56
Leong, Diana, 20, 93, 105–6, 109, 114, 206n61, 209n102
Liberalism, 6, 12–13, 19–20, 29, 34, 52, 100, 107, 137, 172, 192n25. *See also* Neoliberalism
Listening ear, 19, 55, 81, 173
Lordi, Emily, 151
"Love on the Brain" (Rihanna), 111

Mader, Mary Beth, 2, 9–10, 13, 67, 156, 159, 171

241

Materialism, new, 87–118, 203nn10–12, 204n29, 206n66, 207n77; and enclosure, 124; and feminism, 20, 86, 190n79; founding gesture, 20, 93, 100–106, 114–15, 118, 124; and ideal theory, 108–9; and politics of exception, 89, 101–6, 114; and resonance, 92, 95–106, 109; and sonic episteme, 5, 88–89

Math: and acoustics, 1–2, 11, 26–28, 31–33, 60, 104–6, 110, 179–80, 199n44; and chance, 25–26, 30–31, 52, 93–94, 105, 112, 136; and data science, 1; demonic calculus, 6, 21, 131, 146–57, 220n106; Du Bois and, 52; frequency ratio, 2, 4–5, 8–10, 16, 36–37, 49, 51, 60, 94, 161–62, 204n29; Foucault and, 16, 28–31; Gaussian/bell curve, 8, 10, 25–26, 156, 158–59, 172, 188n37; and inequality, 10, 27, 67, 105, 147, 167, 172; and insurance, 118–19, 211n124; and music (as trope), 1–2, 21–22, 36–37, 130, 156–57, 169–73, 185n5; and neoliberal markets, 19, 26–28, 33, 49, 89, 107; and physics, 5, 18, 22, 94, 105, 158–62, 167–73; Plato and, 5, 59, 94, 133–34, 156, 171–72, 217n48; and postdemocracy, 58, 60; and the social, 2, 9, 13; and sophrosyne, 130–31, 134–36, 140, 146–47, 156; wicked, 157, 173–79

Mathematics of black life, 116, 119, 131, 148–50, 156, 174

McKittrick, Katherine, 6, 21, 111, 116, 131, 146–57; and Weheliye, 22, 159, 173–79, 182

Mills, Charles, 17, 89, 108, 201n94, 209n93

Modern/modernity, 7, 28, 78, 95, 163, 177, 186n15, 196n17; aesthetics, 40–41; Afro-modernity, 17; episteme, 3; and inequality, 13, 50, 66, 86, 182; philosophy, 4, 38, 49, 61–62, 88,

135, 203n10; and resonance, 6, 103–5; and subjectivity, 61; and voice, 63

Morgan, Joan, 152

Neoliberalism, 3–7, 9–10, 16, 20–22, 23, 26–30; aesthetic, 40–43, 112, 125–27, 131, 136, 142–43, 147, 178–80; calculus or rationality, 1–5, 8–14, 28–30, 134–35, 146–50, 174, 192n25, 218n56; and capitalism, 1, 23, 49, 180; and classical liberalism, 6, 12–13, 19–20, 29, 34, 52, 100, 107, 137, 172, 192n25; cost/benefit, 4, 8, 48, 58, 93, 127, 135–39, 163–64, 178–79, 218n56; episteme, 3–4, 58, 95, 97, 100; investment, 14, 33–34, 38–41, 136; subjectivity, 6, 15, 38–39, 44, 125, 130, 172, 180, 192n25

Noise, 30–31, 39–45, 49, 51, 58, 64, 87–88, 191n6, 193n45; domestication of, 12–13, 19, 27, 39–40, 49–50, 51, 58, 142–43; feminist, 141–42, 146; signal and, 2, 13, 39, 57, 64, 71, 138, 142–46; sonic, 24–26, 32, 39, 43, 49, 103, 143–44, 199n54, 211n122; speech versus, 67–69, 199n45; white, 129, 146

Nonideal theory, 18, 104, 108–9, 115–17. See also Ideal theory

Normalization, 21, 36, 104–5, 128, 172; and compression, 11; and governmentality, 10–13, 52, 107, 112, 135–36, 163, 166, 188n48, 189n68, 223n21

Ontology, 9, 16, 181, 203n11; materialist, 5, 20, 88–89, 93, 106–7, 158, 204n23, 205n36; ontological turn, 94, 186n12; phonographic, 75–86; political, 5–6, 50–60, 68, 72, 86, 158, 196n17; social, 117, 172; and statistics, 12–13, 168; vibrational, 5, 90, 93, 99–101, 110, 203n10, 204n29, 206n66; vocal, 60–63, 198n43, 200n55

Patriarchy, 41, 108, 115, 142, 154, 181, 186n8, 186n13; ancient Greek, 141; epistemology, 156; and kinship, 121; neoliberal, 14–17, 66–67, 94–96, 143–46; and ontology, 52, 55, 74–75, 82; and perceptual coding, 19, 81, 110, 179; and personhood, 21, 75–79, 152, 156; postfeminist, 21; and privilege, 43, 130, 180; property relation, 7, 11, 52, 75–80, 84, 110, 121–23, 176–77; system, 13, 53, 155, 171–72

Perceptual coding: defined, 11–12; and politics of exception, 16, 19, 52–55, 146, 173–74, 181–82; resistance to, 20–21, 54–55, 74–86, 110–25, 149–50, 156, 177–79. *See also* Compression

Pet Shop Boys, 23–24

Philosophy, 181–83; and audiovisual litany, 95–98; black feminist, 75–77; and enclosure, 90, 110–14, 119–20, 124, 178, 210n111, 213n142; and musicology, 98–99; neoliberal upgrades, 89, 94–95, 100–107, 109, 124; and occularcentrism, 89, 206n51; and phonography, 21, 81–82, 86, 110–15, 119–20, 124–25; sonic episteme and, 27, 37–38, 72–77, 86, 163, 183; and voice, 52, 55, 61, 93; Western, 20, 27, 49, 61, 66, 72–74, 89, 109, 167

Phonography, 7, 18–22, 55, 75–78, 159, 173; in the red, 6, 75, 80–82, 110, 143, 183, 196n8, 202n97, 202n104; and philosophy, 17–19, 75, 82, 86, 90, 110, 125, 181

Physics, 18, 91; astrophysics, 157–59; demonic, 150; quantum, 5, 101, 105, 204n20; and philosophy, 224n55; social, 25, 157, 160–63, 165–74, 177–79, 191n10, 212n13, 223n29; of sound, 1, 7, 26, 65, 211n122; theoretical, 18, 168–69, 173, 179

Plato, 56, 65, 68, 156–57, 216n34, 217nn47–50; Cavarero and, 197n27, 197n29; and epistemology, 135; and

metaphysics of presence, 96, 186n12; theory of divided line, 9–10, 21, 61, 78, 94, 132; and women, 140. *See also* Sophrosyne

Post-identity, 50, 58–60, 163; defined, 12–14; and new materialism, 105–8; and politics of exception, 55, 89, 135; and voice, 66. *See also* Identity

Quetelet, Adolphe, 25, 158–59

Rancière, Jacques, 5, 19, 55–60, 66–68, 131, 200n59, 217n47

Reich, Steve, 8, 25, 40, 65, 198n43, 222n8

Resonance, 5, 16, 50, 86, 105–7, 159–60, 182, 224n54; dysgenic, 102–3; and frequency, 1, 199n44; history of, 7–8; and ideal theory, 108–9; phonographic, 6, 20, 90, 104, 110–17, 124–25; and representation, 3, 20, 55, 97–100, 104–6, 167; sympathetic, 7, 199n54; vibratory, 88–92, 94–96, 103, 203n10, 206n66; vocal, 60–76, 197n27. *See also* Acoustic resonance; Consonance; Dissonance; Harmony

Rihanna, 20, 174, 177–78, 189n71, 202n103; "BBHMM," 82–86, 119; "Love on the Brain," 111; and theory, 17

Risk: 185n5; individual, 40–49, 94, 103, 126–28, 139, 143; disproportionate, 151, 155–57, 178–79, 218n56; probabilistic, 44, 94, 131, 136–39, 147, 164, 188n37, 212n139

Robinson, Zandria, 123, 151, 155

Rosa, Hartmut, 199n54

Sharpe, Christina, 18, 90, 115–19, 182, 211nn121–25, 212n139. *See also* Wake

Shaviro, Steven, 39, 127, 189n71

Signal: and noise, 13, 39, 57, 64, 71, 138, 142–46, 185n2, 191n6

Simone, Nina, 120, 123

243

"6 Inch" (Beyoncé), 151–52

Sonic episteme, 21–22, 31, 40, 181–83, 189n68, 192n17, 199n54; alternatives to, 28; constituents of, 16, 19; defined, 3–8, 18; ideal theory and, 17–18; inequality and, 19, 27; neoliberal markets and, 26–27, 36–37, 47; new materialism and, 88–89, 105; phonography and, 5–6, 74–76, 82, 112, 156, 159, 173–79; politics of exception and, 72, 74, 86; pop science and, 158–59, 162–63, 167–70, 173; Rancière and, 56, 58–60; sophrosyne and, 130, 136, 157; voice and, 52, 55, 65–66. *See also* Episteme

Sophrosyne: ancient Greek/Plato, 5, 21, 59–60, 130–38, 140–41, 146–47, 156, 216n44, 217n50; and math, 59–60, 131, 134–36, 154–56; and music, 133–34, 136–37; neoliberal, 16, 21, 69, 130–31, 134–41, 144–50, 155–56, 217n50; and resonance, 69, 136; and subordination, 130–33, 139, 143, 146–47; and women/gender, 21, 130, 136, 140–43, 146, 155–56

Sound: acoustically resonant, 56, 61–64, 156, 173; and algorithmic culture, 1, 26, 87–88, 160–62; bad, 41–44; and black studies, 17, 225n60; and compression, 11, 30; feminist, 141–46; and gender, 140–41, 155; in the red, 86, 110, 156, 196n8; and math, 1–2, 5, 22, 193n56; misattributed, 171; musical, 15, 38, 84, 150, 170, 185n2, 212n37; phonographic, 17–18, 20, 55, 74–78, 110–25, 173–79; and physics, 26, 169–70; Plato and, 59, 133–34, 197n27, 217nn48–49; and probability, 37, 52; and representation, 19, 49, 81, 98–99, 186n12, 192n17, 206n66; and revolution, 4; and sonic episteme, 5, 8, 17, 159, 181–83, 196n13; synthesis, 32–33, 40; and theory/philosophy, 7, 16, 22, 52, 186n15; and

vision, 3, 55, 61, 89, 95–97, 100; vocal, 57–58, 64–65, 71

Sounding, 6, 20, 55, 79–82, 119, 148; defined, 74–78; Rihanna and, 86

Soundness of mind, 131–32, 134, 137, 140

Sound studies, 3, 17–18, 95, 173, 188n37, 204n23, 209n97

Sound waves, 1, 4, 90–91; consonant and dissonant, 187n34; and neoliberal markets, 36; and physics, 7, 170, 187n31, 223n41, 224n56

Spandau Ballet, 19, 27, 38, 42, 44, 194n79

Spence, Lester, 14–15, 44, 66–72, 89, 101–4, 138–39

Spillers, Hortense, 78–81

String theory, 5, 22, 157–59, 168–74, 224n47

Swift, Taylor, 19, 27, 38, 45–48

Sympathetic resonance, 7, 199n54

Symphony/symphonia, 1–2, 132, 160, 223n41

Thaemlitz, Terry, 211n118, 211nn121–22

Trower, Shelley, 204n29

Vibration, 75, 87–88, 117, 204n29; choreosonic, 90, 110–17, 120, 124; and elemental reality, 5, 20, 86, 88, 90–91, 102, 206n66; and harmony, 65, 91, 223n41; and motion, 7, 63; musical, 22, 59; nonideal theory, 104–9, 124; physical, 168, 210n118; and probability, 93; and quantum strings, 169–70; and sonic episteme, 89, 100–102; and sound, 99, 206n60; and wake, 117. *See also* Ontology, vibrational

Voice, acoustically resonant, 52; feminist, 21, 136, 142–47, 156; grain of, 81; giving to, 88, 93; human, 60, 71, 76, 109, 167; and identity, 69–70; and language, 71, 76; musical, 77–78,